BIRYANI

PRATIBHA KARAN

RANDOM HOUSE INDIA

To
my husband Vijay Karan
who seems to have so snugly
ensconced into my system,
my heart and my soul.

Published by Random House India in 2009
Third impression in 2012

Copyright of text and photographs© Pratibha Karan 2009

China and Flatware Courtesy good earth
celebrating style

Photographs: Anushka Nadia Menon
Food styling: Sujata Sadr
Book design: Alagu Chockalingam

Random House Publishers India Private Limited
Windsor IT Park, 7th Floor, Tower-B,
A-1, Sector-125, Noida-201301, UP

Random House Group Limited
20 Vauxhall Bridge Road
London SW1V 2SA
United Kingdom

978 81 8400 093 1

This book is sold subject to the condition that it shall not, by way of trade or otherwise, be lent, resold, hired out, or otherwise circulated without the publisher's prior consent in any form of binding or cover other than that in which it is published and without a similar condition including this condition being imposed on the subsequent purchaser.

Set in Bookman Adobe Caslon Pro

Printed and bound in India by Aegean Offset Printers, Noida

Contents

Introduction	6
Tips for the reader	9
North	15
South	55
East	125
West	143
Relishes	181
List of recipes	194
Acknowledgements	198

Introduction

If there is such a thing as food of the gods, it is undoubtedly the biryani. No dish can match it in grandeur, taste, subtlety and refinement. The magic of biryani lies in the way rice is transformed into something ambrosial—absorbing the rich flavours of meat and spice, scented with the dizzying aromas of saffron, rose, jasmine or screwpine; the white grains taking on a gem-like mien.

The Indian subcontinent owes a deep debt to the Muslim community, for it is they who introduced the gamut of biryanis and pulaos to us. The dish has since spread through the country and taken many forms. Depending on the place, its culinary history, and the availability of spices, biryanis and pulaos can be markedly different. Some biryanis, for example, lay emphasis upon one particular ingredient or spice, which then lends its own flavour to the dish. In Bengal one finds the use of mustard seeds; the biryanis of southern Maharashtra are famed for their use of chillies. Traditionally too, biryanis would be cooked using the local variety of rice, such as the kaima of Kerala or the kala bhaat of Hyderabad which, when cooked, would permeate an entire home with its seductive aroma. Today, however, most biryanis are made with the famed long grained basmati rice.

In this book, I present before you a dazzling range of such biryanis, from across the length and breadth of the country. When I began researching for this book, one of the first surprises to greet me was the discovery that there are more biryanis in south India than the north, despite being associated with the Mughal and Awadhi culinary culture. And south does not mean just Hyderabad. Tamil Nadu, Karnataka and Kerala have a surfeit of biryanis, with many towns in these states possessing their own signature versions of biryanis. Similarly, western India, especially Mumbai, home to Muslim communities such as the Khojas and Boris, also boasts of a large variety of biryanis. Only the east, with the exception of Kolkata, seems somewhat bereft. With some effort, I was able to locate just one biryani in Assam called the Kampuri Biryani, named after Kampur, the town to which it belongs. In the interest of equitable representation, several biryanis of Delhi, Lucknow, Hyderabad, Kerala etc. had to be left out.

Among all the biryanis, the thoroughbreds are from Hyderabad. It is said that about forty kinds of biryanis alone are made in Hyderabad, which is not surprising on account of its location and history. The cuisine seems to have borrowed something from everywhere, and not just from all over India, but also from Persia and Arabia. Journalist Vir Sanghvi, perhaps India's most famous food writer, was told very categorically in Lucknow that the real biryani was made only in Hyderabad and that Lucknow had only pulaos. He writes that the famous Dumpukht Biryani served in the Dumpukht restaurants in the ITC hotels drew its inspiration not so much from Awadh, but from Hyderabad.

The origin of the word pulao is well known, but the origin of the word biryani seems somewhat hazy. Pulao comes from the Turkish word pilav or pilaf, the Persian word polou and the Spanish word paella. All of them seem to have a common origin. They say that the word biryani comes from the Persian word birinj, meaning rice, which seems quite plausible. But the Dumpukht restaurants in the ITC chain of hotels claim that birinj means frying before cooking. This hardly leads us to the biryani. The hotel chain also claims Taimur the Lame brought biryani to India in the fourteenth century. One is not sure whether the claim is as apocryphal as its claim on the origins of the melting Kakori Kabab—that it was invented for an Awadh king who could not chew as he had lost all his teeth.

In all probability, the pulao (if not the biryani) originated as a war meal. After a day's battle, the cooks could not be expected to organize a meal in courses for the soldiers, except maybe for the generals and the kings. So they would cook rice with meat or poultry and maybe vegetables thrown in, in one huge deg or pot, thus giving the world this delicious dish.

What is pulao, and what is biryani? Talk of their differences is unending, but in actual fact, there is a very fine dividing line between the two. Both are rice dishes cooked with meat, poultry, seafood or even vegetables and both can be absolutely irresistible. Though the procedure of cooking them is quite different, there prevails an amusing mix-up among them, with some pulaos being named as biryanis and vice versa. For instance, the Hyderabadi Doodh ki Biryani is actually made the pulao way. Again, the Hyderabadi Keeme ki Khichdi is not a khichdi but a biryani. And there is one biryani, also outstanding in taste, that is not made with rice but with vermicelli.

Broadly speaking, the following are the distinguishing features of the two. The cardinal principle of a biryani is that it is made by the method of layering in a pan, with rice being the first layer and the last layer, and meat, fish, poultry or vegetables constituting the middle layer. Sometimes, there are just two layers, with rice constituting the first and meat, poultry or fish constituting the upper layer and vice versa. Sometimes rice and meat or poultry or vegetables are also arranged in four alternating layers. In the pulaos, however, there is no layering and the rice and all the other ingredients are cooked together, in a kind of potpourri.

Generally, biryanis are scented with saffron, rose, screwpine or jasmine, whereas pulaos are hardly embellished with any essence. Biryanis also use more spices than pulaos, and are wetter than pulaos. In pulaos, on the other hand, whole spices (khada masala) are used more often. Biryanis are generally made with par-boiled rice whereas pulaos are cooked in just sufficient water and, when done, the rice fully absorbs the water. A lot of pulaos are also made in chicken or mutton stock. Over the years, the pulao has also been vegetarianized in northern India obviously by and for the predominantly vegetarian population in this region. In Delhi and Lucknow, it is widely believed, that pulaos are superior to biryanis. Today, rice dishes flavoured with cumin, onions or only green peas are also called pulaos.

One thing that is common to biryanis and pulaos is that towards the end both are cooked on slow fire. This procedure is called dum. The cover of the pot is either sealed with dough or a heavy stone is placed on top of it. Alternately, hot coals are placed both under the pot and on the lid. In fact, from dum has come the word dumpukht (or dumpokht in Hyderabad), which means sealing the dish tightly, in the process trapping the aroma and flavours inside the pot.

Pratibha Karan
New Delhi
November 2009

Note: Recipes have been ordered by region and within each section the non-vegetarian biryanis appear before the vegetarian ones. All biryanis from a particular place also appear within these groupings together.

Tips for the reader

Broadly, there are no hard and fast rules on cooking. Cooking is an evolving and a continuously creative art and you can rely on your ingenuity, creativity and common sense and on your sense of smells, flavours and textures. Therefore, while being guided by documented knowledge, discussions and observations, it is always possible, given a little interest and inclination, to create something delicious and pleasing to behold.

Never let rigid rules define your attempt at cooking and so never be stuck for want of ingredients. You can generally make do with what you have off the shelf at home. It always helps to keep the basic food provisions, spices and greens readily available at home. Of course, for best results, it helps to cook with the best ingredients. Meat, poultry, fish and vegetables must be fresh and of high quality. Though it may be convenient to buy ready-made spices, fresh ones made at home are always better. For example, lightly roasted and freshly ground cumin seeds and coriander seeds and freshly ground peppercorns can make a world of difference to the flavour of a dish. Similarly home-made garam masala is easily superior to what you get in the market and can richly enhance the flavour of a dish. There is also no parallel to the home-made ghee.

To cook biryani may seem a daunting task. In Hyderabad, the home of biryanis, many housewives shy away from making biryanis for the fear that the end result may turn out to be a disaster, with either the meat remaining undercooked, or rice becoming soggy and the dish becoming a mishmash. A few points, if kept in mind, while making biryani, can make the entire exercise simple and results brilliant.

As stated before, it is important to select good quality and fresh meat, poultry or fish while cooking biryanis. Generally, cuts of a small goat's shoulder are preferred as its meat is tender. Tough meat or a huge chicken will not yield the same results. Different parts of a goat or a combination of some are prescribed in different recipes.

In some recipes like Katchi Biryani, marination for 5–6 hours is recommended. Here, apart from yoghurt and other spices, the pulp and skin of raw papaya is also used for marination as raw papaya has a great tenderizing quality. Additionally, marination helps in absorption of spices, makes the meat tastier and reduces cooking time. In Katchi Biryani, for instance, meat is marinated longer than normal and is then cooked with rice in almost raw form. The timing needs to be delicately balanced so that both meat and rice are fully cooked together, with each grain of rice still remaining separate.

It hardly needs to be mentioned that, in contrast, fish and prawns take very little time to cook. Fish should not be marinated for long as the natural juices of the fish then get released, making the fish drier. Chicken would also normally require lesser time for marination and cooking as compared to meat.

The use of the best quality long grain rice is recommended, as it improves both the flavour and look of the biryani. However, in different regions, different varieties of rice are used, not always because of any exceptional qualities but presumably because of local availability. Therefore, jeera samba or jeerakashala rice are widely used in Kerala and at times even in Tamil Nadu. A highly aromatic rice of Hyderabad called Kala Bhat, whose fragrance would waft and linger in the air, has now disappeared and is no longer available. In many Muslim homes and eateries, golden sela rice is preferred because of its long grain and firm texture. This rice, however, needs to be soaked for a much longer time.

However, the best rice for a biryani is easily the long grain basmati of high quality. Rice should be nicely washed in 3–4 changes of water and soaked well covered with water. The average soaking time can be anywhere between 20 minutes to half an hour. Soaking the rice prior to cooking also prevents it from breaking.

The time taken to cook rice varies from recipe to recipe. Broadly speaking and other things remaining the same, given below are a broad set of guidelines to cook rice:

If you add rice (previously soaked for about 20 minutes) to salted boiling water, the time taken to cook the rice to different degrees of cooking is as follows:
To cook up to 50 percent—about 5 minutes
To cook up to ⅔—about 6–7 minutes
To cook up to 90 percent—about 8–9 minutes
To cook fully—about 9–10 minutes

If the rice is required to be partially cooked, say up to 50 percent or even up to 80 to 90 percent then you need to drain the water immediately after cooking and transfer the rice to a flat pan so that it does not get soft any further on account of the steam. An important and accurate gauge to judge the extent to which rice is cooked is by feeling the grain between your thumb and finger. The addition of a small quantity of say 1 tsp of oil while boiling rice prevents the rice from sticking together. Adding a teaspoon of vinegar or juice of lime gives it a whiter and firmer texture.

While cooking biryani, meat and rice are almost always cooked separately and then layered and cooked on dum. The amount of time taken to cook the dish on dum (a very slow fire) depends on the degree to which it has been cooked before layering. Thus if the meat has been almost fully cooked and rice three fourths done, then it should take a maximum of about 10 minutes of cooking on dum to get it fully ready.

A nice way to serve biryani fresh and hot is to cook and layer it a little in advance and start cooking on dum a little before it is required to be served. Biryani can be heated in the same utensil in which it is cooked by sprinkling a little water, covering it tightly and heating on medium flame for 2–3 minutes. After the biryani is heated, it can be kept warm for a long time if the utensil is kept on a griddle on a very low flame.

Biryani can also be made in a handi-like vessel. To cook on dum, the vessel should be covered with lid and the edges sealed with dough to prevent the steam from escaping. This can also be achieved by covering the dish with a tight fitting lid and by putting a heavy stone on the cover. A rather nice and convenient vessel in which to cook biryani is a heavy aluminium karahi with a well fitting lid. The karahi gives adequate depth and width and makes handling easier.

Biryanis must always be served steaming hot. It should be taken out in large chunks from the sides without mixing the meat and rice so that it is presented in all its multi-hued glory.

North

The Mughals are widely believed to have introduced the tradition of biryanis in India. As their seat of power was in north India, one would have expected more biryanis and pulaos in this part of the country. But the truth is that there are more biryanis in the south, not just in Hyderabad but also in Tamil Nadu and Kerala. One reason for this could be that north Indians are not essentially rice eaters. Also, the north has historically been in the stranglehold of vegetarianism as much of the Hindu north, consisting primarily of Brahmins and Vaisyas, have always been vegetarian. The Jain religion, with its strong culture of non-violence and vegetarianism, has also played a role in keeping the north off the meats, as has the monotheistic Arya Samaj movement that swept over much of Punjab, Haryana, and UP in the nineteenth century. That is why so many Hindu communities like the Jats and the Bishnois are predominantly vegetarian. Despite their robust and warlike ways, the Sikhs have also largely stuck to vegetarianism, especially sects like the Namdhari Sikhs. The Radha Soami movement, that began in Punjab and spread to Haryana, Himachal Pradesh, and Western UP, further strengthened these foundations.

Biryanis did develop in the north, but in the Muslim centres—in the Mughal capital of Delhi, the Awadh centre of Lucknow and in the small principalities ruled by Muslim princes. Though it might be argued that Delhi and Lucknow are traditionally not biryani but pulao places, the fact remains and, as the recipes that follow will show, some of the most exquisite biryanis in the subcontinent are made in these two places today. Both the Mughlai and Awadhi food is highly subtle and refined, as are their pulaos and biryanis. They are also lighter in colour because of the use of yoghurt and dry fruits, especially almonds. During the Mughal era, Hindu vegetarianism also absorbed many of influences of the non-vegetarian dishes. Thus, we find a large number of vegetarian pulaos and some vegetarian biryanis in this region as well.

Gosht Biryani (Lucknow)

Another one of those scented biryanis made with almonds, melon seeds, and cream. Rich and aromatic, it is ideal for special meals.

Preparation time: 20 minutes
Marination time: 30 minutes
Cooking time: 50 minutes
Serves: 8–10

1	kg mutton, cut into medium sized pieces (a mix of meat from the shoulder, a few chops and a few pieces from puth i.e. the backbone)

A
2	cups yoghurt, whisked
3	tbs ginger paste
2	tbs garlic paste
1½	tsp red chilli powder

B *ground to a paste*
8–10	almonds, blanched and skin peeled
2	tbs watermelon and musk melon seeds

C *powdered*
1	tsp caraway seeds
1	tsp peppercorns
	A few mace flakes (3–4)
	A small piece of nutmeg
1	1 inch cinnamon stick
4	green cardamoms

500	gm long grain rice
2	medium onions, ground
½	tsp saffron
2	tbs screwpine water
½	cup warm milk
1	tbs ghee
3	tbs thick cream
½	cup oil
	Salt

1. Marinate the mutton: Wash the mutton and drain it of all water. Mix the meat with all the ingredients at A, B, and C and salt. Marinate for 30 minutes.

2. Prepare the rice: Wash and soak the rice in liberal quantity of water for 15–20 minutes, then drain the water. Boil 2½ litres of water with a little salt. Once the water starts to boil, add the rice and cook for about 5–6 minutes till it is half done. Drain the water and transfer the rice to a wide pan.

3. Cook the mutton: Heat the oil and fry the onions till golden brown. Add the marinated meat and keep stirring till it comes to a boil. Add a little water and cook for 25 minutes till the meat is tender. When done, the meat should have 2 cups of gravy left.

4. Assemble and serve: Take a heavy bottomed pan and smear it with oil. Place two thirds of the rice in it, followed by the cooked meat with the gravy. Cover this with the balance rice. Sprinkle saffron dissolved in screwpine water and milk, ghee, and cream. Cover with a tight fitting lid and cook first on high flame for 1–2 minutes and then on low flame for about 10–15 minutes till the rice is done and steaming. Serve hot.

Ananas ki Biryani (Lucknow)

Preparation time: 30 minutes
Marination time: 1 hour
Cooking time: 50 minutes
Serves: 8

1	kg mutton, cut into medium pieces (a mix of meat from shoulder, chops and puth i.e. meat pieces cut from the backbone)
1	tbs ginger paste
1½	tsp garlic paste
1	tbs green chilli paste
⅓	cup coriander leaves, chopped
¼	cup mint leaves
2	onions, sliced
1½	cups yoghurt, whisked
⅔	cup pineapple, cut into ½ inch pieces

} A

500	gm long grain rice
	Juice of half a lime for rice
3	onions, finely sliced
50	gm khus khus (poppy seeds), ground into a fine paste

There are indeed many fruit biryanis, this one made with pineapple. It not only makes the biryani mildly sweet but also tenderizes the meat.

1. Marinate the mutton: Mix the mutton well with all the ingredients at A and leave it for an hour.

2. Prepare the rice: Wash and soak the rice in water for about 20 minutes, then drain. Boil about 2 litres of water. Once the water starts to boil, add a little salt, the juice of half a lime together with rice. Cook for about 6–7 minutes till the rice is two thirds done.

3. Fry the onions: Take a large heavy bottomed pan and heat the oil. Fry the onions till they turn golden. Remove and set aside. Crush when it cools down.

4. Cook the mutton: In the same oil, add the mutton with the marinade, stirring continuously till the liquids come to a boil. Keep on stirring for another 1–2 minutes, then add salt. Cover and cook on medium flame for about 20–25 minutes till the meat is 90 percent done. Then add the poppy seeds, crushed onions, and the spices at B. Add a little water and cover and cook for another 5 minutes. When done, the meat should have about one glass gravy in it.

1	bay leaf	
2	green cardamoms	
1	black cardamom	
2	1 inch cinnamon sticks	B
4	cloves	
1	small piece of nutmeg	
2–3	mace flakes	
½	tsp caraway seeds	

10	cashew nuts
10–15	raisins
2	tbs ghee
1	cup oil
	Salt

5. Assemble: Take a heavy bottomed pan and smear it with ghee. Place half the rice in it followed by the meat with the gravy. Add the balance rice on top and sprinkle a little water. Now cover this with a tight fitting lid and cook on dum till the dish is steaming hot and the rice done.

6. Garnish and serve: Heat 2 tbs ghee. Fry the cashew nuts till golden and set them aside. Add the raisins and fry till they swell up. Spread the ghee with the cashew nuts and raisins over the rice. Serve hot.

Rose Biryani (Lucknow)

Preparation time: 15 minutes
Cooking time: 1 hour 30 minutes
Serves: 8

250	gm lean mutton, minced
1	tsp grated ginger
1	tsp crushed garlic
1	tsp red chilli powder
½	tsp garam masala
	A few sprigs of fresh green coriander, chopped
	A few mint leaves, chopped
4–5	onions, finely sliced
500	gm boneless mutton pieces, about 2 inches in size, (beaten with a mallet or lightly beaten with the sharp end of a knife to help absorption of spices)
2	bay leaves ⎫
4	green cardamoms ⎬ A
1	inch cinnamon stick ⎭
6–8	green chillies chopped
	A few sprigs of fresh green coriander, chopped
1	tsp yellow chilli powder
1	tsp coriander powder
1	tsp cumin powder
1	cup yoghurt, whisked
2	tbs rose water
500	gm long grain rice

Rose biryani is so named because it is flavoured with rose water and garnished with dried rose petals. It is a delicate biryani, made with mutton balls. How the Mughal biryanis were traditionally made is not really recorded. But obviously, they would have started with meat, which could be mutton, beef or poultry.

1. Prepare the meatballs: Put the minced mutton in a bowl. Add half of the ginger and garlic, red chilli powder, garam masala, coriander, mint, and salt. Mix well. Form into about 12 equal sized meat balls (koftas). Set aside.

2. Cook the meatballs: Heat oil in a saucepan and fry the onions till golden brown. Remove and place on an absorbent paper. When cool, crush half of the onions and reserve. In the same oil, fry the meatballs on medium flame, gently turning them so that they are evenly browned and cooked. Remove and set aside.

3. Cook the mutton: Wash the meat pieces and drain the water. Take a heavy bottomed pan and heat about 60 gm of oil from the same oil in which the onions were fried. Add the whole spices at A and salt followed in a few seconds by the balance ginger and garlic. Fry for a few seconds. Now add the green chillies and fresh coriander followed by red chilli powder, coriander powder, cumin powder and salt and the meat pieces. Fry for 6–7 minutes. Add the yoghurt, and keep stirring vigorously to prevent curdling. Fry till the oil starts to separate from the meat. Add a little water and cook the meat covered for about 25 minutes, till tender. When done, the meat should have about 1 cup gravy left. Sprinkle the crushed onions over the meat together with 1 tbs rose water.

½	tsp saffron, crushed and soaked in ½ cup warm milk
2	tbs ghee
	Oil for frying
	Salt

4. Prepare the rice: Wash and soak the rice in water for about 20 minutes, then drain out the water. Boil 2¼ litres of water with a little salt. Once the water starts to boil, add the rice and cook for about 5–6 minutes till it is half done. Drain the water from the rice.

5. Assemble and serve: Spread the par boiled rice over the meat. Sprinkle the balance rose water, saffron milk and the fried onion over the rice. Dot with ghee. Arrange the fried meatballs over the rice and cover with a tight fitting lid. Cook first on medium-high flame for about 2 minutes till the steam starts to form. Then reduce flame to low and cook on dum for about 25 minutes till the dish is steaming hot and the rice done. Carefully transfer to a nice serving dish and serve hot.

Motiye ki Biryani (Lucknow)

Motiye ki Biryani is called so as it is perfumed with the essence of jasmine or motiya. This is a classic Awadhi biryani, made with saffron and cream.

Preparation time: 20 minutes
Cooking time: 1 hour 10 minutes
Serves: 8–10

1	kg mutton from a small goat, a mix of medium sized pieces from the shoulder, a few chops and a few pieces from the breast
5	onions, sliced
2	bay leaves
4–5	cloves
4	green cardamoms
2	1 inch cinnamon sticks
1½	tbs ginger paste
1½	tbs garlic paste
1	tsp yellow chilli powder
1	cup yoghurt, whisked

A:
- Juice of 2 limes
- Seeds of 4–5 green cardamoms *powdered*
- A small piece of nutmeg *powdered*
- 2–3 mace flakes *powdered*
- 4 tsp thick cream
- 1 tsp saffron, soaked in half cup warm milk
- 2 drops of jasmine essence mixed with 2–3 tbs water

650	gm long grain rice
	Juice of half a lime
1	tbs ginger juliennes
2–3	green chillies, chopped

1. Prepare the mutton: Wash the mutton and put it in a colander for the water to drain. Heat the ghee–oil mixture in a heavy-base pan, large enough to take the meat and rice. Add the sliced onions and fry till golden brown. Remove half and set aside. Add the whole spices, followed in a few seconds by the ginger and garlic paste. After a minute or so, add meat and fry for 3–4 minutes. Add salt and yellow chilli powder and fry for another 1–2 minutes. Then add yoghurt and stir briskly. Continue stirring till the contents come to a boil and for 1 more minute thereafter. Cover and cook till the liquids quite dry up and the oil starts to surface. Now add water and cook covered on medium to slow flame till the meat is tender. When done, the meat should have about 1¼ cup of gravy left. At this stage, put together all the ingredients at A and mix. Add half of these to the meat, mix gently and cover.

2. Prepare the rice: Wash and soak the rice in water for 20 minutes. Bring 3 litres of water to a boil. Drain and add the rice, salt, juice of half a lime, and 1 tsp of oil. Cook for 6–7 minutes till the rice is two-thirds done. Drain the water and transfer the rice to a flat pan.

3. Assemble: Heat the pan with the meat. Spread half of the ginger juliennes, green chillies, fresh coriander, mint, and half of the fried onions over the meat. Cover with half of the rice. Spread the balance of the ingredients at A and ginger juliennes, green chilli, coriander and mint over the rice. Cover with the balance rice. Sprinkle a little water.

⅓	cup fresh green coriander, chopped
	A few mint leaves
1¼	cup ghee–oil, mixed
1	tsp oil
	Salt

Cover the dish with a tight-fitting lid. Cook for the first 2 minutes on high flame and then low for about 15 minutes till the rice is ready and steaming hot.

4. Serve: Take out in large chunks from the sides, without disturbing the layers. Serve steaming hot.

Dumpukht Biryani (Lucknow)

A slow-fire biryani, it is cooked with tomato puree as the base and scented traditionally with saffron and screwpine water. A gentle sprinkling of powdered nutmeg and mace further enhances the flavour.

Preparation time: 20–30 minutes
Marination time: 4–5 hours
Cooking time: 1 hour 10 minutes
Serves: 8–10

1	kg boneless mutton, cut into medium sized pieces

A:
10–12	green chillies, chopped
⅓	cup fresh green coriander, chopped
2	tsp red chilli powder
½	tsp turmeric powder
1	tsp garam masala
2	cups hung yoghurt, whisked
1	tbs raw green papaya paste (pulp and skin ground together)

4–5	tomatoes, chopped
500	gm long grain rice
4	medium onions, finely sliced
2	tsp ginger paste
2	tsp garlic paste
2	tbs muskmelon seeds } ground to a fine paste
2	tbs poppy seeds
½	tsp nutmeg, powdered
½	tsp mace, powdered
2	tbs ghee
½	tsp saffron, lightly roasted and crushed
2	tbs screwpine water
⅔	cup warm milk
60	gm oil
	Salt

1. Marinate the meat: Mix the mutton with all the ingredients at A and salt. Rub the mixture well into the meat. Leave it to marinate for 4–5 hours.

2 Prepare the tomato puree: Add ½ cup of water to the tomatoes and boil covered, till tender. When cool, strain to extract tomato puree.

3. Prepare the rice: Wash and soak the rice in water for about 20 minutes. Boil 2 litres of water with a little salt. Add rice and cook till for about 5–6 minutes till it is half done. Drain the water and transfer the rice to a wide pan and set aside.

4. Assemble and serve: Heat oil in a heavy-base pan, large enough to take the meat and rice. Fry the onions till golden brown. Add the ginger and garlic paste and fry for 1–2 minutes. Add the ground seeds and fry for another 1–2 minutes. Then add the tomato puree, a little salt, and cook till the oil starts to surface. Add the marinated meat to the cooked puree and mix. Arrange half the rice over the meat mixture. Sprinkle nutmeg and mace powder. Cover with balance rice and sprinkle with ghee. Mix together saffron, screwpine water and milk and sprinkle over the rice. Cover with a tight fitting lid. Now place the pan with the meat and rice over a girdle and cover tightly by or placing a heavy stone over the cover to prevent the steam from escaping. Cook for the first 1–2 minutes on high flame, then on dum, for about 50 minutes till the meat and rice are done. Serve hot.

Purani Dilli ki Ande aur Sabzion ki Biryani (Delhi)

Preparation time: 25 minutes
Cooking time: 30 minutes
Serves: 8

500	gm long grain rice
1	tbs garlic paste
1	tbs ginger juliennes
2	onions, chopped coarsely
250	gm shelled peas
2	potatoes, cut into medium sized pieces
3	carrots, cut into about ½ inch to ¾ inch pieces
½	tsp yellow chilli powder
3–4	green chillies, slit
4	green cardamoms, cracked open
4–5	cloves
1	1 inch cinnamon stick
2	bay leaves
2	tomatoes, chopped
4	hard-boiled eggs
½	tsp saffron, soaked in ⅓ cup milk
2	tbs melted ghee
50	gm oil
	Salt

This is an example of a biryani made like a pulao. A vegetable biryani, it is made with carrots, potatoes and peas and enriched with ghee and eggs.

1. Soak the rice: Wash and soak rice in liberal quantity of water for 15–20 minutes, then drain.

2. Cook the vegetables: Heat oil in a heavy bottomed pan. Add garlic paste followed in a few seconds by ginger juliennes. Add the chopped onions, followed in a few seconds by the chopped vegetables. After frying the vegetables for 2–3 minutes add the yellow chilli powder, green chillies, the whole spices and salt. Fry for 2–3 minutes and add the chopped tomatoes. Mix well and cook on medium flame for 2–3 minutes.

3. Assemble and serve: Add the previously soaked rice, mix and add hot water up to 1 inch over the surface of rice. Cook covered first on high flame for 1–2 minutes and then on medium-slow flame for about 2–3 minutes. Reduce flame to low. When the rice is more than half done, add the hard-boiled eggs, ghee, and saffron milk. Mix gently and reduce flame. Cook covered for about 10 minutes till the rice is done, yet each grain separate. Let the biryani rest, tightly covered, for 5 minutes. Serve hot.

Purani Dilli ki Gosht ki Biryani (Delhi)

This is a recipe from the Turkman Gate area of old Delhi. It is made with golden sella rice, a long grained variety of basmati rice, usesd in the making of biryanis.

Preparation time: 10 minutes
Soaking time: 2 hours
Cooking time: 1 hour 10 minutes
Serves: 8

1	kg mutton from the raan (leg) of a small goat, cut into medium sized pieces
2	onions, quartered
3	tsp garlic paste
1	tsp yellow chilli powder
500	gm golden sella rice, soaked in liberal quantity of water for 2 hours
5	cloves
5	green cardamoms, cracked open
1	1 inch cinnamon stick
1	cup yoghurt, whisked
1	tbs ginger juliennes
5–6	green chillies, slit
½	tsp saffron, crushed
1½	tbs kewra water (screwpine water)
	A pinch of saffron-coloured edible food colour
2	tbs ghee
60	gm ghee/oil
	Salt

1. Prepare the mutton: Wash the meat and put it in a colander for the water to drain. In a heavy bottomed pan, heat ghee or oil, whatever you may wish to use. Add the mutton, quartered onions, garlic paste, yellow chilli powder, and salt and fry covered for about 7–8 minutes on medium-slow flame. Add about 1½ glasses of water and cook covered on slow flame for about 20–25 minutes till the meat is about 90 percent cooked. There should be about ½ a cup of gravy left when the meat is 90 percent done.

2. Prepare the rice: Meanwhile, boil about 2 litres of water. Add cloves, cardamom, cinnamon, and salt. Once the water starts to boil, add the previously soaked rice and cook for 7–8 minutes till it is 80 percent done.

3. Assemble and serve: Mix yoghurt with ginger julienne, green chillies, saffron and a very small pinch of edible saffron coloured food colour. Spread the yoghurt over the meat. Do not mix with meat. Spread the par-boiled rice over the yoghurt, again without mixing. Sprinkle kewra water and 2 tbs ghee. Add a little hot water so as to reach 1 inch above the surface of rice. Cover tightly and cook on high flame for about 2 minutes and then on dum for about 20–30 minutes till both the meat and rice are done. Mix and serve hot.

Kofta Biryani (Delhi)

Kofta Biryani is a biryani of mince balls cooked in mutton stock and flavoured with saffron.

Preparation time: 30 minutes
Cooking time: 50 minutes
Serves: 4–6

300	gm mutton mince
250	gm long grain rice

A:
1	onion, finely chopped
2	tbs fresh green coriander, chopped
6–8	green chillies, finely chopped
½	tsp garam masala
1	tsp red chilli powder
2	heaped tbs roasted gram, without skin, powdered

B:
4	medium onions, finely sliced
1	bay leaf
6	cloves
4	green cardamoms
1	1 inch cinnamon stick

3 –3½	glasses mutton stock
½	tsp saffron
1	tbs ghee
	Oil to fry
	Salt

1. Prepare the mince mutton: Grind the minced mutton on a sil batta to make very fine mince.

2. Soak the rice: Wash and soak the rice in water for about 15 minutes. Drain and set aside.

3. Prepare the mince balls: Mix the mince with all the ingredients at A and salt. Take a heaped tablespoon and make it into a round ball about 2 inches by 2 inches in size. Repeat the procedure and make balls or koftas out of the remaining mince. Heat oil in a heavy bottomed pan. Fry the mince balls, a few at a time, to a rich golden brown. Remove and set aside.

4. Assemble and serve: Keep about 50 gm oil from the same oil in which the koftas were fried and remove the rest. Heat the oil and fry the onions till they turn pink. Then add the whole spices at B and fry till the onions are golden brown. Add rice and fry for 1–2 minutes. Add mutton stock, salt, ghee and saffron. The stock should come 1¼ inches over the surface of the rice. Once the liquid comes to a boil, cook covered on medium-slow flame for 7–8 minutes till the rice is two thirds done. At this stage, add the fried koftas and mix gently. Cover tightly and cook on dum for about 10 minutes till the rice is done. Serve hot.

Mutton Biryani (Delhi)

Though called a biryani, the process of cooking this dish is more pulao-like. Mutton and rice are not marinated but boiled and cooked in mutton stock on slow fire. Also, there is no use of saffron or screwpine water.

Preparation time: 15 minutes
Cooking time: 50 minutes
Serves: 8–10 minutes

1	kg mutton (a mix of medium sized pieces from the shoulder, a few mutton chops and a few marrow bones with meat on)

A:
2	medium sized onions, quartered
4	garlic cloves
1	bay leaf
4	green cardamoms, crushed open at the end
1	black cardamom, opened
1	1 inch cinnamon stick
1	tsp peppercorns

500	gm long grain rice
4	onions, finely sliced
½	tsp garam masala
½	tsp pepper powder
4	glasses mutton stock

B:
A few sprigs of fresh green coriander, chopped
A few mint leaves
2–3 green chillies, slit

1	heaped tbs ghee
½	cup oil
	Salt

1. Prepare mutton stock: Wash the mutton. Place the mutton in a pressure cooker with all the ingredients at A and 6 glasses of water. Pressure cook on high flame till it whistles once. Lower heat and cook for about 10–15 minutes till the meat is tender. Once the pressure subsides a little, open the pressure cooker. Strain to get a clear stock. Pick out the meat pieces and set aside.

2. Soak the rice: Simultaneously, wash and soak the rice in water for about 20 minutes. Drain and set aside.

3. Assemble and serve: In a heavy bottomed pan, heat the oil and fry the onions till they turn pale gold. Add garam masala, pepper powder, and the meat pieces and fry for 2–3 minutes. Add the rice and fry for another 1–2 minutes. Then add the mutton stock and all the ingredients at B, till the liquid is 1 inch over the surface of rice and meat. Cook tightly covered, first on high flame till the stock comes to a boil and then on dum for about 10–15 minutes till the rice is done with each grain separate. Serve hot.

Babu Shahi's Matka Peer Biryani (Delhi)

Near the old fort, not far from the Delhi Zoo, is the ancient shrine of a Muslim saint called Matka Peer. An old tree near the shrine is laden with matkas (clay pots) containing offerings by devotees of the saint. Near the shrine is the small restaurant of Babu Shahi, a frail ninety year old man, who looks like a saint himself. A gentle soul with a flowing white beard and proud bearing, he patiently spelled out this famed biryani recipe to me.

Preparation time: 10 minutes
Soaking time: 2 hours
Cooking time: 1 hour
Serves: 8

1	kg golden sela rice
1	kg mutton, a mix of medium sized mutton pieces from the leg of a small goat, a few chops and a few pieces from puth (the backbone)
1	tbs garlic paste
1	tbs ginger paste

A:
- 10 green cardamoms
- 10 cloves
- 2 1 inch cinnamon sticks
- ½ tsp peppercorns
- 2 black cardamoms
- 3–4 bay leaves
- 6 dry whole red chillies
- 1 tsp chilli powder

100+50 gm yoghurt, whisked
A pinch of yellow edible food colour
50 gm ghee
100 gm oil
Salt

1. Soak the rice: Wash and soak the rice in water for about 2 hours.

2. Prepare the mutton: Wash and place the meat in a colander for the water to drain out. Heat 100 gm oil in a heavy bottomed pan large enough to take both the meat and the rice. Add the garlic paste. Once it turns golden brown, add the meat, and all the ingredients at A and fry for about 5 minutes. Then add the 100 gm whisked yoghurt. Mix and stir continuously till the contents come to a boil and then cook for another 1–2 minutes thereafter. Add salt and continue cooking on medium slow flame for about 6–8 minutes till the spices blend and become homogeneous and the oil starts to surface. Add a little water (about 3 glasses) and cook covered till the meat is almost tender. Mix the yellow food colour with 50 gm whisked yoghurt and add to the meat. Mix and cook for a further 2 minutes. When done, the meat should have about 1 cup gravy left.

3. Prepare the rice: Heat about 4 litres of water with salt for the rice. Once the water starts boiling, add the previously soaked rice and cook for 7–8 minutes till it is three fourths done. Drain the water from the rice.

4. Assemble and serve: Spread the rice over the meat and cook tightly covered, for the first 2 minutes on high flame and then on low flame for about 10 minutes till the meat and rice are fully done. Take care that the rice doesn't get soggy and that each grain is separate. When done, pour the ghee over the rice. Take out the biryani from the sides in large chunks without mixing the meat and the rice. Serve hot.

Santare ki Biryani–I (Delhi)

A unique biryani made with oranges, this has a distinct edge as it is made not just with the juice but also with the rind of the fruit.

Preparation time: 10 minutes
Cooking time: 50 minutes
Serves: 8

500	gm long grain rice
2	oranges
1	kg mutton, cut into medium sized pieces
2	bay leaves
2	black cardamoms, crushed
2	1 inch cinnamon sticks
¼	tsp grated nutmeg
2	tbs ginger juice
½	tsp saffron, crushed and dissolved in 2 tbs water
½	cup ghee–oil, mixed
	Salt

Ingredients marked A: bay leaves, black cardamoms, cinnamon sticks, grated nutmeg.

1. Prepare the rice: Wash and soak rice in water for 15–20 minutes, then drain out the water. Boil 2 litres of water. Once the water starts to boil, add the rice with a little salt, and cook for about 5–6 minutes till it is half done. Drain and transfer the rice to a wide pan. Set it aside.

2. Prepare the orange juice: Squeeze the juice of two oranges. Remove the inner white thread-like part from the peel. Slice the peel of half an orange finely into medium sized pieces. Boil with just 1 cup water for about a minute. Drain the water and set aside.

3. Prepare the mutton: Wash and place the meat in a colander and let the water drain out completely. In a heavy pan, large enough to take the meat and rice, heat ghee–oil mix. Add all the ingredients at A along with the meat and fry for about 7–8 minutes. Add just sufficient water and cook till the meat is tender and somewhat dry. Add the orange juice and the rind and also the ginger juice to the meat. Cover with par-boiled rice. Sprinkle saffron dissolved in water over the rice.

4. Assemble and serve: Cover with a tight fitting lid and cook for the first 2 minutes on medium-high flame to heat up the dish and the initial steam to form and then on low flame for about 10–15 minutes till the rice is done. Serve hot.

Santare ki Biryani–II (Delhi)

Preparation time: 15–20 minutes
Cooking time: 1 hour
Serves: 8–10

1	kg mutton, cut into medium sized pieces
2	medium onions, roughly chopped
1	tbs ginger paste
1½	tsp peppercorns
4–5	medium-large onions, finely sliced, fried golden brown and crushed when cool
500	gm long grain rice
1	bay leaf
2–3	green cardamoms
¾	cup orange juice
1	tbs rind of orange, sliced into small pieces
½	tsp saffron, dissolved in half cup warm milk
2	tbs rose water
12–15	almonds, blanched and slivered
1	tbs ghee
½	cup oil
	Salt

In this biryani, the sharpness of the orange juice and the orange rind is tempered with rose water, saffron and slivers of almonds.

1. Cook the mutton: Wash and drain the mutton pieces of water. Heat the oil, add the mutton and fry for about 5–6 minutes, after which add onions, ginger paste, peppercorns, salt and fry for another 5 minutes. Add a little water and cook till the meat gets tender. Add the crushed onions and fry for another 1–2 minutes. When done, the meat should have a sufficient coating of gravy on it.

2. Prepare the rice: Wash and soak the rice for about 20 minutes. Boil about 2 litres of water with the bay leaf, 2–3 green cardamoms, and salt. When the water starts to boil, add the rice and cook for 7–8 minutes till it is three fourths done. Drain the water and transfer the rice to a wide dish.

3. Assemble and cook on dum: Smear a heavy bottomed pan with a little oil. Spread half of the rice on it. Place the cooked meat over the rice. Pour the orange juice over the meat and also sprinkle the orange rind. Cover it with the balance rice and sprinkle the saffron milk and rose water over the rice. Also add the slivered almonds and then dot it with ghee. Cover with a tight fitting lid and cook for the first 3 minutes on medium-high flame till the steam starts to form, then reduce the heat to low and cook on dum for about 10 minutes till the dish is steaming hot and rice done without getting mushy. Serve hot.

Kabab Biryani (Delhi)

This is an extraordinary biryani made with barbecued mutton brushed with butter, cream, saffron and beaten eggs. The most unusual feature of this biryani is the subtle tandoori flavour of the tender kabab fused with fragrant rice.

Preparation time: 15–20 minutes
Marination time: 3 hours
Cooking time: 1 hour
Serves: 8–10

1	kg boneless mutton, cut into medium sized pieces (about 1½"–2")

A:
2	medium onions, ground
1½	tsp ginger paste
1½	tsp garlic paste
1½	tsp freshly ground pepper powder
1	tbs raw green papaya paste (pulp and skin ground together)
	Juice of 2 limes

500	gm long grain rice

B (Mixed Together):
50	gm butter
2	tbs cream
½	tsp saffron, lighly roasted and crushed
2	eggs, beaten
½	tsp freshly ground pepper powder
1	tbs butter

½	tsp cassia buds powder
	A few mint leaves
	Oil
	Salt

1. Marinate the meat: Wash the meat and drain the water out. Mix the meat with all the ingredients at A together with 3 tbs oil and salt, and leave it to marinate for 3 hours.

2. Prepare the rice: Wash and soak rice in water for 20 minutes. Boil about 2 litres of water with salt. When the water starts to boil, add the rice and cook till tender. Put the rice in a colander and drain the water. Return rice immediately to the pan. Mix the beaten eggs with pepper and butter and add it to the rice, mixing gently. Cover and let the rice simmer on low heat for about 2 minutes.

3. Make the kabab: Pass a skewer(s) through the marinated meat pieces and barbeque over live charcoals of medium-low intensity. Baste with butter, cream and saffron mix as at B, while grilling the meat for a few minutes till tender and brown. Remove from skewers, cover and set aside.

4. Assemble and cook on dum: Take a heavy bottomed pan and place half the rice in the pan. Spread the grilled meat over it, sprinkle cassia buds powder and cover with the balance rice. Sprinkle a little water, then cover tightly and let the dish simmer on dum for about 5 minutes.

5. Garnish and serve: Gently take out the rice from the sides and serve hot in a largish platter, garnished with just a few mint leaves. Serve hot.

Moti Pulao (Delhi)

Preparation time: 10 minutes
Cooking time: 1 hour
Serves: 6

1	kg mutton bones (for stock only)

1	tsp peppercorns	
8–10	cloves	
2	bay leaves	A
1	1 inch cinnamon stick	
2	black cardamoms	
2	green cardamoms	

400	gm long grain rice
½	kg boneless mutton, finely minced

1	egg white, beaten	
1	tbs cornflour	
6–8	green chillies, finely chopped	
¼	cup fresh green coriander, chopped	B
½	tsp garam masala	

3–4	silver leaves (chandi ke warq) to coat the meatballs
2	medium onions, finely sliced

Moti Pulao is called so because the meatballs coated with the silver leaves glow like pearls in the rice. A refined and aromatic dish, it is gently flavoured with saffron and screwpine essence.

1. Prepare the stock: Place the mutton bones and the spices at A together with salt in a pressure cooker. To this, add 6 glasses of water and pressure cook it on high flame for 1–2 whistles and then cook it further on low flame for about 15 minutes. Remove from stove and when the pressure subsides a little, strain and keep aside the mutton stock.

2. Prepare the rice: While the stock is getting ready, wash and soak the rice in water for about 20 minutes. Then drain. Heat about 4–5 glasses of mutton stock. Once the stock comes to a boil, add the rice and 1 tsp oil. Cook for 6–7 minutes till the rice is two thirds done. Put the rice in a colander and drain the excess stock. Now transfer the rice to a wide pan. Reserve.

3. Fry the meatballs: Mix the mince with all the ingredients at B, and salt and make small marble sized balls. Heat the oil in a frying pan and deep fry the balls, a few at a time, till they turn golden brown. Remove and place them on an absorbent paper. Spread out the silver leaves on a piece of paper and roll over half of the fried mince balls to coat them well with the silver leaf.

4–5	cloves
1½	tsp ginger paste
1½	tsp garlic paste
1½	tsp red chilli powder
1	tbs musk and watermelon seeds, finely ground
1	cup yoghurt, whisked
½	tsp saffron
½	cup milk
1	tbs kewra (screwpine) water
1–2	silver leaves
3	tbs cream
1	tbs ghee
50	gm oil for frying
	Salt

4. Cook the meatballs: Heat oil and fry the onions till golden brown. Add the cloves, ginger and garlic paste and fry for a few seconds. Sprinkle a little water and add red chilli powder and the ground musk and watermelon seeds. Fry for just about a minute, and add yoghurt and mix, stirring continuously to avoid curdling till the contents come to a boil. Add salt and the fried meatballs uncoated with silver leaves. Add a little water and cook covered for about 5 minutes. When done there should be about 1 cup gravy left.

5. Assemble and serve: Take a heavy bottomed pan and smear it with oil. Arrange two thirds of the par-boiled rice in the pan followed by the mince balls with gravy over the rice. Cover the meatballs with the balance rice. Sprinkle saffron mixed with milk, kewra water, ghee and cream. Cover with a tight fitting lid and cook for the first 1–2 minutes on high flame and then on low flame for about 10 minutes till the rice is done. Take out the steaming hot pulao gently from the sides in large chunks without disturbing the layers. Garnish with silver coated meatballs and silver leaves.

Muthanjan Pulao (Delhi)

Muthanjan is a corruption of the Arabic word 'muttajjan', which means 'fried in a pan'. A highly celebrated pulao of the Mughal era, Muthanjan Pulao is made with mutton, sugar, butter, and nuts. Here kababs are made out of mutton mince and coated with gold leaves. This is one of the few pulaos that use gold and not silver leaves.

Preparation time: 45 minutes
Cooking time: 2 hours 15 minutes
Serves: 8–10

750	gm mutton, cut into medium pieces

A:
1	black cardamom
4	green cardamoms
5	cloves
1	tsp peppercorns
1	1 inch cinnamon stick
2	bay leaves
1	onion, quartered
3–4	cloves of garlic
2–3	mace flakes
1	small piece of nutmeg

1	tsp ghee
5	cloves
1	litre full cream milk
100	gm almonds, blanched, skin removed and ground
500	gm long grain rice

B:
2	medium sized onions, finely sliced
1	tbs chopped ginger
½	cup yoghurt, beaten
1	tsp coriander powder
1	tsp chilli powder
½	tsp garam masala

1. Prepare the mutton stock: Boil the meat with all the ingredients at A, salt and 5–5½ glasses of water for about 30 minutes till the meat is tender. Strain the meat pieces and keep the stock aside. When done, you should be left with about 4 glasses of clear mutton stock. Heat 1 tsp ghee, add 5 cloves, and fry till dark brown. Add the ghee and the cloves to the stock and cover.

2. Prepare the milk: Bring milk to a boil and continue boiling, stirring every now and then till the consistency of milk is reduced to ¼. Add the ground almonds, mix, and set aside.

3. Prepare the rice: Wash and soak rice in liberal quantity of water for about 20 minutes. Drain the water and set aside. Heat about 4 glasses of mutton stock. Add the rice, 1 tbs ghee and salt for rice. The level of stock should be 1 inch above the surface of rice. Adjust the level of stock accordingly. Cook first on medium-high flame and then on low flame for about 10 minutes till the rice is 80 percent done and liquids absorbed.

4. Prepare the mutton: Heat 50 gm ghee–oil. Add onions and fry till golden brown. Add the boiled mutton pieces with all the ingredients at B and salt. Sprinkle a little water now and then and fry till the meat is browned. Keep aside.

250	gm mutton mince
2	tbs split grams
1	tsp red chilli powder
2–3	green chillies, finely chopped
100	gm raisins
50	gm pistachios, unsalted
1	cup powdered sugar
	Juice of 2 limes
2	tbs milk
2–3	tbs kewra (screwpine) water
½	tsp saffron
	Few golden leaves (sone ke varq)
50	gm ghee–oil, mixed, for mutton
	Oil to fry
	Salt

5. Prepare the kababs: Boil the mince with very little water, split gram and salt till the mince is tender. Raise the heat so that all the water from the mince is dried then add red chilli powder and green chillies. To make the kababs, take about 1½ tsp of the mince and shape it into a sausage. Repeat the process for the rest of the mince. Heat oil. Deep fry the kababs, a few at a time, on medium flame till they are golden brown. When cool, wrap them with golden leaves. Set aside.

6. Assemble the dish: Take a heavy bottomed pan. Smear with oil. Arrange half of the cooked meat in it. Spread one third of the rice over the meat. Spread half of the thickened milk over the rice. Scatter half of the raisins and pistachios over the milk. Then sprinkle half of the sugar and lime juice. Cover with another third of rice. Spread the remaining milk over the rice and the remaining raisins and pistachios, sugar and lime juice. Cover with the rest of the rice. Sprinkle milk mixed with kewra water and saffron. Cover with a tight fitting lid and cook for the first 1–2 minutes on high flame and then cook on dum for about 20–25 minutes till the dish is steaming hot, the rice done and individual grains still separate.

7. Garnish and serve: Serve hot, garnished with gold leaf wrapped kababs.

Pork Chops Pulao (Delhi)

Pork was traditionally never used in the pulao as it was a Muslim innovation. However, with time, other variations on the meat started being used by the other communities to satisfy their palate. The dish acquires its own richness on account of pork being naturally rich in fat.

Preparation time: 10 minutes
Cooking time: 1 hour
Serves: 8

500	gm long grain rice
1	kg pork chops
1½	tsp ginger paste
1½	tsp garlic paste
2	bay leaves
3–4	cardamoms
2	1 inch cinnamon sticks
4–6	cloves
½	tsp caraway seeds
1	heaped tbs peppercorns
2–3	medium onions, finely sliced
½	tsp garam masala
1	tsp butter
1	cup oil
	Salt

(Ingredients from ginger paste to peppercorns marked as A)

1. Soak the rice: Wash and soak rice in water for 20 minutes.

2. Prepare the pork: Wash pork and drain the water out. Boil the chops in about 6–6½ glasses of water with all the ingredients at A and salt. Cook for about 30 minutes till the chops are almost tender. Strain to get clear meat stock and keep the pork chops aside.

3. Assemble and serve: Heat oil in a heavy base pan and fry the onions till golden brown. Add rice and fry for about 3–4 minutes, then add the pork chops and fry for another 2–3 minutes. Add meat stock, garam masala, a little salt and butter. The level of stock should be 1' over the surface of rice. Cover the pan with a tight fitting lid and cook for the first 1–2 minutes on high flame and then cook on dum for about 20–25 minutes till the rice is done with individual grains separate. Serve hot.

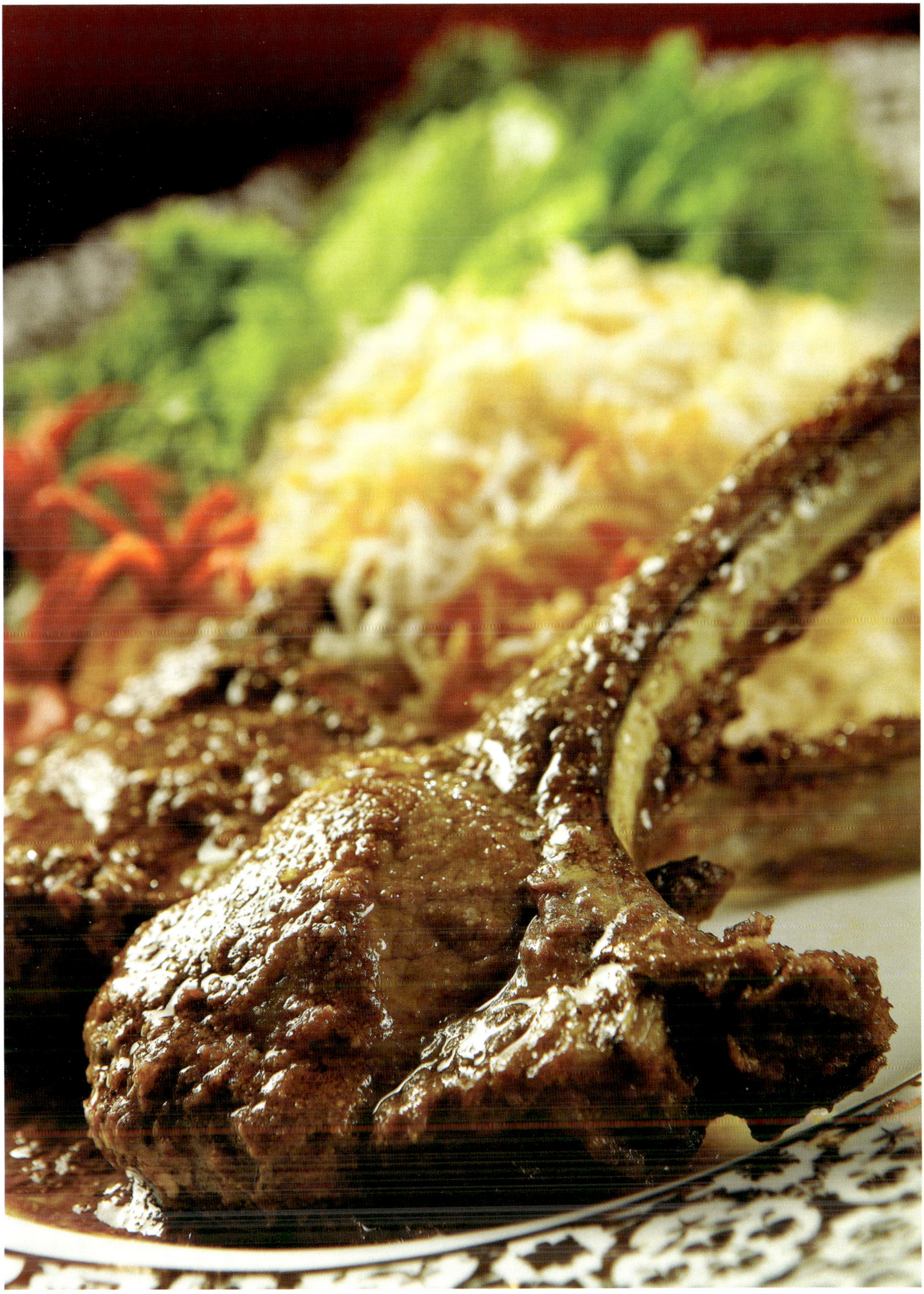

Baradar Oval Platter courtesy Good Earth

Maya's Biryani (Delhi)

This is a recipe given to me by Maya, a Nepali from Uttarakhand. She learnt cooking during her stints in various Delhi homes, honing her skills in the house of Neelam and Tarun Vadhera. Her biryani is much sought after and a rave with all who savour it.

Preparation time: 15 minutes
Cooking time: 1 hour
Serves: 8–10

1	kg mutton, from the leg or shoulder of a goat, cut into medium sized pieces
2–3	medium onions, finely sliced
1	tbs ginger paste
1	tbs garlic paste
1	tsp chilli powder
1	tsp garam masala
2	tbs coriander powder
¼	tsp nutmeg powder
1	cup yoghurt, whisked
600	gm rice
6	glasses mutton stock
	Juice of 3 limes
½	tsp saffron
2	tbs screwpine water
½	cup fresh green coriander, chopped
⅓	cup mint leaves
6–8	green chillies, chopped
60	gm ghee
	Oil for frying
	Salt

1. Cook the mutton: Wash and put the meat in a colander for the water to drain. Heat 2 tbs of oil in a heavy base pan. Add the onions and fry till golden brown. Add ginger and garlic paste and fry for a minute. Then add the meat and salt and fry for about 7–8 minutes till the moisture evaporates. Then add the chilli powder, garam masala, coriander powder, and nutmeg powder. Mix and fry for a few seconds. Add about 1½ glasses of water and cook covered on medium-slow flame for about 10 minutes till the meat is done. Now add 1 cup of yoghurt and mix and cook, stirring briskly till the contents come to a boil and oil starts to surface. Cook till just about ½ cup gravy is left.

2. Prepare the rice: Wash and soak the rice for 20 minutes. Boil rice in 6 glasses of mutton stock. Cook covered first on high flame and then on low flame. Cook for about 12–15 minutes till the rice is cooked fully and the stock absorbed. Cook the rice after the meat has been cooked, as we would need fresh and steaming hot rice to assemble the dish. Add ghee, juice of 3 limes, saffron, and 2 tbs of screwpine water and salt to the rice as soon as it is ready.

3. Heat the mutton: Sprinkle a little water and heat the meat and keep it ready heated up.

4. Assemble and serve: Place half the rice in a serving platter. Arrange the cooked meat over the rice. Mix the chopped coriander and mint with the balance rice and cover the meat with this balance rice. Serve hot immediately.

Mutton Pulao (Kashmir)

A typical Kashmiri pulao, this dish is lusciously flavoured with spices such as dry ginger (sonth), asafoetida and dry fruits such as walnut and almond, all of which are used in Kashmiri cooking.

Preparation time: 10 minutes
Cooking time: 50 minutes
Serves: 8

1	kg mutton (from the shoulder) cut into 2 inch pieces

A:
1	tsp dry ginger powder (sonth)
1	tsp aniseed powder
	A pinch of asafoetida

500	gm long grain rice

B:
2–3	bay leaves
2	1 inch cinnamon sticks
6	green cardamoms, crushed open at the end
3	black cardamoms, crushed open at the end
6–8	cloves
50	gm walnuts
50	gm almonds blanched and skin peeled
½	tsp saffron

4–5	glasses mutton stock
½	cup ghee–oil, mixed
	Salt

1. Prepare the mutton stock: Mix mutton with all the ingredients at A and salt. Boil the mutton in about 6 glasses of water and cook the meat for about 25–30 minutes till almost done. Strain to get clear mutton stock set aside the mutton pieces.

2. Soak the rice: Meanwhile, wash and soak rice in liberal quantity of water for 15–20 minutes, then drain and set aside.

3. Assemble and serve: Heat ghee–oil in a heavy bottomed pan, large enough to take the meat and the rice. Add all the ingredients at B along with the cooked mutton and fry for about 2–3 minutes. Add rice and fry for another 1–2 minutes. Add the mutton stock so that the level of stock is 1 inch above the surface of rice and meat. Once the liquids come to a boil, reduce heat and cook on dum covered for about 20 minutes till the rice is done and each grain separate. Serve hot.

Mutton Biryani (Kashmir)

Preparation time: 10 minutes
Marination time: ½ an hour
Cooking time: 1 hour
Serves: 8

1	kg mutton, cut into medium pieces
2	cups of yoghurt, whisked
⅓	tsp turmeric powder
2	tsp red chilli powder
¼	nutmeg, powdered
500	gm long grain rice
	Juice of half a lime
25	gm raisins
25	gm walnuts

A:
	Seeds of 2 black cardamoms
2	green cardamoms
2	1 inch cinnamon sticks
1	tsp caraway seeds
2	bay leaves
2	tsp coriander powder
1	tsp garam masala

½	tsp saffron, crushed and dissolved in half cup warm milk
	A few mint leaves
1	tbs ghee
½	cup ghee–oil (mixed)
	Salt

This dish is cooked with mutton and yoghurt on slow fire. Dry fruits like raisins and walnuts native to the beautiful state of Kashmir, add a distinctive flavour to it.

1. Marinate the meat: Mix the meat well with yoghurt, turmeric, red chilli powder, nutmeg powder and salt and marinate for ½ an hour.

2. Cook the rice: Wash and soak rice in water for 20 minutes, then drain out the water. Bring 2 litres of water to a boil along with salt and juice of lime. Add rice and cook for about 6–7 minutes till it is two thirds done. Drain the water and transfer the rice to a flat pan. Set aside.

3. Cook the meat: In a heavy base pan, heat the ghee–oil and add the raisins. When they swell up, remove and keep aside. Add walnuts and fry till golden. Remove and keep aside. Now, in the same ghee–oil add all the spices at A together with salt and after a few seconds add the marinated meat with the marinade. Stir and fry till the liquids are absorbed and the meat turns brown. Then add a little water and cook covered for about 25–30 minutes, stirring now and then, till the meat is tender. When done, the meat should have 1 cup of gravy left.

4. Assemble and serve: Spread the par-boiled rice over the meat. Sprinkle saffron milk, the fried raisins, walnuts, and mint over the rice. Dot it with ghee. Cover the dish with a tight fitting lid and cook for the first 1–2 minutes on moderate to high flame to heat up the dish, then on very slow flame or dum for 15–20 minutes till the dish is steaming hot and rice done. Serve hot.

Raw Mango Sq Platter and Raw Mango Bowl, 5" courtesy Good Earth

Vegetable Biryani (Lucknow)

Preparation time: 15–20 minutes
Cooking time: 50 minutes
Serves: 8

400	gm long grain rice
100	gm carrots, cut into 1½ inch finger sized pieces
100	gm French beans, cut into 1½ inch sized pieces
100	gm cauliflower, cut into medium sized florets
100	gm shelled peas
3–4	medium sized onions, finely sliced
1	tsp ginger paste
1	tsp garlic paste
6–7	green chillies, each sliced into 2
	A few sprigs of fresh green coriander, chopped
	A few mint leaves
100	gm yoghurt, whisked
⅓	tsp turmeric powder
½	tsp crushed dry red chillies
4	cardamoms
6–8	cloves
2	1 inch cinnamon sticks
2–3	mace flakes
½	tsp saffron, crushed and soaked in ½ cup warm milk
2	tbs screwpine (kewra) water
1	tbs melted ghee
100	gm ghee–oil, mixed
	Salt

(cardamoms, cloves, cinnamon sticks, mace flakes = A)

Despite the overarching dominance of Mughal culture over much of North India, especially Lucknow, it is home to some wonderful vegetable biryanis. Beans, peas, cauliflower, and carrots are cooked with rice to create this delicious dish.

1. Soak the rice: Wash and soak rice in water for about 20 minutes. Drain and set aside.

2. Cook the vegetables: Put together all the vegetables in a pan. Add about 1 cup water and lightly steam the vegetables for about 2 minutes. Take a heavy bottomed pan, large enough to take the rice and the vegetables, and heat the ghee–oil mix. Add the sliced onions and fry till golden brown. Add the ginger and garlic paste and fry for a few seconds. Then add the green chillies, coriander, and mint and fry for a few seconds. Next add the whipped yoghurt and bring to a boil, stirring continuously. Then add salt, turmeric, crushed red chillies, and the steamed vegetables. Mix and cook for 1–2 minutes.

3. Cook the rice: Boil 2 litres of water with the whole spices at A and a little salt. When the water starts boiling, add rice and cook for about 7–8 minutes till two thirds done. Drain the water from rice.

4. Assemble and serve: Spread the rice over the vegetables and sprinkle saffron milk and screwpine water over the rice. Also pour melted ghee. Now cover with a tight fitting lid and cook for the first 1–2 minutes on high flame and then on dum for about 10–15 minutes till the rice is steaming hot and done. Serve hot.

Aloo Aur Tamater Ka Pulao (Lucknow)

This is a vegetarian pulao of tomatoes and potatoes.

Preparation time: 15 minutes
Cooking time: 30 minutes
Serves: 6

300	gm long grain rice
½	tsp turmeric powder
1	tsp red chilli powder
1	tsp coriander powder
½	tsp cumin powder
½	tsp garam masala
2	large onions, sliced
2	large potatoes, cut into medium pieces
4	tomatoes, chopped
60	gm oil
	Salt

A = turmeric, red chilli, coriander, cumin, garam masala

1. Soak the rice: Wash and soak the rice in a liberal quantity of water for 20 minutes. Drain and set aside.

2. Prepare the spice paste: Mix together all the spices at A with a little salt and water and make a paste.

3. Assemble and serve: Heat oil in a heavy bottomed pan. Fry the onions till golden, add the potatoes and fry for about 5 minutes. Then add the tomatoes and fry for another 2–3 minutes. Add the paste to this and in a minute or so add the rice. Stir and fry for a minute, then add water about 1 inch above the surface of rice. Once the water starts to boil, cover and cook first on medium flame for about 2 minutes and then on low flame for about 10–12 minutes till the rice and potatoes are done. Serve hot.

Mewa Pulao (Delhi)

Mewa means dry fruit in Hindi. As the name suggests, Mewa Pulao has a wide assortment of nuts and dry fruits, which makes it somewhat sweet in taste. It is made with almonds, raisins, pistachios and walnuts, and flavoured with saffron and screwpine water. This pulao is particularly popular in Rajasthan.

Preparation time: 5–10 minutes
Cooking time: 20–25 minutes
Serves: 6–8

300	gm long grain rice

A:
25	gm almonds, soaked, peeled and slivered
25	gm raisins
25	gm pistachios, unsalted
50	gm walnuts

B (coarsely crushed):
8	green cardamoms
8	cloves
2	inch cinnamon sticks, broken in 2–3 pieces
¼	tsp nutmeg
2–3	flakes of mace

2	cups milk
150	gm sugar
2–3	drops of screwpine (kewra) essence mixed with a little water or 2–3 tbs of screw pine water
½	tsp saffron, crushed and dissolved in ⅓ cup milk
½	cup ghee

1. Soak the rice: Wash and soak rice in water for 20 minutes. Drain and set aside.

2. Assemble and serve: Heat ghee in a heavy bottomed pan. Lightly fry the ingredients at A. Remove and set aside. Now add all the ingredients at B. Fry for a few seconds. Add the rice and fry for 2 minutes. Add 2 cups milk and a little water so as to reach 1 inch above the surface of rice. Cook covered, first on high flame for about 1–2 minutes till the water comes to a boil and then on medium slow flame for about 20 minutes till the rice is done. At this stage, add sugar, dry fruit, saffron milk, and mix gently. Cook on low flame for 2–3 minutes. Serve hot.

Verona Water Goblet, Red courtesy Good Earth

Guchchi Biryani (Delhi)

This is a vegetable biryani made with morels or guchchis. Rice is cooked with guchchis and whisked yoghurt, and flavoured with saffron, screwpine water, mace, and cardamom powder.

Preparation time: 10–15 minutes
Cooking time: 45 minutes
Serves: 6

350	gm long grain rice
1	bay leaf
3–4	cloves
2–3	cardamoms
	Juice of half a lime
8–10	guchchis (morels)
½	tsp cumin seeds
2	onions, finely sliced
1	tsp yellow chilli powder
4–5	green chillies, chopped
	A few sprigs of fresh green coriander, chopped
	A few mint leaves
1	tsp cumin powder
2	tbs yoghurt, whisked
1	tbs cream
½	tsp saffron, crushed and dissolved in ½ cup milk
½	tsp mace and cardamom powder
1	tbs screwpine water
2	tbs cream
100	gm oil
	Salt

1. Prepare the rice: Wash and soak the rice in water for about 20 minutes, then drain. Boil about 1¾ litres of water with bay leaf, cloves, cardamom, juice of half a lime, and a little salt. When the water starts to boil, add the rice and cook for about 6–7 minutes till it is two thirds done. Drain and transfer the rice to a wide pan. Set it aside.

2. Prepare the guchchis: Wash and soak the guchchis in warm water for about 10 minutes. Then slice them vertically into 2 pieces and set it aside.

3. Cook the guchchis: Heat the oil and add cumin seeds followed in a few seconds by the sliced onions. When the onions turn golden brown, add the guchchis. Also add yellow chilli powder, green chillies, fresh coriander and mint, cumin powder and salt. Mix and sauté for 1–2 minutes. Add ½ cup water, then cover and cook on medium slow flame for about 4–5 minutes. Mix yoghurt and cream and add to the guchchis. Mix well and cover. Simmer for just about a minute.

4. Assemble and serve: Take a heavy bottomed pan and smear it with oil. Place half of the par–boiled rice in it. Arrange the guchchis over the rice and cover it with the balance rice. Sprinkle the saffron milk over the rice followed by mace and cardamom powder. Add 1 tbs screwpine water and dot with cream. Cover with a tight fitting lid. Cook over high flame for 1–2 minutes to heat up the dish and then on dum for about 10 minutes till the rice is done and steaming hot. Remove the cover and serve hot.

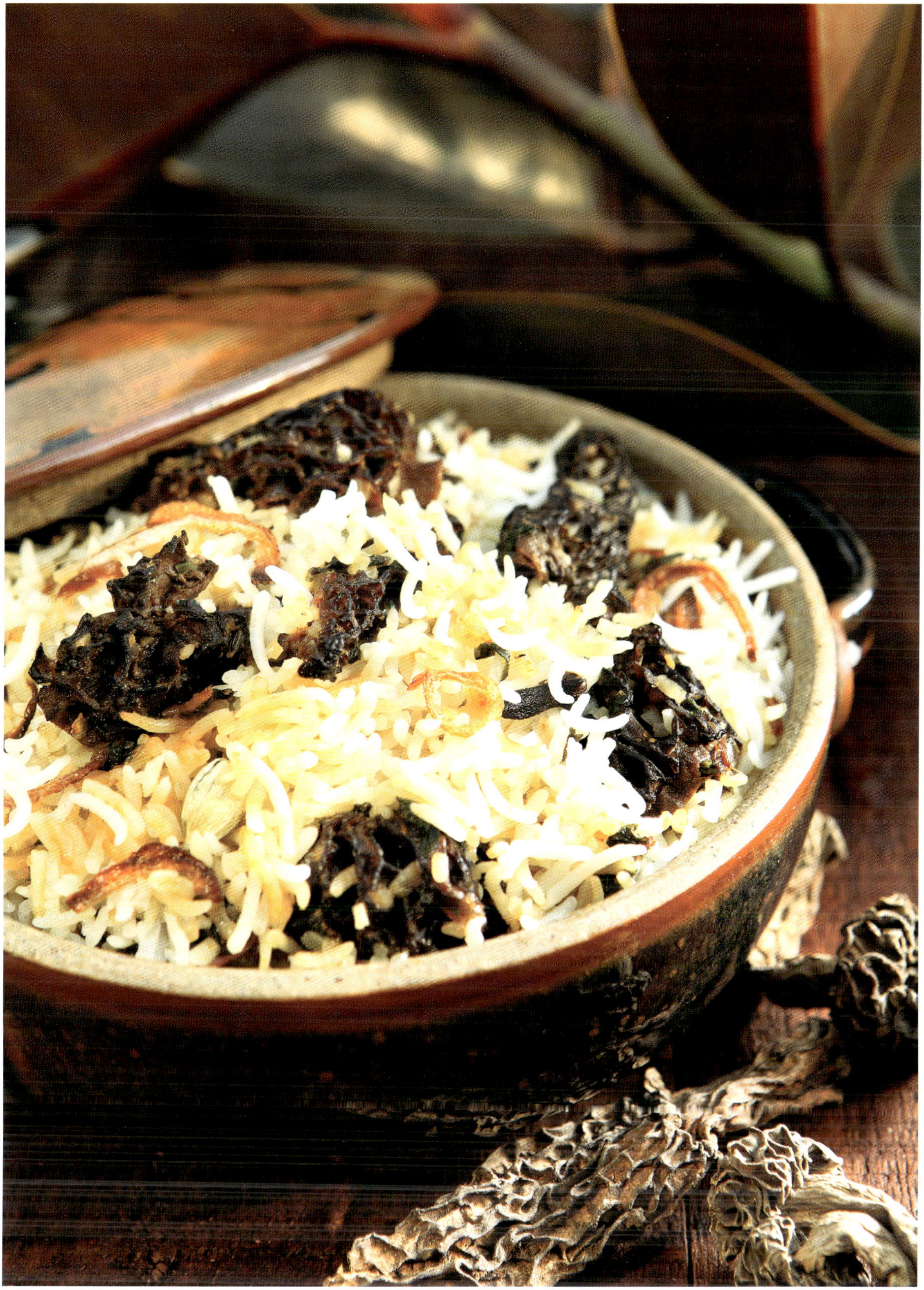

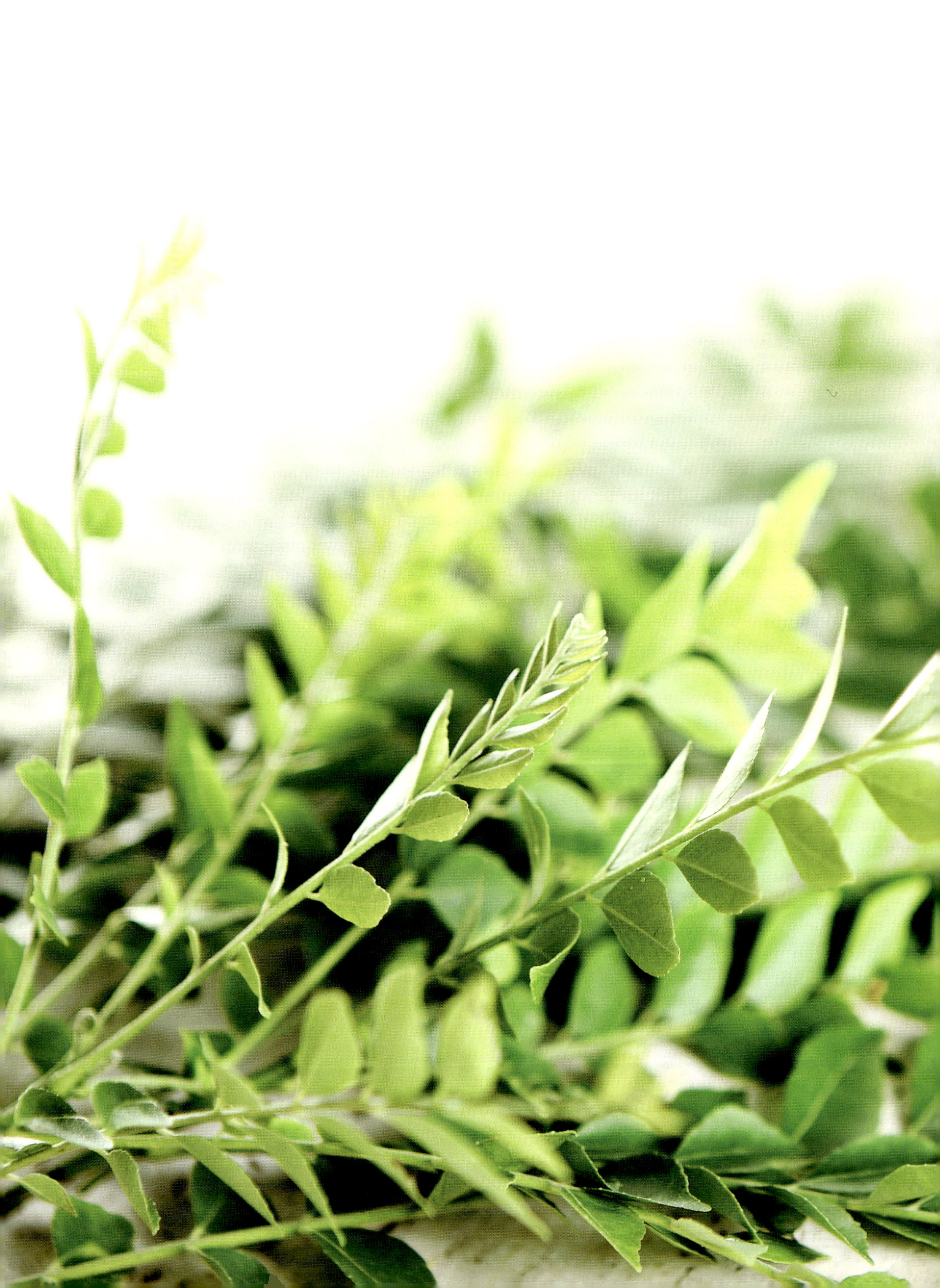

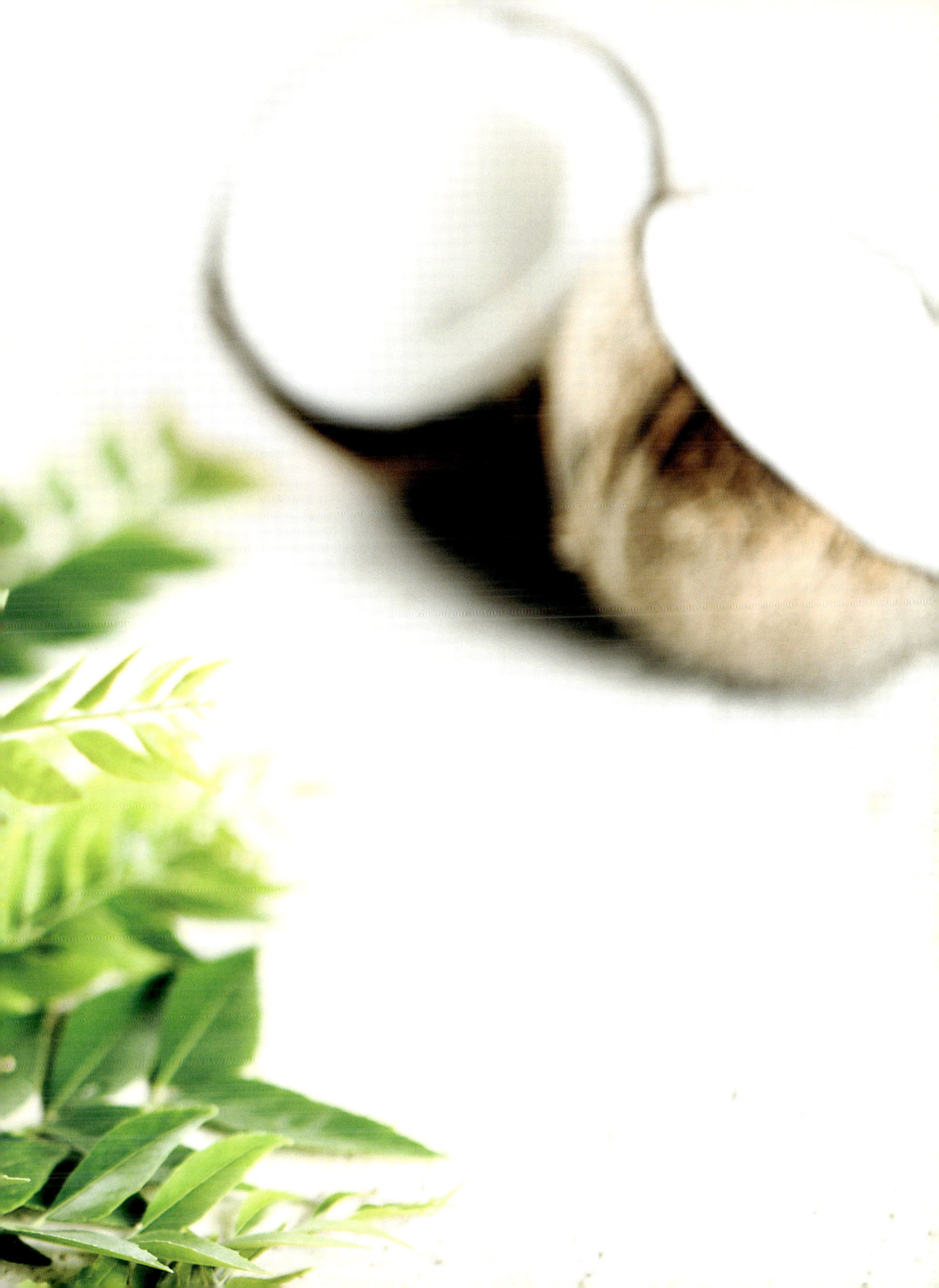

South

Biryanis, as I have said, are more common in south India than in the north. The south Indian being essentially a rice eater, and with the biryani being a meal by itself, is perhaps why it found ready and immediate acceptance. The biryanis in the south are, in particular, marked by their usage of spices although each state has its own distinct style.

Hyderabad, of course, has its own iconic status as the home of true blue-blooded biryanis. You will find many of these in this section, unusual and elegant dishes such as Dumpokht Biryani, Doodh ki Biryani, Korme ki biryani and Pasande ki Biryani. Pulaos are almost nonexistent in the south, except in Hyderabad. But, unlike the north, Hyderabad hardly has any vegetarian pulaos.

Though Tamil Nadu cannot boast of any significant Muslim dynasty, many of its towns are famous for their biryanis. The Chettinad region of Tamil Nadu has a rich tradition of fiery non-vegetarian dishes, biryani being one among them. Most of the smaller Tamil Nadu towns also have their signature biryanis. They include Dindigul, Salem, and Aambur biryanis among others. These biryanis may seem the same but possess subtle differences in aroma and flavour. And yes, each town is fiercely proud of its own biryani.

Karnataka too has a wide variety of biryanis that include not just the Coorgi Mutton biryani, but Bhatkali Biryani and the South Canara Chicken Biryani, but seafood varieties such as the Mangalore Fish Biryani and the Karwar Prawn Biryani. Only the Andhra region of Andhra Pradesh does not seem to have many biryanis.

Kerala is in a separate league. It boasts of several chicken, mutton and seafood biryanis. It has a strong Muslim presence and it's worth noting that Islam did not really come here from the north but largely, like Christianity, via the sea. In addition, God's own country, as it calls itself, has been blessed with the finest spices, including cardamom, cinnamon, cumin, cloves, peppercorns, etc. No other Indian state, except maybe to some extent Tamil Nadu and Karnataka, can claim this privilege. Because of this, unusual spices such as star anise have made their way into the biryanis of the state.

Gosht Biryani–I (Hyderabad)

One of the many iconic biryanis of Hyderabad cooked on dum (slow fire), both the mutton and rice are cooked together after the mutton is tenderized with papaya paste. The biryani is then enriched with cream and ghee.

Preparation time: 20 minutes
Marination time: 1 hour 10 minutes
Cooking time: 1 hour
Serves: 8

1	kg mutton, cut into medium pieces
1	tbs ginger paste
1	tbs garlic paste
1	tbs green papaya paste (pulp and skin ground together)
5–6	medium onions, sliced and fried golden brown

A {
1	tsp red chilli powder
½	tsp caraway seeds
4	green cardamoms
4–6	cloves
2	1 inch cinnamon sticks *ground*
2–3	mace flakes
8–10	green chillies
⅓	cup fresh green coriander, chopped
¼	cup mint leaves, chopped
1	cup hung yoghurt, beaten
	Juice of 2–3 limes

500	gm long grain rice

B {
½	tsp caraway seeds
2	green cardamoms
2–3	cloves
½	tsp saffron, dissolved in ½ cup warm milk
3	tbs ghee
3	tbs thick cream

4	hard-boiled eggs
	Oil
	Salt

1. Marinate the meat: Wash the meat pieces and put in a colander for the water to drain. Apply ginger, garlic, and the papaya paste to the meat pieces. After 10 minutes, lightly beat the mutton pieces all over with a mallet. Then add half of the fried onions and all the ingredients at A to the meat. Mix and marinate for 1 hour.

2. Prepare the rice: Wash and soak rice in water for 20 minutes and then drain. Bring 2 litres of water to a boil and add drained rice along with the spices at B and a little salt. When the rice is about 20 percent done, remove from flame and drain the water. Transfer the rice to a wide dish. Stir with a fork to separate the grains.

3. Assemble and serve: Take a heavy bottomed pan. Heat 4 tbs oil and add the marinated meat. Cover with par-boiled rice. Spread the balance of fried onions over the rice. Sprinkle saffron milk. Dot with ghee and cream. Also sprinkle a little water. Cover with a tight fitting lid and cook for the first about 1–2 minutes on medium-high flame to allow the initial steam to form and then on dum (a very low flame) for about 40 minutes till the dish is steaming hot and meat and rice done. Serve hot garnished with hard-boiled eggs halved.

Bater ki Biryani (Hyderabad)

Game, whether of animals or birds, was vastly popular before Independence, especially with the Indian royalty and the aristocracy. But thereafter their indiscriminate slaughter and the near disappearance of several species led to a total ban of hunting. The policy has worked and there has been an explosion in the population of several game birds and animals. The quail, commonly known as bater, is one such bird. Simultaneously, quail farming also picked up through Japanese technology. As a result, biryani of quails is an exotic and much sought after dish.

Preparation time: 15 minutes
Marination time: Half an hour
Cooking time: 1 hour
Serves: 8

8	quails (bater), dressed
1	tbs ginger juice
1	tsp garlic, ground
2	tbs red chilli powder
1/3	tsp turmeric powder
500	gm long grain rice
2	bay leaves
4	cloves
2	green cardamoms
1	1 inch cinnamon stick
5	medium onions, finely sliced
1	cup yoghurt, beaten well
1	tsp garam masala
	Juice of 2 two limes
1/2	tsp saffron, mixed in ½ cup warm milk

1. Marinate the quails: Wash the quails and dry completely. Apply ginger juice, garlic, red chilli powder, turmeric powder, and salt. Mix well and leave for half an hour.

2. Prepare the rice: Soak rice in water for about 20 minutes. Drain. Boil with about 2 litres of water with bay leaves, cloves, cardamom, and cinnamon. Once the water comes to a boil, add rice with one tsp oil and salt and cook for about 6–7 minutes till two thirds done. Drain the water and transfer the rice to a wide dish. Run the fork through it to separate the grains.

3. Fry the onions: Heat oil in a heavy bottomed pan. Fry the onions till golden brown. Remove. Crush two thirds of the onions, when cool. Set aside. Reserve the remaining onions.

	A few sprigs of fresh green coriander, chopped
	A few mint leaves
2	tbs ghee
	Oil
	Salt

4. Cook the quails: Leave a little less than ½ cup oil in which the onions were fried and remove the rest. Heat the oil and add the marinated quails. Fry till the water dries up and the quails are somewhat browned. Add the beaten yoghurt and keep stirring to prevent it from curdling. After it comes to a boil, cook further for about 5 minutes. Add a little water and cook till the quails are tender. Add the crushed onions, garam masala, and juice of one lime and cook further for 1–2 minutes. When done, the quails should have about one cup gravy left.

5. Assemble and serve: Now spread the par-boiled rice over the quails. Squeeze the juice of lime over the rice. Sprinkle the saffron milk. Also sprinkle coriander and mint. Dot the rice with ghee. Cover with a tight fitting lid. Cook first for about 2 minutes on moderate to high flame. Then cook on low flame for about 15 minutes till the rice is steaming hot and done. Serve hot.

Rajah Place Setting courtesy Good Earth

Murgh Ki Biryani (Hyderabad)

Hyderabad has many fine biryanis. This one is made with chicken and is flavoured with fresh coconut, a distinct South Indian influence.

Preparation time: 20 minutes
Cooking time: 50 minutes
Serves: 8–10

1	chicken, cut in to 10–12 pieces
1	fresh coconut
1	tbs ginger paste
1	tbs garlic paste
1	tbs green chilli paste
2	onions finely sliced, fried golden brown and crushed when cool
½	tsp garam masala
½	cup yoghurt, whisked
6–10	cashew nuts } *ground to a*
1	tbs poppy seeds } *fine paste*
	Juice of 2 limes
500	gm long grain rice

1. Wash the chicken: Wash and drain the chicken of water.

2. Prepare coconut milk: Grate the coconut and add 1½ cups of warm water. Churn it in a blender. Add a little water and squeeze to extract about 1½ glasses of coconut milk. Set aside.

3. Cook the chicken: Heat the ghee and add ginger and garlic paste. Fry for just about 1 minute, then add the green chilli paste, and fry for another minute. Now add salt and the chicken pieces and fry for 5–6 minutes. Add about 1 cup water and cook on moderate-low flame for about 7–8 minutes till the chicken is about two thirds done. At this stage, add the crushed onions and the garam masala. Cook for another 2 minutes. Mix together the coconut milk, yoghurt, the ground cashew nuts, and poppy seeds. Add to the chicken and bring it to a boil. Simmer for about 5–10 minutes. Squeeze the juice of lime and mix. When done, the chicken should have about 1 cup gravy left.

3	green cardamoms	
2	bay leaves	
4	cloves	
1	1 inch cinnamon stick	
½	tsp caraway seeds	A
½	cup milk	
	Juice of 1 lime	
3	tbs cream	

	A few mint leaves
½	cup ghee
2	tbs ghee
1	tsp oil
	Salt

4. Prepare the rice: Soak the rice in water for 20 minutes, then drain. Boil about 2 litres of water and add all the ingredients at A along with 1 tbs oil and salt and cook for about 6–7 minutes till the rice is two thirds done. Drain the excess water and transfer the rice to a wide dish.

5. Assemble and serve: Take a heavy bottomed pan and smear it with oil. Place half of the par-boiled rice in it. Place the chicken over it. Cover it with the balance rice and sprinkle milk over it. Now squeeze the juice of a lime, dot the rice with ghee and cream, and sprinkle the mint leaves. Cover with a tight fitting lid. Cook for the first 2 minutes on moderate to high flame to heat up the dish. Then lower the flame and cook further for another 10 minutes till the dish is steaming hot and rice done. Serve hot.

Fenugreek and Chicken Biryani (Hyderabad)

Preparation time: 15 minutes
Cooking time: 50 minutes
Serves: 8

1	chicken, cut into medium sized boneless pieces
400	gm long grain rice
½	tsp caraway seeds
2	bay leaves
	Juice of half a lime
2	medium onions, sliced
1½	tsp ginger paste
1½	tsp garlic paste
1	cup fresh fenugreek leaves, plucked, washed and chopped coarsely
⅓	tsp turmeric powder
1½	tsp red chilli powder
1	tsp garam masala
2	tomatoes, chopped
½	cup milk
1	tbs butter
1	tbs cream
2	hard-boiled eggs, sliced
½	cup oil
	Salt

This biryani from Hyderabad is made with boneless chicken and garnished with hard-boiled eggs. However, what sets it apart is fresh fenugreek, which gives the dish an irresistibly unique flavour.

1. Wash the chicken: Wash the chicken pieces and put them in a colander for the water to drain.

2. Prepare the rice: Wash and soak the rice for about 20 minutes, then drain out the water. Boil 1½ litres of water along with caraway seeds, bay leaves, juice of lime, and salt. When the water starts boiling, add rice and cook till for 6–7 minutes till it is two thirds done. Drain out the water and transfer the rice to a flattish pan.

3. Cook the chicken: Heat the oil and fry the onions till golden brown. Add the ginger and garlic paste, followed in a few seconds by 2 tbs of fresh fenugreek leaves. After about 20 seconds add salt, turmeric, red chilli powder, and ½ tsp garam masala. In a few seconds, sprinkle a little water and add the chopped tomatoes. Cook for 2–3 minutes. Then add the chicken pieces and fry for about 5 minutes. Add a little water and cook the chicken for 7–8 minutes till it is half done. At this stage, leave about 2 tbs fenugreek leaves for later use and add the rest of it to the chicken. Mix and cook covered till the chicken is tender. When done there should be about ¾ cup gravy left.

4. Assemble and serve: Take a heavy bottomed pan and smear it with oil. Spread two thirds of the par-boiled rice in the pan. Place the chicken with the gravy over the rice. Spread the balance fenugreek over the chicken and cover with the balance rice. Sprinkle milk and the balance garam masala. Now dot with butter and fresh cream and cover with a tight fitting lid. Cook for the first 1–2 minutes over medium-high flame to heat the dish, then on low flame for about 15–20 minutes till the rice is steaming hot. Garnish with hard-boiled eggs and serve hot.

Gosht Biryani–II (Hyderabad)

A rich Hyderabadi biryani, this is made with mutton and flavoured with chironji, an exotic seed, poppy seeds and a liberal quantity of cashew nuts. The chironji, also called the buchanania or cuddapah almond, is locally available and appears to be a cross between a lentil and a nut. It is used in rare dishes in Hyderabad.

Preparation time: 20 minutes
Cooking time: 1 hour
Serves: 8–10

1	kg mutton, cut into medium sized pieces
1	tbs ginger paste
1	tbs garlic paste
500	gm long grain rice
5	medium onions, finely sliced

A:
1	bay leaf
6–8	cloves
1	1 inch cinnamon stick

B — *lightly dry roasted and ground to a fine paste*:
2	tbs *chironji*
1	tbs poppy seeds (*khus khus*)
10–12	cashew nuts
½	tsp caraway seeds
½	tsp peppercorns

½	tsp turmeric powder
1½	tsp red chilli powder
1½	cups yoghurt, whisked

C:
5–6	green chillies, chopped
	A few sprigs of fresh green coriander, chopped
	A few mint leaves

1. Prepare the mutton: Wash the mutton and drain the water out. Mix it well with ginger and garlic paste and salt, then set it aside.

2. Prepare the rice: Wash and soak the rice in a liberal quantity of water for 20 minutes, then drain. Boil about 2 litres of water with a little salt. Add the rice and cook for about 5–6 minutes till it is half done. Drain out the water and transfer the rice to a flattish pan. Set it aside.

3. Fry the onions: Heat the ghee–oil mixture. Fry the onions till golden brown. Remove and set aside. Crush when cool.

4. Cook the mutton: Take half of the ghee–oil in which the onions were fried. Add the spices at A followed by the paste at B. After a few seconds add the mutton, turmeric, and red chilli powder and fry for about 5 minutes. Add half of the crushed onions and mix. Next add the yoghurt and the greens at C. Mix and cook, stirring all the time till the contents come to a boil. Cover and simmer till the oil surfaces. Add a little water and cook till the meat is tender. Add the juice of 1 lime to the meat. When done the meat should have 1 cup gravy left.

	Juice of 2 limes
½	tsp garam masala
½	tsp saffron
1	cup ghee–oil, mixed
	Salt

5. Assemble and serve: Take a heavy bottomed pan and smear it with the balance of ghee–oil mix left. Place two thirds of the par-boiled rice. Now spread the cooked meat over the rice. Mix the garam masala, saffron, and the remaining crushed onions with the juice of 1 lime. Spread this mixture over the meat and cover it with the balance rice. Sprinkle a little water. Cover with a tight fitting lid and cook for the first 1–2 minutes on high flame, then on dum for about 15 minutes till the rice is done and each grain separate. Serve hot.

Dumpokht Biryani (Hyderabad)

This dish is a fine demonstration of the art of slow fire cooking, the highlight being that although raw mutton and rice are cooked together yet at the end, each grain of rice is separate. While the process is known as dumpukht in Lucknow, it is called dumpokht in Hyderabad.

Preparation time: 20–25 minutes
Marination time: 2 hours
Cooking time: 30 minutes
Serves: 8–10

1	kg mutton (cut into medium sized pieces)

A (ground):
250	gm onions, ground
1½	tbs ginger paste
1	tbs skin and pulp of raw green papaya, ground
½	tsp saffron
1	tbs peppercorns
1	tsp cumin seeds
6–8	cloves
	Seeds of 2 black cardamoms

4	cups yoghurt, whisked
500	gm long grain rice
½	cup milk
½	cup ghee–oil, mixed
2	tbs ghee
	Salt

1. Marinate the meat: Wash and drain the mutton of all water. Mix all the ingredients at A and half the quantity of yoghurt and rub the mixture well into the meat. Marinate for at least a couple of hours.

2. Soak the rice: Wash and soak rice in liberal quantity of water for 10–15 minutes. Drain and set aside.

3. Assemble and serve: Take a heavy bottomed pan and place the meat in it. Separately heat the ghee–oil mixture and pour it over the meat. Mix rice with the balance of yoghurt and 1 glass of water and a little salt. Cover the meat with rice and add a little water so that the level of water is 1½ inches over the surface of rice. Cover the pan with a tight fitting lid and seal it with dough or place a heavy stone over the lid to prevent the steam from escaping. Cook first on high heat for about 5 minutes and then on dum i.e. low flame, for about 20 minutes. When the dish is almost done, uncover and sprinkle ghee and milk over the rice. Cover again and cook further on dum till the meat is tender and rice done. The meat should be tender and each grain of rice, though fully cooked, should stand out separately. Serve steaming hot.

Masoor Dal Mutton Biryani (Hyderabad)

Preparation time: 20 minutes
Marination time: 1 hour
Cooking time: 1 hour
Serves: 8

750	gm mutton, cut into medium pieces

2	inch ginger piece	
1	pod garlic	ground
10–12	green chillies	to a fine
1	tsp cumin seeds	paste
1	tbs coriander seeds	

½	tsp turmeric powder
5	onions, finely sliced
100	gm red lentils (masoor dal)
¼	tsp turmeric
400	gm rice
½	tsp caraway seeds
½	tsp oil
1	1 inch cinnamon stick
4	cardamoms
6	cloves
2	tsp melted ghee
	A dash of garam masala
	Juice of 2 limes
	Oil for frying
	Salt

Unlike the masoor dal biryani from Tamil Nadu, this one is a non-vegetarian dish made with mutton. It uses only green chillies and is somewhat milder in taste. The fusion of the dal, mutton and rice makes it very nutritious.

1. Marinate the mutton: Rub the mutton with two thirds of the ground masala, salt and turmeric powder, and leave it for an hour.

2. Fry the onions: Heat oil and fry the onions till golden brown. Remove and set aside. When cool, crush two thirds of the onions. Reserve the balance for garnish.

3. Prepare the rice and the lentils: Boil the lentils with salt and turmeric till almost done. Drain any excess water and set aside. Now boil the rice with a little salt, caraway seeds, and ½ tsp oil for about 7–8 minutes till it is three fourth done. Drain any excess water. Transfer to a flattish pan.

4. Cook the mutton: Take half a cup of oil from the oil in which onions were fried and heat it. Add cinnamon, cardamom and cloves. Put in the balance of the ground masala and after 1–2 minutes add the crushed onions. Then add the mutton and fry for 7–8 minutes. Add a little water and cook for another 15–20 minutes till tender. When done, the mutton should be left with a little gravy.

5. Assemble and serve: Take a heavy bottomed pan and smear it with ghee. Spread the rice in the pan in a layer. Place the cooked mutton with the gravy over it. Cover the mutton with the boiled lentils. Put the ghee over the lentils. Sprinkle the garam masala and squeeze the juice of lime. Cover and cook on dum for a 3–4 minutes till steam forms. Serve hot garnished with fried onions.

Doodh ki Biryani (Hyderabad)

Doodh ki Biryani, as the name suggests, is cooked in milk. Another unique feature of this recipe is that the herbs and spices are not directly added to the dish but introduced in potlis (small bundles of muslin cloth) to impart a subtle flavour. This is one of the more celebrated of the Hyderabadi biryanis: light, not too spicy and fit for all seasons.

Preparation time: 20 minutes
Cooking time: 1 hour 10 minutes
Serves: 8–10

1	kg mutton (inclusive of chops, marrow bones and medium sized meat pieces)	
4	onions, sliced	
75	gm ginger, coarsely chopped	A
60	gm garlic, coarsely chopped	
50	gm green chillies, chopped	
1	cup fresh green coriander, chopped	B
½	cup mint leaves	
1	tsp caraway seeds	
2	1 inch cinnamon sticks	
6	green cardamoms	
2	large black cardamoms	C
6	cloves	
1	small piece of nutmeg	
2–3	mace flakes	
5	glasses milk	
1	glass water	
500	gm rice	
3	tbs thick cream	
3	tbs ghee	
	Salt	

1. Cook the mutton: Wash and drain the water out from the mutton. Coarsely crush the ingredients at A, B, and C in three separate lots and tie them in three separate bundles of muslin cloth. Cook the meat in 5 glasses of milk and 1 glass of water with all the three bundles. Keep stirring frequently. A minute after the liquid starts to boil, add salt and continue stirring for 3–4 minutes. Then cook covered on medium-slow flame, stirring now and then till the meat is tender. Squeeze out the liquids from the bundles into the meat and remove the bundles. When done, the dish should have about 1½ glasses of liquid left. Take out three fourths of a glass for later use.

2. Prepare the rice: Soak the rice for about 20 minutes. Drain it. Boil 2 litres of water with a little salt. Once the water starts to boil, add the rice and cook for 5–6 minutes till the rice is half done. Drain and transfer to a flat dish.

3. Assemble and serve: Take a heavy bottomed pan, smear it with ghee. Place a little more than half the par-boiled rice in the pan. Take out the cooked meat and place it over the rice. Spread the liquid in the meat over it. Cover with the balance rice and sprinkle the three fourth glass reserved liquid from the meat over the rice. Dot with ghee and cream. Cover tightly and place a heavy stone on the dish to prevent the steam from escaping. Cook for the first 2 minutes on high flame to heat the dish and then on medium-slow flame for about 10–15 minutes till the rice is cooked. Serve hot.

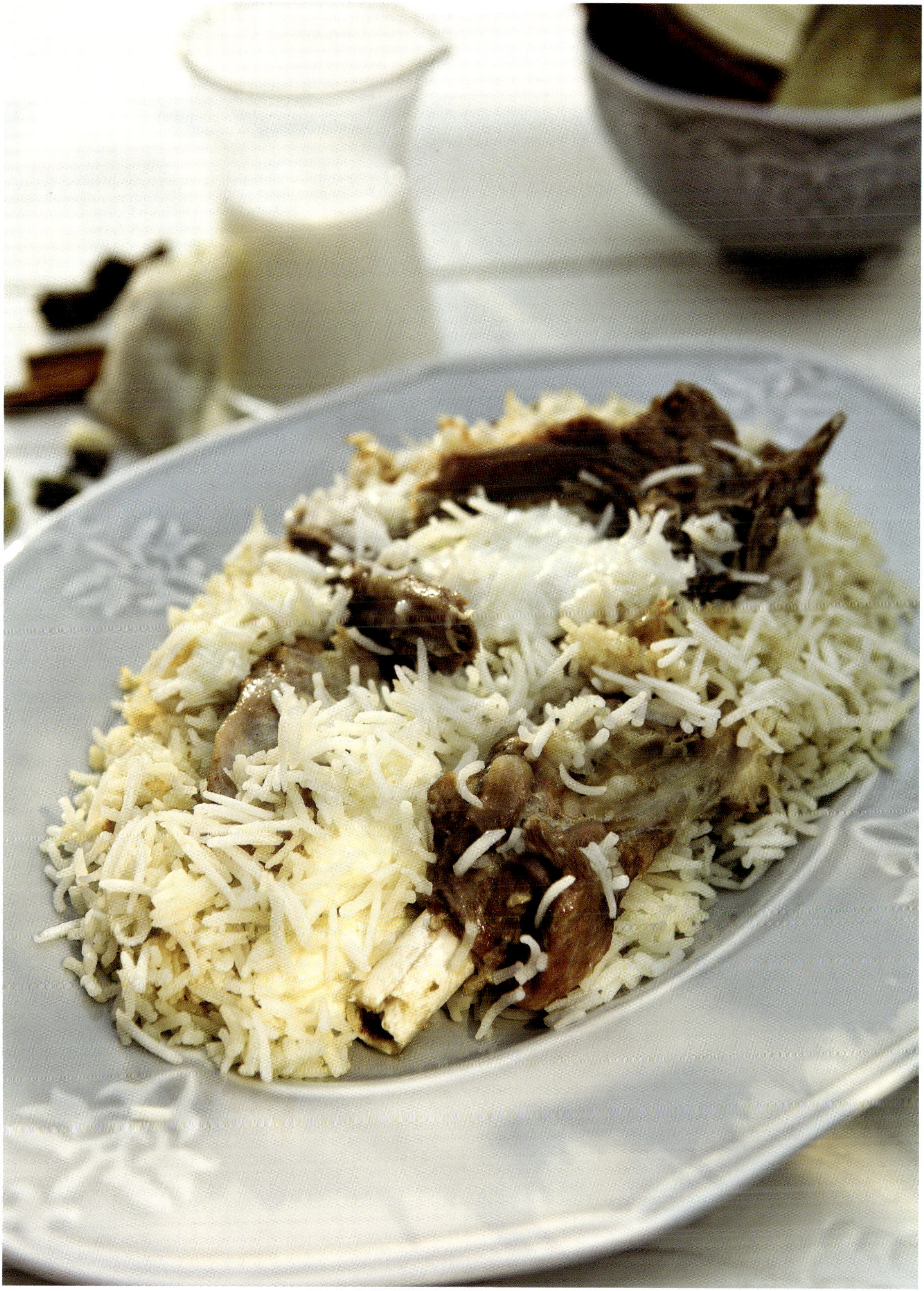

Kairi Ki Biryani (Hyderabad)

Hyderabadi cuisine is famous for the gamut of souring agents used in its food such as lemon, tamarind, yoghurt, tomato, vinegar, sour citrus fruits, roselle leaves, star fruit, etc. The green mango, locally called kairi, is one of them. It is much sought after during the summer season and various dishes, including the biryani, is cooked with them. Somewhat mildly soured, this particular biryani is an excellent summer dish.

Preparation time: 15 minutes
Cooking time: 1 hour
Serves: 6–8

750	gm mutton from shoulder, cut into medium pieces
4	onions, finely sliced
¼	cup curry leaves
1½	tsp ginger, ground
1½	tsp garlic, crushed
⅓	tsp turmeric powder
1½	tsp red chilli powder
1	tsp coriander powder
2	onions, ground
1	tsp garam masala
3–4	raw green mangoes (kairi) weighing about 350 gm, skinned and grated and stone discarded
1	tsp sugar
500	gm long grain rice
½	tsp caraway seeds
2	bay leaves
7–8	green chillies, chopped
	A few mint leaves
½	cup milk
1	tbs ghee
	Oil for frying
	Salt

1. Prepare the meat: Wash the meat in a colander and leave it for a few minutes so that the water is well drained.

2. Cook the meat: Heat oil in a heavy base pan, large enough to take the meat and rice, and fry the onions till golden brown. Remove and allow it to cool. Crush the onions with hand and set aside. Leave about 60 gm of oil and take out the rest. Now heat the oil again and add the curry leaves. After a few seconds, add the ginger paste and crushed garlic. Fry for just about a minute, then add the meat pieces along with turmeric powder, red chilli powder, coriander powder, and salt. Fry for about 8–10 minutes till the meat is browned. Add the ground onions and fry for another 3 minutes. Add a little water and cook for another 15–20 minutes till the meat is tender. Add the crushed onions, garam masala, grated mango and sugar, and cook further for 4–5 minutes. When done, the meat should have about 1 cup of gravy left.

3. Prepare the rice: Wash and soak rice in water for about 20 minutes, then drain. Boil about 2 litres of water with caraway seeds, bay leaves, oil, and salt. When the water starts to boil, add rice and cook for 7–8 minutes till it is two thirds done. Drain the water from the rice.

4. Assemble and serve: Now spread the rice over the meat. Sprinkle the chopped green chillies, mint leaves, and milk over the rice. Dot with ghee. Cover with a tight fitting lid. Cook for the first about 2 minutes on medium-high flame to heat up the dish. Then cook on slow flame for about 15–20 minutes till the rice is done and steaming hot. Serve hot.

Korme ki Biryani (Hyderabad)

Preparation time: 15–20 minutes
Cooking time: 1 hour
Serves: 8–10

1	kg mutton, cut into medium pieces
4	medium sized potatoes, cut in 4 pieces each
4	onions, finely sliced
½	tsp caraway seeds
4	green cardamoms
1	1 inch cinnamon stick
1½	tsp ginger paste
1½	tsp garlic paste
⅓	tsp turmeric powder
2	tsp red chilli powder
2	cups yoghurt, whisked

1	tbs musk and watermelon seeds	A *ground to a fine paste*
8–10	cashew nuts	
1	tbs desiccated coconut	

A few sprigs of fresh green coriander, chopped
A few mint leaves
2–3 green chillies, chopped
½ tsp saffron, lightly roasted, crushed and dissolved in half cup warm milk
500 gm long grain rice

Korma is essentially a yoghurt-based curry to which muskmelon seeds, watermelon seeds and cashew nuts have been added. It is to this curry that rice is added to make an exquisite biryani.

1. Prepare the mutton: Wash the mutton pieces and put them in a colander for the water to drain. Heat oil in a heavy bottomed pan, which should be large enough to take the meat and rice. Fry the potatoes till pale gold. Remove and set aside. In the same oil, fry the onions till golden brown. Remove and set aside and crush when cool. Reserve. Leave about ½ cup oil and remove the rest. Heat the oil again and add caraway seeds, cardamom, and cinnamon and in a few seconds, the ginger and garlic paste. After just about half a minute add salt, turmeric, and red chilli powder and sprinkle a little water. Add the meat pieces and fry for about 5 minutes. Add yoghurt and keep stirring till it comes to a boil. Then add the ground paste at A. Fry for a minute. Add a little water and cook covered on medium-slow flame for about 15–20 minutes. When the meat is three fourths done, add the fried potatoes and the crushed onions and cook till the meat and potatoes are tender. Sprinkle the chopped coriander, mint, and green chillies and also add the saffron milk. When done, the mutton should have about 1 cup gravy left.

2. Prepare the rice: Soak the rice for about 20 minutes. Drain. In a large vessel, boil about 2 litres of water with all the ingredients at B along with 1 tbs oil and salt. When the water comes to a boil, add rice and cook till about two thirds done. Drain the water.

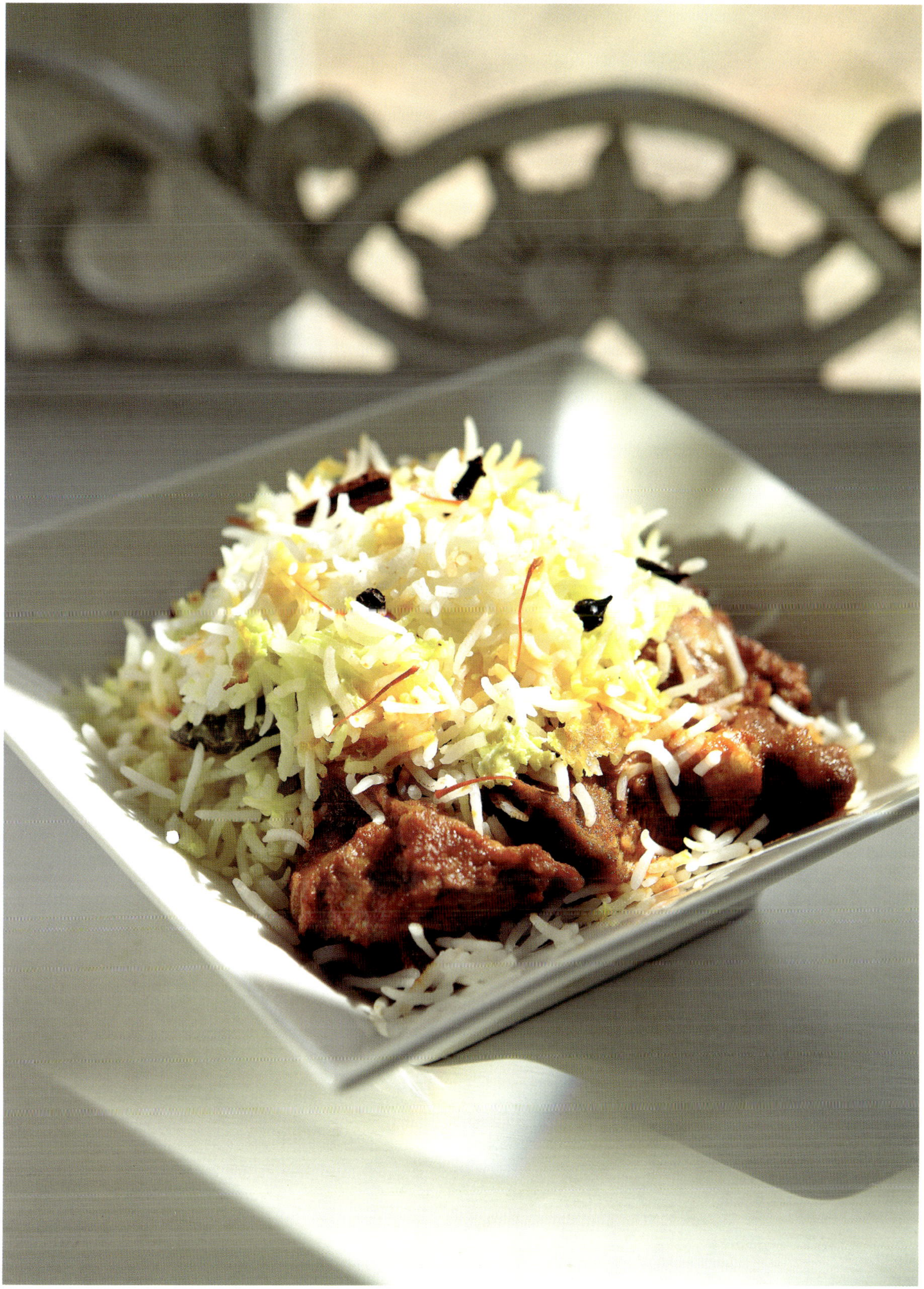

½	tsp peppercorns	
1	1 inch cinnamon stick	B
4	cloves	

⅓	cup milk
	Juice of 1½ limes
1	tbs cream
1	tbs ghee
	Oil for frying
	Salt

3. Assemble and serve: Place the par-boiled rice over the korma (the cooked meat and gravy). Sprinkle milk and juice of lime over the rice. Dot it with ghee and cream. Cover with a tight fitting lid and cook for the first 2 minutes on medium-high flame to heat up the dish. Then reduce flame to low and cook till the dish in steaming hot and rice done. Take the rice and meat out from the sides in large chunks and serve hot in a nice wide serving dish.

Paye ka Pulao (Hyderabad)

Trotters are a delicacy not only in the north but also in Hyderabad. The jelly-like mutton, the bone and the lighter marrow in the bones make this dish chewy and highly enjoyable.

Preparation time: 20 minutes
Cooking time: 50 minutes
Serves: 6–8

1	dozen cleaned trotters, each cut horizontally into three pieces (a butcher will do it for you)
2 ½	glasses milk
1	tsp caraway seeds
4–6	cloves
4	green cardamoms
1	1 inch cinnamon stick
1	small piece of nutmeg
2–3	mace flakes
1	tsp peppercorns

A — *crushed and tied in a bundle in muslin cloth*

500	gm long grain rice
4	medium onions, finely sliced
1	tsp ginger paste
1	tsp garlic paste
8–10	green chillies, ground
⅓	cup fresh green coriander, chopped
¼	cup mint leaves, chopped
2	tbs ghee
½	cup oil
	Salt

1. Prepare the trotters: Boil the cleaned and washed trotters in 2 glasses of milk and a little water along with the bundle of crushed spices, stirring now and then. Once the liquid comes to a boil add salt and stir for another 1–2 minutes. Cover tightly and cook till the trotters are tender. Uncover and boil away the excess liquid.

2. Prepare the rice: Soak rice in liberal quantity of water for about 15 minutes, and then drain out the water. Boil about 2 litres of water. Once the water starts to boil add the rice and a little salt and cook for 7–8 minutes till the rice is two thirds done. Drain the water and transfer the rice to a flattish pan, then set aside.

3. Assemble and serve: Heat oil in a heavy bottomed pan and fry the onions till they turn golden brown. Remove half and reserve. Add ginger, garlic, ground green chillies, and half of the coriander and mint. After a few seconds add the cooked trotters mix, the par-boiled rice, and mix gently. Smoothen the surface and sprinkle the remaining ½ glass milk, the reserved onions, balance coriander, and mint. Dot with ghee and cover with a tight fitting lid and cook first on high flame for about 1–2 minutes and then on low flame for 15–20 minutes till the rice is done and steaming. Serve hot.

Katchi Biryani (Hyderabad)

Preparation time: 25–30 minutes
Marination time: 5–6 hours
Cooking time: 1 hour 15 minutes
Serves: 8–10

1	kg mutton, a mix of medium sized pieces from the goat's shoulder, a few chops and a few marrowbones with some meat on
1	tbs ginger paste
1½	tbs garlic paste
1	tbs raw green papaya (skin and pulp together), ground fine

A:
- 4 onions, finely sliced
- 15 green chillies, ground
- ½ cup fresh green coriander, chopped
- ⅓ cup mint leaves
- 1 tsp garam masala
- 500 gm yoghurt, whisked
- Juice of 3 limes

650	gm long grain rice
	A liberal pinch of saffron soaked in ½ cup milk
2	tbs ghee
150	gm oil
	Salt

This is perhaps Hyderabad's most renowned biryani. Both the rice and the meat are layered in an almost raw form in the pan (katchi means raw in Hindi). Therein lies its unbelievable magic. Many claim Katchi Biryani is the ultimate biryani dish.

1. Marinate the meat: Wash the meat and put it in a colander for the water to drain. Add ginger, garlic, and papaya paste. Mix and rub it well into the meat. Set it aside. Heat 150 gm oil. Add the sliced onions and fry till golden brown. Remove and allow to cool slightly, then crush the onions. Add the crushed onions, the ingredients at A and salt to the meat. Also add the oil in which the onions were fried. Mix and leave to marinate for 5–6 hours.

2. Prepare the rice: Wash and soak the rice in water for about 20 minutes. Boil 3½ litres of water with salt and 1 tsp of oil. Once the water starts boiling, add the rice and cook for about 3 minutes till it is 20 percent done. Drain the water and transfer the rice to a flat pan.

3. Assemble and serve: Take a heavy bottomed pan and transfer the marinated meat with the marinade to the pan. Start cooking on high flame, stirring continuously, till the contents come to a boil. Cover and cook for about 10 minutes. Add 1 cup of water and when the dish starts to boil again, lower heat and spread the rice over the meat. Cover with a tight fitting lid and place a heavy stone on it to prevent the steam from escaping. Cook on dum for about half an hour. Sprinkle the saffron milk over the rice and dot the rice with ghee. Cover once again with a tight fitting lid. Cook further on slow flame for about 15 minutes till the meat and rice are done and steaming hot. Take out the biryani in large chunks from the sides without mixing to retain its multi-hued glory. Serve steaming hot.

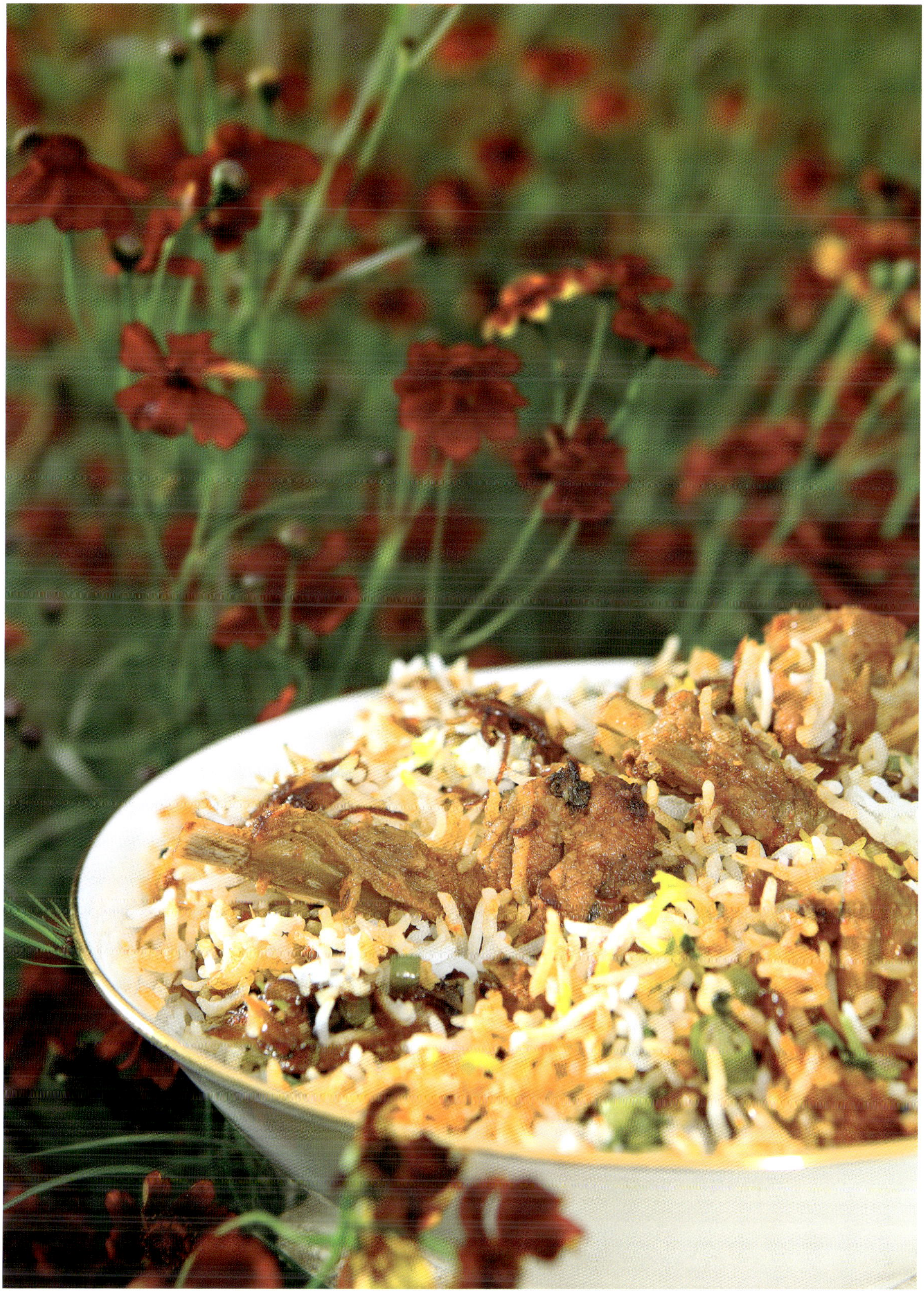

Rajah Katori courtesy Good Earth

Seviyon ki Biryani (Hyderabad)

Preparation time: 20 minutes
Cooking time: 45 minutes
Serves: 6–8

250	vermicelli
250	gm keema (minced mutton)
⅓	tsp turmeric
1	fresh coconut
5–6	sprigs of curry leaves
2	1 inch cinnamon sticks ⎫
4–5	cardamoms ⎬ A
6	cloves ⎭
3–4	onions, finely sliced
1	tsp ginger paste
1	tsp garlic paste
6–8	green chillies, ground
1	tsp red chilli powder
50	gm cashew nuts, ground
½	cup yoghurt, whisked
	A dash of garam masala
	Juice of 1–2 limes
	A few sprigs of fresh green coriander, chopped
1	tbs ghee
60	gm oil
	Salt

Unlike the vermicelli biryani from Rajasthan, this one is cooked with minced meat, coconut milk, and curry leaves, giving it its marked southern flavour. It's a great example of the fusion of the north and the south in Hyderabad.

1. Fry the vermicelli: Take a heavy bottomed pan. Heat the ghee and fry the vermicelli till pale brown. Remove and set aside.

2. Boil the mince: Place the mince in the pan with salt, turmeric and a little water for about 8–10 minutes. Set aside.

3. Prepare coconut milk: Grate the coconut and add a little warm water to it. Put it in a blender and churn. Strain to extract 2–3 glasses of coconut milk.

4. Cook the mince: Heat the oil and add the curry leaves and the spices at A. In a few seconds, add the onions and fry till golden brown. Add the ginger and garlic paste followed in a minute by the green chilli paste. After a minute, add the red chilli powder and ground cashew nuts and fry for a minute. Then add yoghurt and fry for 3–4 minutes. At this stage, add the keema and fry for 4–5 minutes. Add the coconut milk and bring to a boil.

5. Assemble and serve: Add vermicelli to the keema and mix gently. Cover and cook on dum for 10–15 minutes till ready. Sprinkle the garam masala on top. Squeeze the juice of lime and sprinkle the chopped coriander. Cover and simmer for a couple of minutes. When done the vermicelli should be tender and yet not sticky. Each strand of vermicelli should stand out separately. Serve hot.

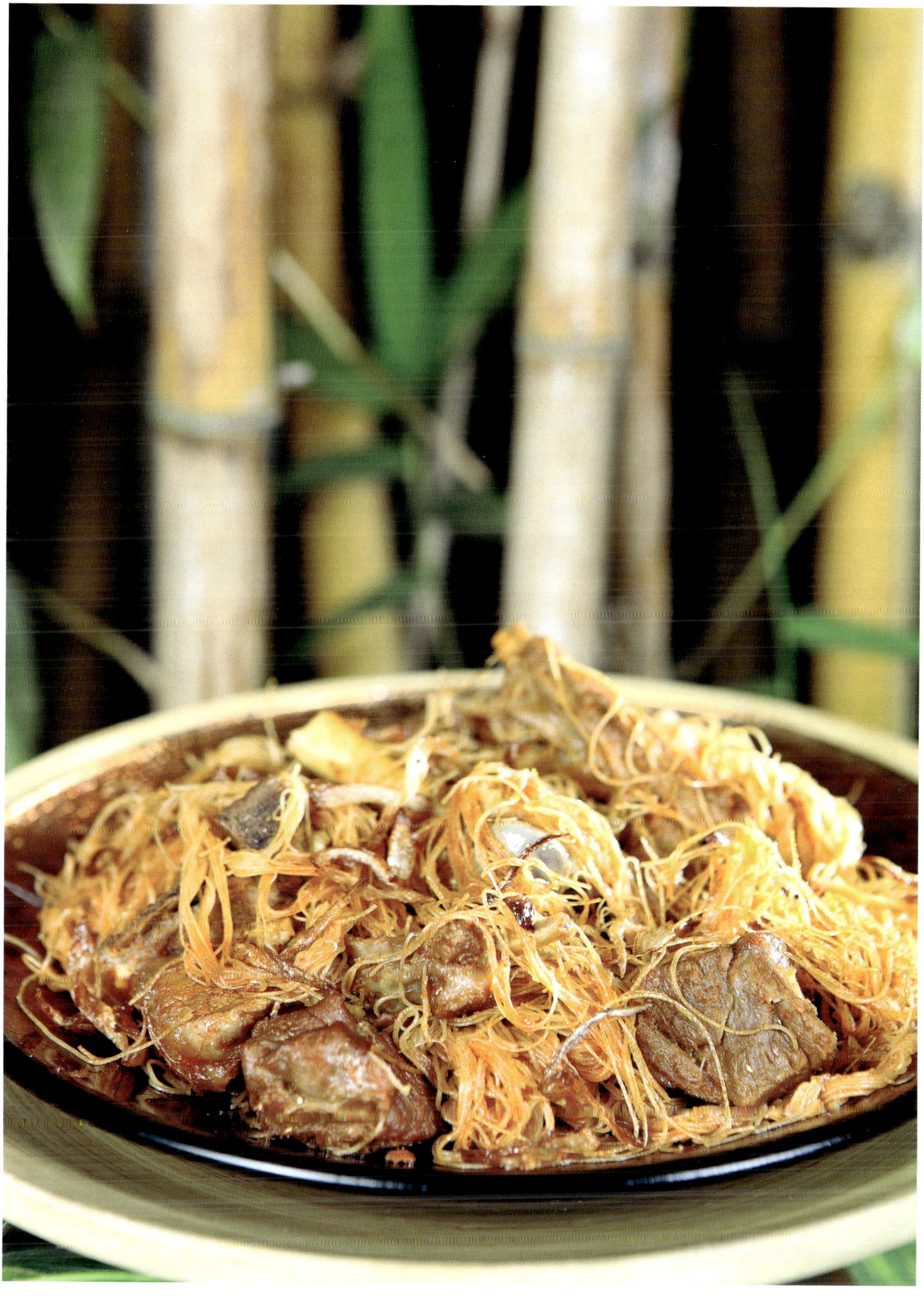

Bone Marrow Pulao (Hyderabad)

This biryani is specially made for expectant mothers, as it is very nutritious. Bone marrow is usually a favourite with children as well. Make sure you have a marrow spoon to extract the bone marrow in order to relish this dish to the fullest.

Preparation time: 10 minutes
Cooking time: 50 minutes
Serves: 8

½	kg marrowbones with some meat on
½	kg mutton, from leg or shoulder, cut into medium pieces

1	tsp peppercorns	
6	cloves	
2	1 inch pieces cinnamon	
2	bay leaves	
½	tsp cumin seeds	A
2	black cardamoms, crushed open at the end	
1	small piece nutmeg	
1–2	mace flakes	
1	large onion, quartered	
4–5	garlic cloves	
1	inch ginger piece, chopped	

400	gm long grain rice
3	onions, finely sliced
5–6	cloves
2–3	bay leaves
3	green cardamoms
1	1 inch cinnamon stick
1	tbs ghee
60	gm ghee–oil, mixed
	Salt

1. **Prepare the marrow:** Wash the marrowbones and mutton pieces. Add all the ingredients at A and salt to the marrowbones and mutton pieces along with 5–6 glasses of water. Cover tightly and cook for about 25–30 minutes till the meat is almost tender. Strain the meat to get clear mutton stock. Pick the marrowbones and mutton pieces and set them aside. Discard the residue.

2. **Prepare the rice:** Wash and soak rice in water for about 20 minutes. Drain and set aside.

3. **Assemble and serve:** Heat the ghee–oil mix in a heavy bottomed pan. Add the sliced onions and fry till they are pink. Then add cloves, bay leaves, cardamom, cinnamon, and fry till the onions turn golden brown. Then add the marrowbones and mutton and fry for 4–5 minutes. Add rice and salt and fry for another 2 minutes. Now add mutton stock till it is 1 inch over the surface of mutton and rice and add ghee. Cover with a tight fitting lid and cook, first on high flame for 2 minutes till the contents come to a boil and then on low flame for 15–20 minutes till the stock is absorbed and rice done. Serve the dish hot and keep 1–2 marrow spoons handy.

Keeme ki Khichri (Hyderabad)

Preparation time: 10 minutes
Cooking time: 50 minutes
Serves: 6–8

½	kg minced mutton (taken out from the mince machine only once to prevent the keema from getting too pasty or fine)
½	tsp saffron soaked in ⅓ cup warm milk
3	onions, finely sliced
1½	tsp ginger paste
1	tbs garlic paste
6–8	green chillies, ground
½	cup fresh green coriander, chopped (reserve a little for garnish)
⅓	cup fresh mint leaves (reserve a little for garnish)
⅓	tsp turmeric powder
1	tsp red chilli powder
1	cup yoghurt, whisked
	Juice of 2 limes
500	gm long grain rice
	Juice of half a lime
½	tsp garam masala
	A few sprigs of fresh green coriander, chopped
	A few mint leaves
2–3	green chillies, chopped
2	tbs thick cream
2	tbs ghee
60	gm oil
1	tsp oil
	Salt

Although a mince biryani, it is called a khichri deliberately because it has the look of a khichri, with the mince simulating the lentils.

1. Cook the keema: Wash the keema and put it in a colander for all the water to drain. Soak saffron in ⅓ cup warm milk and set aside. Heat oil. Add onions and fry till golden brown. Add ginger and garlic paste and fry for just about a minute. Add green chilli paste and fry further for a few seconds. Add fresh coriander and mint followed in a few seconds by salt, turmeric, and red chilli powder and then the keema. Mix and fry till the liquids dry up. Add yoghurt and continue cooking, stirring all the time till the contents start to boil and become homogenous. Add a little water and cover till the keema is cooked. Squeeze the juice of 2 limes. When done the keema should be a little juicy without being runny.

2. Prepare the rice: Wash and soak the rice in water for 15–20 minutes. Drain the water. Boil 2 litres of water with juice of half a lime, 1 tsp oil, and salt. When the rice is two thirds done, drain the water, and transfer the rice to a flat dish.

3. Assemble and serve: Take a heavy bottomed pan and brush it with oil. Place half of the par-boiled rice in the pan. Arrange the cooked keema over the rice and cover with balance rice. Sprinkle the saffron soaked milk, garam masala, green coriander, mint, and green chillies. Also pour the ghee and cream over the rice. Now cover the rice with a tight fitting lid and cook for 2 minutes on high flame and then on low flame for about 10 minutes till the rice is done. Serve steaming hot.

Keeme ki Biryani (Hyderabad)

Preparation time: 20 minutes
Marination time: 1 hour
Cooking time: 50 minutes
Serves: 8

750	gm minced mutton

2	inch piece ginger	
½	pod garlic	
10–12	green chillies	
⅓	cup coriander leaves	
⅓	cup fresh mint leaves	
¼	tsp garam masala	A
¾	cup yoghurt, whisked	
	Juice of 2–3 limes	
1	tbs green papaya paste (pulp and skin ground together)	
⅓	tsp turmeric powder	

ground to a fine paste

400	gm long grain rice
½	tsp caraway seeds
4–5	onions, finely sliced
½	tsp saffron, crushed and dissolved in ⅓ cup warm milk
3	tbs oil
1	tsp oil
	Oil for frying
3	tbs ghee
	Salt

In this biryani, typical to the princely state of Hyderabad, minced mutton is layered with rice, and flavoured with saffron and finely sliced browned onions.

1. Marinate the meat: Mix the mince with all the ingredients at A, 3 tbs oil, salt and marinate for an hour.

2. Prepare the rice: Soak the rice in water for 20 minutes, then drain out the water. Bring about 2 litres of water to a boil and then add rice, a little salt, caraway seeds, and 1 tsp oil and cook for about 3–4 minutes till the rice is 20 percent done. Then drain the water and transfer the rice to a paraat (a flattish pan) and set aside.

3. Fry the onions: Heat oil and fry the onions golden brown. Set aside.

4. Assemble and cook on dum: Take a heavy bottomed pan and smear with oil. Spread half of the fried onions and the marinated mince over the onion. Sprinkle the balance onions over the mince and spread the rice over it. Sprinkle saffron milk and a little water and dot with ghee. Cover with a tight fitting lid and cook first on medium-high flame for about 2 minutes to allow the dish to get hot and then on dum (a very low flame) for about 30 minutes till the dish is steaming. Serve hot.

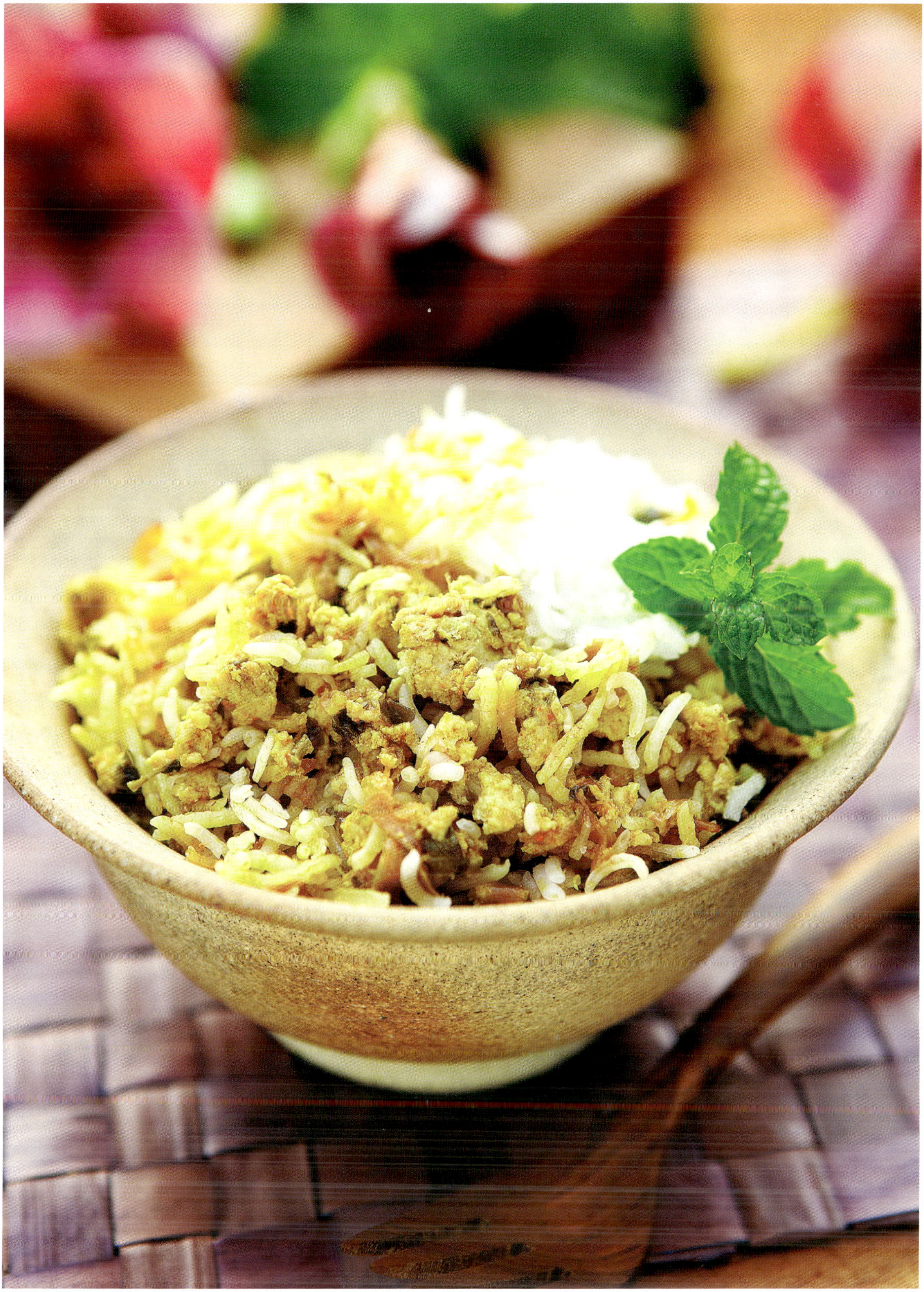

Karonde ki Biryani (Hyderabad)

In this Hyderabadi biryani, Carissa caranda, also called karonda in India, is used as the souring agent. This biryani is overwhelmingly sour, so bite into the karonda pieces somewhat sparingly.

Preparation time: 20 minutes
Cooking time: 1 hour
Serves: 8–10

1	kg keema (mutton mince), taken out just once from the mince-machine so that it does get too fine and pasty
4	onions, finely sliced
1½	tbs ginger paste
1½	tbs garlic paste
2	tbs green chilli paste
⅓	cup fresh green coriander, chopped
¼	mint leaves
1	tsp turmeric powder
1	tsp red chilli powder
1½	cups yoghurt, whisked
125	gm karondas (*Carissa caranda*) washed, deseeded and each karonda cut into 4 pieces. (Reserve 7–8 karondas cut into half, deseeded, for garnish)
750	gm long grain rice
2–3	green cardamoms
2	1 inch cinnamon sticks
4–6	cloves
1	bay leaf
	A few mint leaves
2	tbs melted ghee
¾	cup oil
	Salt

1. Prepare the keema: Wash the keema and put it in a colander for the water to drain out completely. Heat oil in a heavy bottomed pan. Add onions and fry till golden brown. Add the ginger and garlic paste and fry for 1–2 minutes, after which add the green chilli paste and fry for just about a minute. Then add coriander, mint, salt, turmeric, and red chilli powder and mix well. Add keema, mix, and cook for about 10 minutes. Now add the yoghurt and cook for another 5 minutes, stirring continuously. When the gravy gets slightly thick, add a little water, and cook covered for about 6–7 minutes till the keema is 85–90 percent done. Add the chopped karondas, fry a little and cook covered for further 5–7 minutes.

2. Prepare the rice: Meanwhile, soak the rice in water for about 20 minutes. Boil 3½ litres of water with the whole spices. To this, add the rice and salt and cook for about 7–8 minutes till two thirds done. Drain and set it aside.

3. Assemble and serve: Smear a heavy bottomed pan with oil and place half the rice in it. Arrange the cooked keema over the rice and cover it with the balance rice. Pour melted ghee and sprinkle the mint leaves followed by a little water. Cover with a tight fitting lid and cook for the first 2 minutes on high flame and then on low flame for about 10 minutes till the rice is done and steaming hot. Serve hot garnished with the reserved karondas.

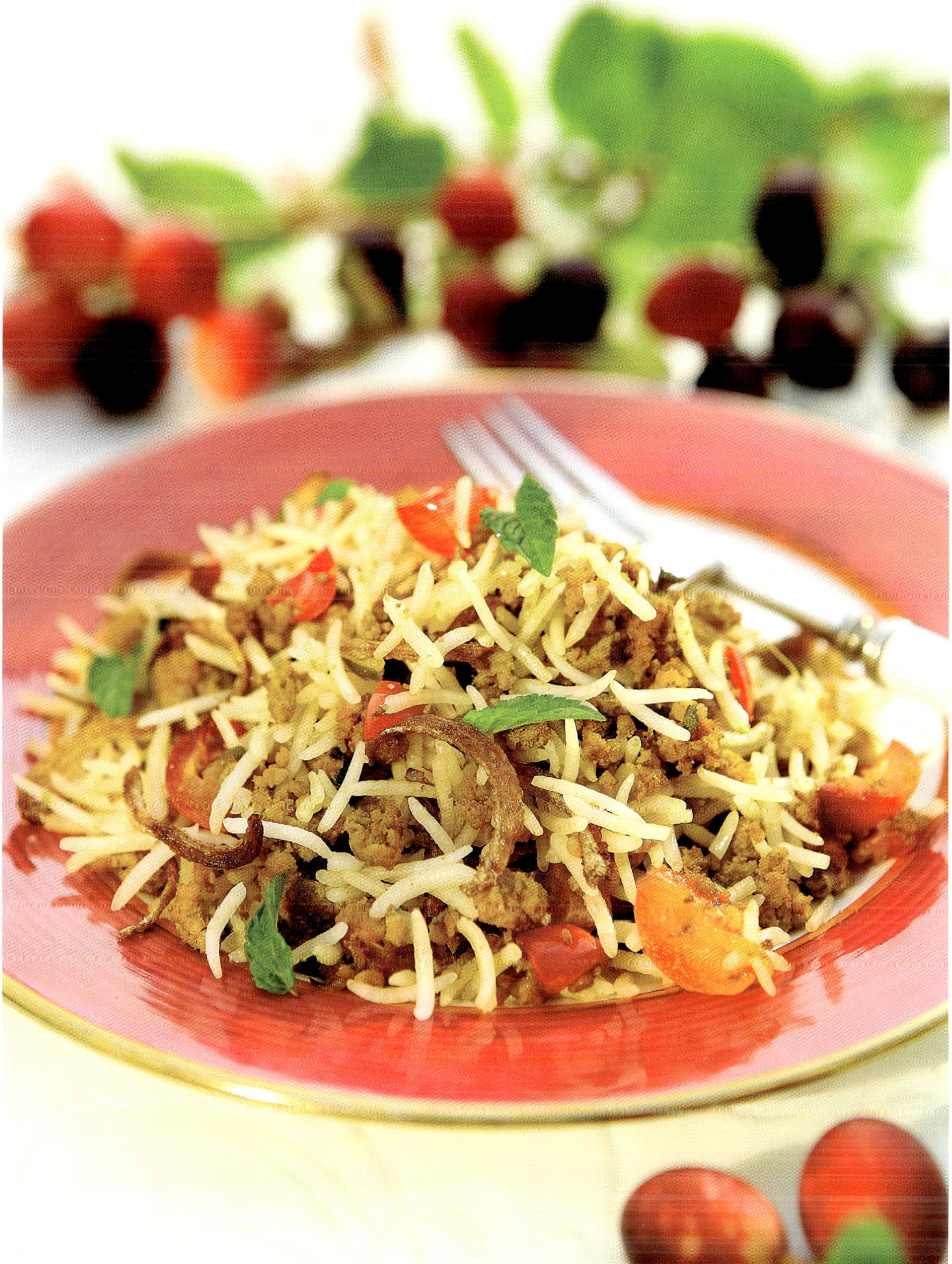

Boote aur Keeme ki Biryani (Hyderabad)

Preparation time: 15 minutes
Cooking time: 1 hour
Serves: 8

750	gm minced mutton (keema)
350	gm fresh green gram (boote or cholia)
2	medium onions, finely sliced
1	tbs ginger paste
1	tbs garlic paste
50	gm green chillies, ground
½	tsp turmeric powder
1	tsp red chilli powder
½	cup fresh green coriander, chopped
¼	cup fresh mint leaves
1	cup yoghurt, whisked
	Juice of 2–3 limes
500	gm long grain rice

A:
- 2 bay leaves
- 1 1 inch cinnamon stick
- 4 cloves
- 4 green cardamoms
- Juice of half a lime

This is a mince-meat biryani made with green gram commonly called boote or cholia. Hyderabadis love green gram and cook it both with vegetables and minced meat.

1. Wash the gram and the mutton: Wash the mutton mince, put it in a colander and drain the water completely. Also wash the green gram and set these aside.

2. Cook the mutton: Heat oil in a heavy based pan. Fry the onions till golden brown. To this add ginger and garlic paste and fry for a minute, then add the ground green chillies and fry for another couple of minutes. Now add turmeric powder and red chilli powder. Reserve 1 tbs green coriander and a few mint leaves and add the rest to the pan. Also add salt. Stir and mix and cook for a few seconds. Then add the keema and cook for about 5–6 minutes. Add the whipped yoghurt and mix well, stirring continuously. Once the yoghurt is mixed well and the dish starts to boil, add a little water, lower the heat and cook covered for about 7–8 minutes till the keema is 80 percent cooked. At this stage, add the green gram and cook further for about 6–8 minutes till the keema and green gram are cooked. Add the juice of lime. Mix and set aside.

½	tsp garam masala
3	tbs fresh cream
½	tsp saffron, dissolved in ⅓ cup warm milk
2	green chillies, chopped
1	tbs melted ghee
100	gm oil
	Salt

3. Prepare the rice: Wash and soak the rice in water for about 20 minutes. Drain and set aside. Boil about 2½ litres of water along with all the ingredients at A. Once the water starts to boil, add rice and cook for 7–8 minutes till it is two thirds done. Drain and transfer to a flattish pan.

4. Assemble and serve: Smear a heavy bottomed pan with oil. Place half of the par-boiled rice in it followed by the mince and green gram over it. Cover with balance rice. Pour the melted ghee over the rice and sprinkle the garam masala. Also dot with fresh cream, saffron milk, and the remaining fresh green coriander, mint, and green chillies. Cover with a tight fitting lid. Put a griddle over high flame and place the biryani pan over it. Cook covered on high flame for about 5 minutes and then on dum for about 10–15 minutes till the dish is steaming hot and rice done. Serve hot.

Salem Biryani (Tamil Nadu)

Preparation time: 15 minutes
Cooking time: 1 hour
Serves: 8–10

1	kg mutton, cut into medium sized pieces
½	tsp turmeric
500	gm long grain rice
3	onions, finely sliced

A:
2	bay leaves
6–8	cloves
3–4	green cardamoms
1	star anise
2	1 inch cinnamon sticks

ground to a fine paste:
25	gm ginger
25	gm garlic
1	tbs poppy seeds (khus khus)(washed and soaked in warm water for 10–15 minutes)
1	small onion
	A few sprigs of fresh green coriander

3–4	green chillies, slit
2	large tomatoes, chopped
1	tsp garam masala
1½	tsp coriander powder
1½	tsp red chilli powder
2	cups yoghurt, whisked
	Juice of 2 limes
	A few mint leaves
3	tbs ghee
100	gm oil
	Salt

The state of Tamil Nadu has some really celebrated biryanis, all invariably evolved in its smaller towns. Thus you have the Salem Biryani, the Chettinad Biryani, the Dindigul Biryani, and the Aambur Biryani. If folklore is to be believed, Salem Biryani developed in a particular hotel, possibly a military hotel, as restaurants serving non-vegetarian food are commonly known in Tamil Nadu.

1. Prepare the meat: Wash and cook meat with turmeric and salt in just sufficient water for about 10–15 minutes till two thirds done.

2. Prepare the rice: Wash and soak rice in water for about 15 minutes, then drain. Heat 2 tbs ghee in a pan. Add rice and fry for 2 minutes. Set aside.

3. Cook the meat: Heat oil in a heavy bottomed pan, large enough to take meat and rice. Add the sliced onions and fry till they turn translucent. Then add the whole spices at A and fry till the onions turn golden brown. Add the ground paste and fry a little so that oil starts to surface. Then add green chillies and tomatoes and fry till the tomatoes are soft. Add meat and cook for a few minutes till the moisture is somewhat absorbed. Add the garam masala, coriander and chilli powder and the yoghurt and mix well. Continue stirring till the contents come to a boil. Cook covered till the meat is tender. Squeeze the lime juice.

4. Assemble: Now evenly spread the rice over the cooked meat. Sprinkle mint leaves. Add water to come 1 inch above the surface of rice. Also add 1 tbs ghee. Cover with a tight fitting lid and cook first on high flame for a few minutes till the contents come to a boil, and then on low flame till the rice is done with each grain separate.

Aambur Biryani (Tamil Nadu)

Preparation time: 20 minutes
Marination time: 1 hour
Cooking time: 1 hour
Serves: 6–8

750	gm mutton, cut into medium pieces	
¾	cup hung yoghurt	
3	tomatoes, roughly chopped	
1	tsp ginger paste	
1	tsp garlic paste	A
⅓	tsp turmeric powder	
	A few sprigs of fresh green coriander, chopped	
	A few mint leaves	
400	gm jeera samba (a variety of rice available in South India) or long grain rice	
2	bay leaves	
6	cloves	B
4	green cardamoms	
4	medium onions, finely sliced	
2	tsp red chilli powder	
2	tsp coriander powder	
1	tsp oil	
½	cup oil	
1	tbs ghee	
	Salt	

Aambur is a town in the district of Vellore in northern Tamil Nadu. Its signature biryani is made with jeera samba rice, mutton, tomatoes, and hung yoghurt.

1. Marinate the meat: Wash the meat and drain the water out. Add all the ingredients at A together with salt and mix well. Leave it to marinate for an hour.

2. Prepare the rice: Wash and soak the rice in water for 20 minutes. Drain out the water. Boil about 2 litres of water with half the spices at B, salt, and 1 tsp oil. When the water starts to boil, add the rice and cook for about 7–8 minutes till it is two thirds done. Drain the water and transfer the rice to a wide dish.

3. Cook the meat: Heat the oil and add onions, the balance of spices at B and fry till the onions are golden brown. Add the marinated meat and keep stirring till the contents come to a boil. Cook further till the oil starts to surface. Add red chilli powder, coriander powder and salt, and cook for another 4–5 minutes. Add a little water and cook for about 25 minutes till the meat is tender. When done there should be about 1 cup gravy left.

4. Assemble and serve: Now add the par-boiled rice and mix gently. Spread 1 tbs melted ghee over the rice. Cover with a tight fitting lid and cook on slow flame till the rice is done and steaming. Serve hot.

Egg Biryani (Tamil Nadu)

Preparation time: 10 minutes
Cooking time: 45 minutes
Serves: 6

300	gm long grain rice
2	bay leaves
2	green cardamoms
2	cloves
1	1 inch cinnamon stick

(A)

1	tsp oil
8	hard-boiled eggs
	A pinch of garam masala
6	tomatoes, roughly chopped
1½	inch piece ginger
7–8	garlic cloves
6–8	green chillies

ground to a paste

2	onions, finely sliced and fried to a golden brown
50	gm ghee–oil, mixed
	Oil
1	tbs ghee
	Salt

An easy, wholesome biryani, this is made with hard-boiled eggs, green chillies, ginger, garlic, pureed tomatoes, and layered with rice.

1. Prepare the rice: Wash and soak the rice in water for 20 minutes, then drain out the water. Boil the rice with all the ingredients at A, 1 tsp oil and a little salt with water 1 inch above the surface of rice. When done the rice should have fully absorbed the water and each grain should stand out separately.

2. Prepare the egg: Cut 6 hard-boiled eggs horizontally into half. Heat 1 tbs of oil in a non-stick pan and lightly fry the hard-boiled eggs. Sprinkle a little salt and garam masala over the eggs while frying. Remove and set aside. Slice the remaining 2 eggs into rounds and reserve.

3. Make the tomato puree: Add ½ cup water to the tomatoes and cook for about 5 minutes. When cool, churn in a mixer and strain to get tomato puree. Set aside.

4. Assemble and serve: Heat the ghee–oil mixture and add the ground paste. Fry for 1–2 minutes. Add the tomato puree and salt and fry for 5–6 minutes till the mixture gets homogenous and oil starts to surface. Add the lightly fried eggs to the tomato mixture and mix gently. Now take a heavy bottomed pan and smear with oil. Spread half the quantity of rice. Place the hard-boiled egg mixture over the rice and cover with balance rice. Sprinkle a little water and also one tbs ghee and cover and cook on medium flame for 5–6 minutes till steaming hot. Serve hot garnished with egg slices and fried onions.

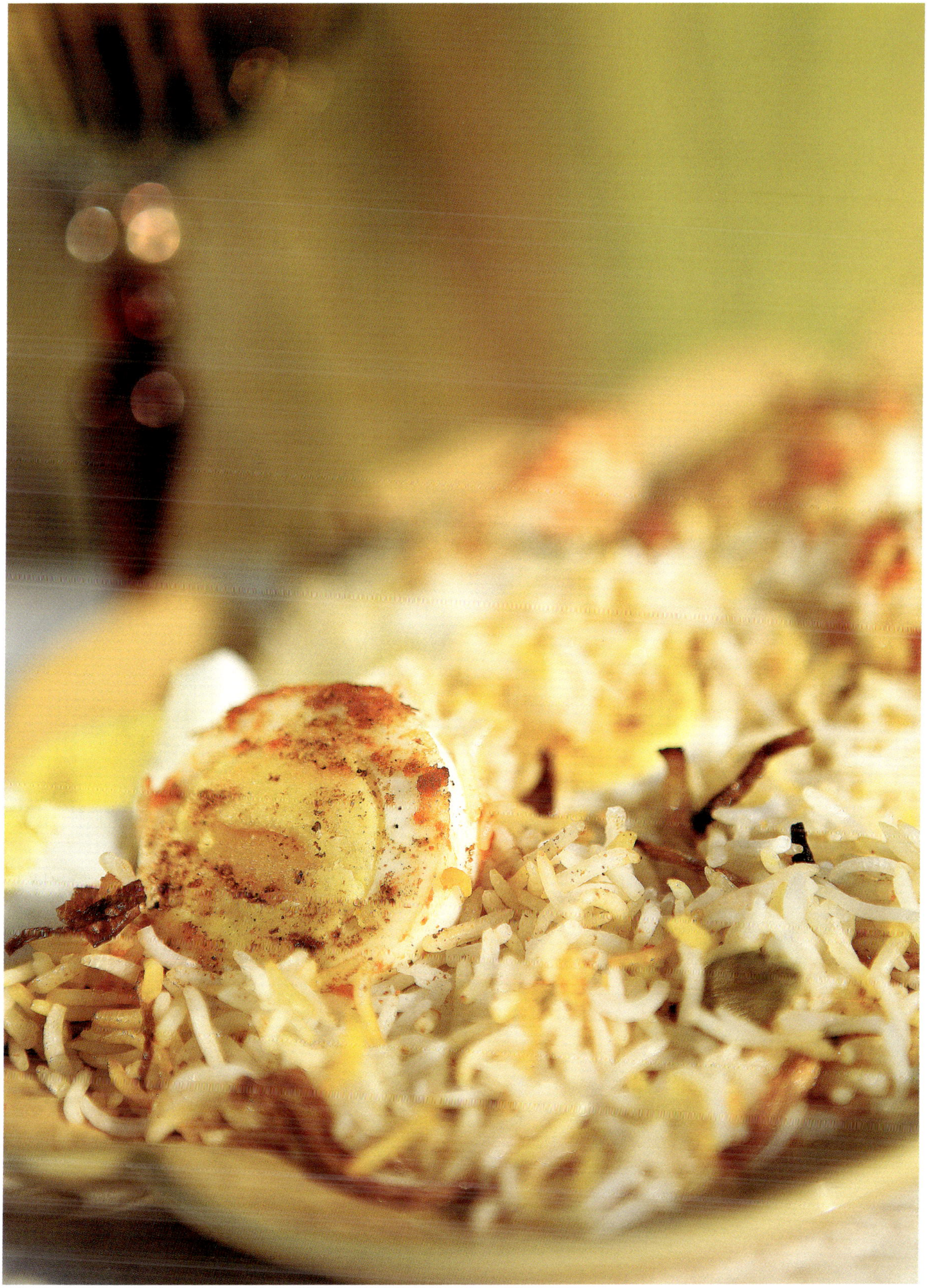

Chettinad Mutton Biryani (Tamil Nadu)

The Chettinad region of Tamil Nadu, home of the Tamil Chettiars (the Vaisyas of the south) is celebrated for its fiery, irresistible cuisine. Unlike the Vaisyas of the north who are staunch vegetarians, the Chettiars are avid mutton eaters. This is an entirely different kind of biryani: its process is pulao-like with no layering and, since the Chettiars like it hot, it has plenty of ground green chillies. Most interestingly, it is the rice that is marinated here instead of the meat, and that too with ghee, which lends it its unique flavour.

Preparation time: 20 minutes
Marination time: 1 hour
Cooking time: 1 hour
Serves: 8

1	kg mutton, cut into medium pieces, preferably from the shoulder

A:
1	tbs ginger paste
1	tbs garlic paste
15	green chillies, ground
½	cup fresh green coriander leaves, chopped
4	tomatoes, chopped
½	cup yoghurt, whisked

500	gm long grain rice
4	onions, finely sliced

B:
1	bay leaf
6–8	cloves
3–4	green cardamoms
2	1 inch cinnamon sticks

½	cup oil
1	tbs ghee
	Salt

1. Marinate the mutton: Wash and drain the mutton of all water. Mix it well with all ingredients at A and salt, and leave it for an hour.

2. Marinate the rice: Wash the rice well. Drain the water and mix with 1 tbs ghee. Set aside for 1 hour to marinate.

3. Cook the meat: Heat the oil and add the sliced onions along with all the spices at B. Fry till the onions turn golden brown, then add the marinated meat. Cook till the contents come to a boil, stirring frequently. When the oil starts to surface add a little water and cook it covered for 30 minutes, stirring now and then till the meat is tender.

4. Assemble and serve: Add rice, salt and hot water so as to reach 1 inch above the surface of meat and rice. Cook it covered first on medium and then on slow flame for about 10–15 minutes till the rice is done. Serve hot.

Dindigul Biryani (Tamil Nadu)

This biryani is from Dindigul in Tamil Nadu. It uses whole spices instead of ground ones and is spiced with both red and green chillies. Its yellow colour sets it apart from the traditional white, brown, and saffron appearance.

Preparation time: 20 minutes
Cooking time: 1 hour
Serves: 8

1	kg mutton, cut into medium sized pieces
4	onions, finely sliced
1	bay leaf
2	1 inch cinnamon sticks
4	green cardamoms
6	cloves
1½	tsp ginger paste
1½	tsp garlic paste
6	green chillies, chopped
4	tomatoes, chopped
⅓	tsp turmeric powder
2	tsp red chilli powder
3	tsp coriander powder
⅓	cup fresh green coriander, chopped
¼	cup mint leaves, chopped
1	cup hung yoghurt, whisked
500	gm long grain rice
	A few drops yellow food colour, mixed with a little water
30	gm ghee + 70 gm oil, mixed
	Salt

1. Prepare the mutton: Wash and drain the mutton of all water. Heat the ghee–oil mix and add the onions along with bay leaf, cinnamon, cardamom, and cloves. When the onions turn golden, add ginger, and garlic paste and fry for a few seconds after which add the green chillies and sauté it for a few seconds. Then add the mutton and fry it for 4–5 minutes. Add tomatoes and fry till they are soft. Then add salt, turmeric, red chilli powder, and coriander powder. Mix well. Add fresh coriander, mint, and then the hung yoghurt. Mix and stir continuously till the contents come to a boil and the oil starts to surface. Add a little water and cook for about 20 minutes till the mutton is 95 percent done.

2. Assemble and serve: Add rice and water to the mutton so that the water is 1 inch above the surface of meat and rice. Cook tightly covered, for the first 2–3 minutes on high flame and then on low flame for about 15 minutes. When the rice is almost done, sprinkle the yellow food colour mixed with a little water and cook further for 2–3 minutes till the rice is done with individual grains separate. Serve hot.

Mangalore Fish Biryani (Karnataka)

Preparation time: 20 minutes
Cooking time: 45 minutes
Serves: 8–10

600	gm seer fish, cleaned, scales removed and cut straight across into 4 pieces, weighing 150 gm each
⅓	tsp turmeric powder
	Juice of half a lime
800	gm long grain rice
3–4	onions, finely sliced
2	tomatoes, chopped

8	dry whole red chillies	
½	fresh coconut, grated	
1	tbs poppy seeds	
6	cloves	
1	1 inch cinnamon stick	**A** *ground to a fine paste*
6	cardamoms	
1	tbs fennel seeds	
1	tbs ginger piece	
10	garlic cloves	
4–5	sprigs curry leaves	

100	gm coconut oil
100	gm vegetable oil
	Salt

Very coastal, very south Indian, this somewhat heady biryani is flavoured with a little more of coconut, garlic cloves, curry leaves, and ground whole red chillies.

1. Prepare the fish: Wash the fish and apply salt, turmeric, and lime juice. Set aside for 5–10 minutes.

2. Soak the rice: Wash and soak rice in water for about 15 minutes. Drain the water.

3. Cook the fish: Heat the coconut and vegetable oil together in a heavy bottomed pan large enough to take fish and rice. Add the onions and fry till golden brown. Add and fry the tomatoes till they blend with the onions. Then add the ground paste and salt and fry for 3–4 minutes. Add fish and cook for 2–3 minutes. Gently turn over the fish and cook further for 2–3 minutes. Remove the fish from the masala and set aside.

4. Cook the rice: Now add the previously soaked rice and mix with the masala. Add water so as to come 1 inch above the surface of rice. Cook first on high flame and when the water starts to boil, cover, and cook on medium slow flame for about 12–15 minutes till the rice has absorbed the water.

5. Assemble and serve: Arrange the fish on top of the rice and cover tightly with a lid. Cook on dum (very slow flame) for 5–10 minutes till the fish and rice are done. When done, each grain of rice should be separate. Serve hot.

Karwar Prawn Biryani (Karnataka)

Preparation time: 15–20 minutes
Marination time: 15 minutes
Cooking time: 40 minutes
Serves: 8–10

1	kg medium sized prawns, cleaned and deveined
1	cup yoghurt, whisked
1	tsp chilli powder
800	gm long grain rice
3–4	medium sized onions, finely sliced
8	dry whole red chillies
2	tomatoes, chopped
1	tbs coriander powder

6	green cardamoms	
1	1 inch cinnamon stick	
6	cloves	**A**
1	tsp cumin seeds	*ground*
1	tsp peppercorns	*to a fine*
1	inch ginger piece	*paste*
10	garlic cloves	

200 gm oil
Salt

Karwar is a coastal district in the northwestern part of Karnataka and is famed for its seafood. Though called a biryani, this is made in the pulao way. Since Karwar is not far from southern Maharashtra, where the food is known to be highly spicy, this prawn biryani too has a fiery flavour.

1. Marinate the prawns: Wash and marinate the prawns with yoghurt, chilli powder, and salt for about 15 minutes.

2. Soak the rice: Wash and soak the rice in water for 20 minutes. Drain and set it aside.

3. Assemble and serve: Heat 200 gm of oil in a heavy bottomed pan. Fry the onions with the dry red chillies till golden brown. Add the chopped tomatoes and coriander powder and cook till the oil starts to surface. Add the ground masala and salt and fry for 4–5 minutes. Add the previously soaked rice. Mix and fry for 1–2 minutes. Now add the hot water so it reaches 1 inch above the surface of rice. Cook rice for about 5 minutes. Add the marinated prawns and mix. Cover and cook first on medium-slow flame and then on slow flame for about 10 minutes till the rice and prawns are done. Serve hot.

Coorg Mutton Biryani (Karnataka)

Preparation time: 10–15 minutes
Marination time: 2 hours
Cooking time: 1 hour
Serves: 8

750	gm mutton, cut into medium sized pieces

2	inch ginger piece	
10	green chillies	
1	pod garlic	**A** ground to a paste
2	inch pieces of fresh green papaya with skin	
1	cup freshly grated coconut	

1	tsp cumin seeds	
2	tsp coriander seeds	
	Seeds from 1 black cardamom	**B**
6	cloves	
1	2 inch cinnamon stick	

400	gm long grain rice
2	bay leaves
1	tsp oil for rice
15	cashew nuts
1	tbs desiccated coconut, sliced
½	cup oil
2	tbs ghee
	Salt

A biryani with a marked coastal flavour, this is made with fresh and desiccated coconut. Fresh green papaya paste is used to tenderize the mutton.

1. Marinate the mutton: Wash and drain the mutton. Apply the ground paste at A together with salt to the mutton and marinate it for half an hour. Lightly dry roast all the ingredients at B and grind to a fine paste. Add to the meat and marinate further for 1½ hours.

2. Prepare the rice: Wash and soak the rice in water for 20 minutes. Drain. Boil 2 litres of water with bay leaves and salt. Once the water starts to boil, add the rice, and cook for about 5–6 minutes till it is half done. Drain out the water using a colander and transfer the rice to a wide pan. Set it aside.

3. Assemble and serve: Heat the oil in a heavy bottomed pan. Fry the cashew nuts and the desiccated coconut till they turn golden. Remove and set aside. In the same oil, add the marinated meat and fry for about 10 minutes. Add a little water and cook covered till the meat is tender. Let 1 cup of liquid remain. Now spread the par-boiled rice over the meat and pour 2 tbs ghee over it. Sprinkle a little water and cover with a tight fitting lid, cooking for the first 2 minutes on medium-high flame to heat up the dish and then on slow flame for about 15–20 minutes till the dish is steaming hot and the rice done. Serve hot garnished with fried cashew nuts and coconut.

Belgaum Chicken Biryani (Karnataka)

Preparation time: 20 minutes
Marination time: 1 hour
Cooking time: 1 hour
Serves: 8

1	chicken, cut into 10–12 pieces
⅓	cup fresh green coriander, chopped
¼	cup fresh mint leaves
15	green chillies
1	small piece ginger
½	pod garlic
1	small onion

A — ground to a fine paste

½	cup yoghurt, whisked
1	tsp garam masala
500	gm long grain rice
1	tsp oil
350	gm small potatoes
4–5	onions, finely sliced
½	tsp saffron
½	cup warm milk
2	tbs melted ghee
3	tbs thick cream
1	tsp oil
	Oil to fry
	Salt

This is a signature biryani from Belgaum, cooked with baby potatoes, and flavoured with saffron and cream.

1. Marinate the chicken: Wash the chicken. Drain. Rub the ground paste at A on the chicken pieces. Add the whisked yoghurt, garam masala, and salt, and mix. Leave to marinate for 1 hour.

2. Prepare the rice and the potatoes: Simultaneously, wash and soak rice for about 20 minutes. Drain. Boil about 2 litres of water. To this, add the rice together with 1 tsp of oil and salt. Cook for about 7–8 minutes till the rice is two thirds done. Drain and transfer to a wide pan. Wash the potatoes. Do not peel the skin but prick them all over with a fork. Rub salt into the potatoes with your hands. Set it aside for 10 minutes. Heat oil and fry the potatoes for about 5–7 minutes till half cooked. Remove and set aside.

4. Cook the chicken: Keep about two thirds cup of oil and remove the rest. Fry the onions till golden brown. Remove half and set aside. To the balance onions add the marinated chicken. Fry stirring frequently and let the contents come to a boil. Continue frying on medium flame till the oil starts to surface. Add a little water and cook covered for about 15 minutes till the chicken is two thirds done. Now add the fried potatoes and cook on slow flame for 5–7 minutes till the chicken and potatoes are tender. When done, there should be at least 1–1½ cups gravy left.

5. Assemble: Spread the rice over the chicken. Sprinkle saffron mixed with warm milk, melted ghee, and fried onions. Dot with cream. Cover with a tight fitting lid and cook for 1–2 minutes on high flame, then on slow flame for about 15 minutes till the rice is done.

South Canara Chicken Biryani (Karnataka)

A unique biryani from the Dakshin Kannad (South Canara) district of Karnataka, this is made neither like the biryani nor the pulao. Instead the rice is first cooked with the gravy of the chicken. The chicken is then placed on a bed of rice and both are cooked together again on dum. The ingredients include fennel, star anise, and poppy seeds.

Preparation time: 20 minutes
Cooking time: 40 minutes
Serves: 8

1	chicken, cut into 10 pieces
600	gm long grain rice
1	inch cinnamon stick
2	star anise
½	cup fresh green chopped coriander leaves
¼	cup mint leaves
8	green chillies
1	tbs poppy seeds
1	tbs fennel seeds
1	tsp cumin seeds
2	inch piece ginger, chopped
10	garlic cloves

ground to a fine paste

4–5	medium sized onions, finely sliced
3	tomatoes, chopped
150	gm oil
	Salt

1. Prepare the chicken: Wash and put the chicken in a colander for the water to drain.

2. Soak the rice: Wash and soak the rice in water for 15–20 minutes, then drain.

3. Fry the masala: Heat 50 gm of oil. Add the ground ingredients and fry on medium slow flame for 2–3 minutes. Set aside.

4. Cook the chicken: Heat 100 gm of oil. Add the onions and fry till golden brown. Then add the ground paste and mix. Add the chopped tomatoes and fry till the oil starts to surface. Add chicken and salt and cook on slow flame for about 20 minutes till it is 90 percent ready.

5. Assemble and serve: Take out the cooked chicken from the gravy and set it aside. Add the previously soaked rice and mix. Add water up to 1 inch above the surface of rice. Cook first on high flame for about 2 minutes and then low flame for about 8–9 minutes till the rice has almost absorbed the water. Now place the chicken over the rice and cook tightly covered on low flame for about 8 minutes till the chicken and rice are done. Serve hot.

Rajah Place Setting courtesy Good Earth

Prawn Biryani with Curry leaves and Aniseed (Kerala)

The curry leaf is extremely common in South Indian food but much less so in the food of north. It is hardly used in biryanis except in some southern-inspired biryanis such as this one. Curry leaves, aniseeds, and coconut milk impart a special flavour to this prawn biryani.

Preparation time: 15 minutes
Cooking time: 40 minutes
Serves: 6–10

750	gm medium sized prawns, shelled and deveined
	Juice of 1 lime
¼	tsp turmeric powder
3	onions, sliced
5–6	twigs of curry leaves

ground to a fine paste:
¼	fresh coconut
6	dried whole red chillies
2	inch piece ginger
6–8	cloves garlic
1	aniseed

	Juice of 1 lime
2	tbs yoghurt, whisked
400	gm long grain rice

A:
1	tbs ghee
2	bay leaves
3–4	green cardamoms
2	1 inch cinnamon sticks
½	tsp peppercorns
½	cup coconut milk

	Juice of 1 lime
	A few sprigs of fresh green coriander, chopped
	A few mint leaves
1	tbs ghee
60	gm oil
	Salt

1. Marinate the prawns: Marinate the prawns with salt, lime juice, and ¼ tsp turmeric for 10 minutes. Wash and set aside.

2. Cook the prawns: Heat the oil and fry the onions till they turn light golden. Add the curry leaves, the ground paste, and salt and fry for about 4–5 minutes. Now add the prawns and fry for 2–3 minutes. Add a little water and cook covered for another 2–3 minutes till the prawns are tender. Add the lime juice and yoghurt and cook gently for another 1–2 minutes.

3. Prepare the rice: Wash and soak the rice in water for about 20 minutes, then drain. Boil 6 glasses of water with all the ingredients at A and salt. Once the water comes to a boil add the rice and cook for about 7–8 minutes till the rice is two thirds done. Drain the water and transfer the rice to a flattish pan.

4. Assemble and serve: Take a heavy bottomed pan and smear it with oil. Place half the quantity of the par-boiled rice in it followed by the prawns with the masala over it. Cover it with the balance rice, dot with ghee, and squeeze the juice of 1 lime. Sprinkle a little water, coriander, and mint. Cover with a tight fitting lid and cook on dum (low flame) for about 10–12 minutes till the rice in done. Serve hot.

Mutton Biryani (Kerala)

This is a slow-fire mutton biryani inspired by the Mughal process of dum cooking. The use of the local kaima rice is much recommended. The pinkish and somewhat sweet rice adds a distinctive colour and taste to the dish.

Preparation time: 15 minutes
Cooking time: 45 minutes
Serves: 8

1	kg boneless mutton, cut into medium pieces
6–7	medium onions, sliced
2	inch piece ginger ⎫
1	pod garlic ⎬ *pounded*
10–15	green chillies ⎭
3	tomatoes, roughly chopped
1	tsp garam masala
	A few sprigs of fresh green coriander, chopped
	A few mint leaves
1	tsp garam masala
	Juice of 2 limes
500	gm kaima or long grain rice
10–15	cashew nuts, broken
3–4	sprigs of curry leaves
2	1 inch cinnamon sticks
5–6	green cardamoms
6	cloves
60	gm ghee–oil, mixed
½	cup ghee–oil, mixed
	Salt

1. Prepare the mutton: Wash and drain the mutton of all water. Heat almost 60 gm of the ghee–oil in a heavy bottomed pan. Add a third of the sliced onions and fry till they become soft and pink. Add crushed ginger, garlic, green chillies, and salt and fry a little. Add chopped tomatoes and sauté for about 5 minutes. Add coriander, mint, and curry leaves. Now add the mutton and fry on medium–slow flame for about 25–30 minutes, sprinkling a little water now and then, till almost done. Add garam masala and juice of lime.

2. Prepare the rice: Heat ½ cup ghee–oil. Fry a third of the sliced onions till they turn golden brown. Remove and set aside. Now fry the cashew nuts till golden. Remove and set aside. In the same ghee–oil, fry the remaining third of the onions for 3–4 minutes till they become soft. Add curry leaves, cinnamon, cardamom, and cloves. Fry for a few seconds after which add the washed and drained rice. Fry for about 5 minutes. Add water, almost double the quantity of rice, and cook for about 10 minutes till the rice absorbs all the water.

3. Assemble and serve: Spread rice over the mutton. Spread the remaining browned onions and cashew nuts over the rice. Cover with a tight fitting lid and cook on dum (a very slow fire) for about 15 minutes till steam forms. Serve hot with coconut and raw mango chutney and thick yoghurt relish made with chopped cucumber, onion, mint, fresh coriander, and green chillies.

Chemeen Biryani (Kerala)

Chemeen means prawns in Malayalam. This one is a wonderful prawn biryani from God's own country.

Preparation time: 20 minutes
Cooking time: 30 minutes
Serves: 6

12	medium sized prawns, cleaned and deveined
	Juice of half a lime
250	gm long grain rice
3	onions, finely sliced
1	tsp garam masala
1	tbs ginger paste ⎫
1	tbs garlic paste ⎪
1	tsp turmeric powder ⎬ A
3	tsp red chilli powder ⎪
6	green chillies, slit ⎪
4	dry whole red chillies ⎭
2	tomatoes, chopped
½	cup yoghurt, whisked
	A few sprigs of fresh green coriander, chopped
	A few mint leaves
2	tbs ghee
4–5	tbs thick cream
50	gm ghee–oil, mixed
	Salt

1. Marinate the prawns: Wash and drain the prawns. Mix the prawns with lime juice and a little salt and marinate for 5–10 minutes. Wash and drain the water and set aside.

2. Soak the rice: Soak rice in water for about 15–20 minutes. Drain and set aside.

3. Cook the prawns: Heat ghee–oil in a heavy bottomed pan and fry the onions till golden brown. Add garam masala followed by all the ingredients at A, salt, and the prawns. Fry for about a minute, then add the chopped tomatoes and fry for 1–2 minutes. Add yoghurt, salt, and about 1 glass of water and cook.

4. Assemble and serve: When the liquid gets reduced by about 25 percent add rice, chopped coriander and mint, and mix. Also add a little water up to 1 inch above the surface of rice. Once the water starts to boil, cover and cook first on medium flame for 2–3 minutes and then on slow flame for about 15–20 minutes till the rice is done. Top it with 2 tbs ghee, 4–5 tbs cream, then cover and let it stand for 5 minutes. Open and serve hot.

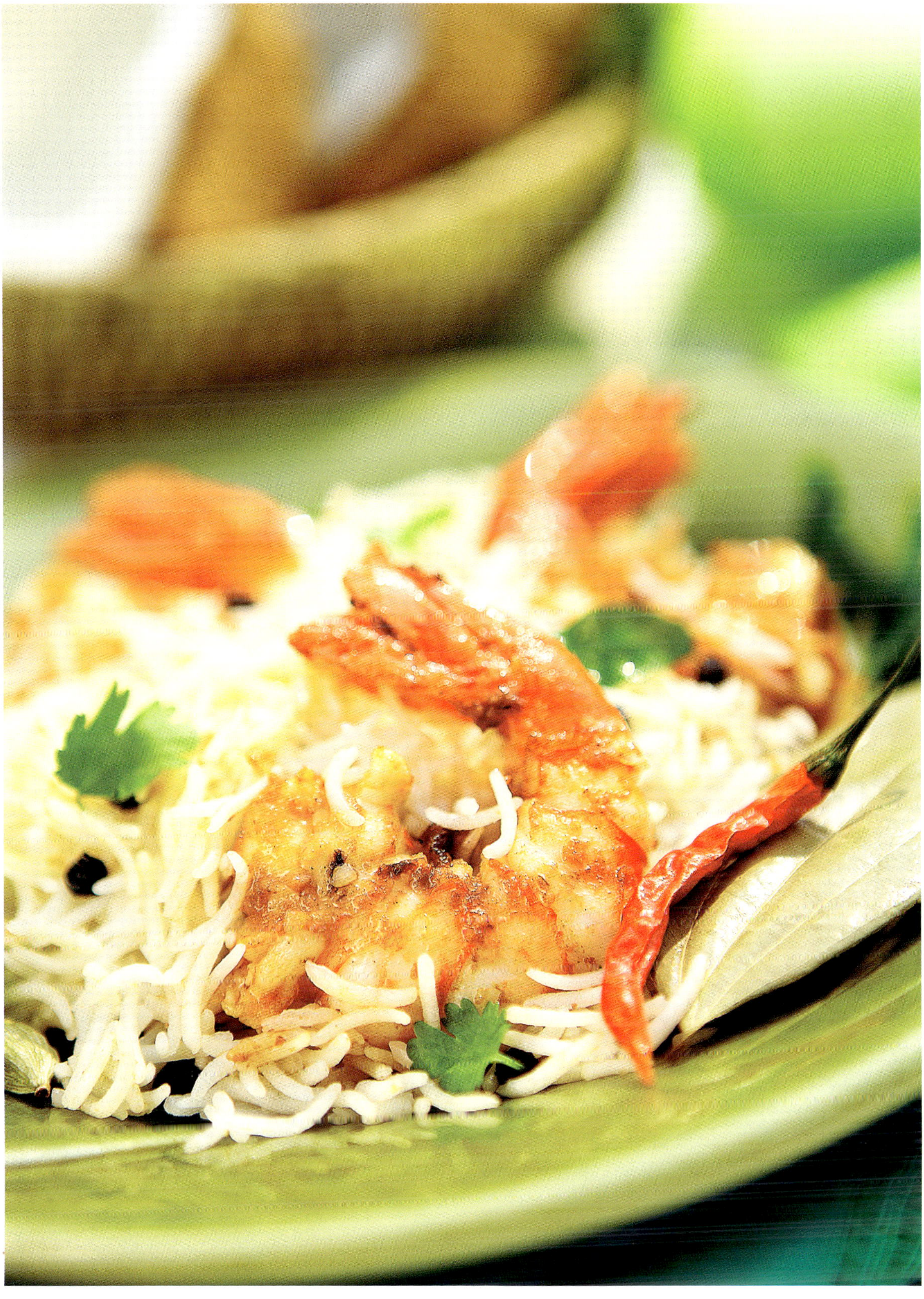

Meen Choru (Kerala)

A fish biryani—meen means fish and choru means rice in Malayalam. The rice used here is kaima, a small-grained sweetish rice native to Kerala. The fish is cooked on dum, garnished with cashew nuts, raisins, and fried onions. Long grain basmati rice can be used if kaima rice is not available.

Preparation time: 15 minutes
Cooking time: 50 minutes
Serves: 6–8

750	gm fish, seer fish or pomfret (cleaned and cut straight across into 2 inch thick pieces)
2–3	tsp red chilli powder
1	tsp turmeric powder
	Juice of 1 lime
3	medium sized onions, sliced
5–6	green chillies, crushed
1	tbs ginger, crushed
2	medium tomatoes, chopped
⅔	cup yoghurt, whisked
	A few sprigs of fresh green coriander, chopped
	A few mint leaves
400	gm kaima rice or long grain basmati rice

1. Prepare and marinate the fish: Get the fish cut, cleaned, and washed. Marinate with red chilli powder, turmeric and salt and juice of one lime for about 10 minutes. Heat oil. Deep fry the fish. Set aside.

2. Soak the rice: Wash rice and soak in water for about 20 minutes. Drain and set aside.

3. Cook the fish: Keep 50 gm oil from the same oil in which the fish was fried and remove the rest. Add sliced onions and fry till transparent. Add crushed green chillies and ginger and fry for a few seconds. Add tomatoes and fry till tomatoes are done. Add whisked yoghurt. Keep stirring for 2–3 minutes. Add fresh coriander, mint, and lime juice. Add the fish to the above masala and simmer for 4–5 minutes. Set aside.

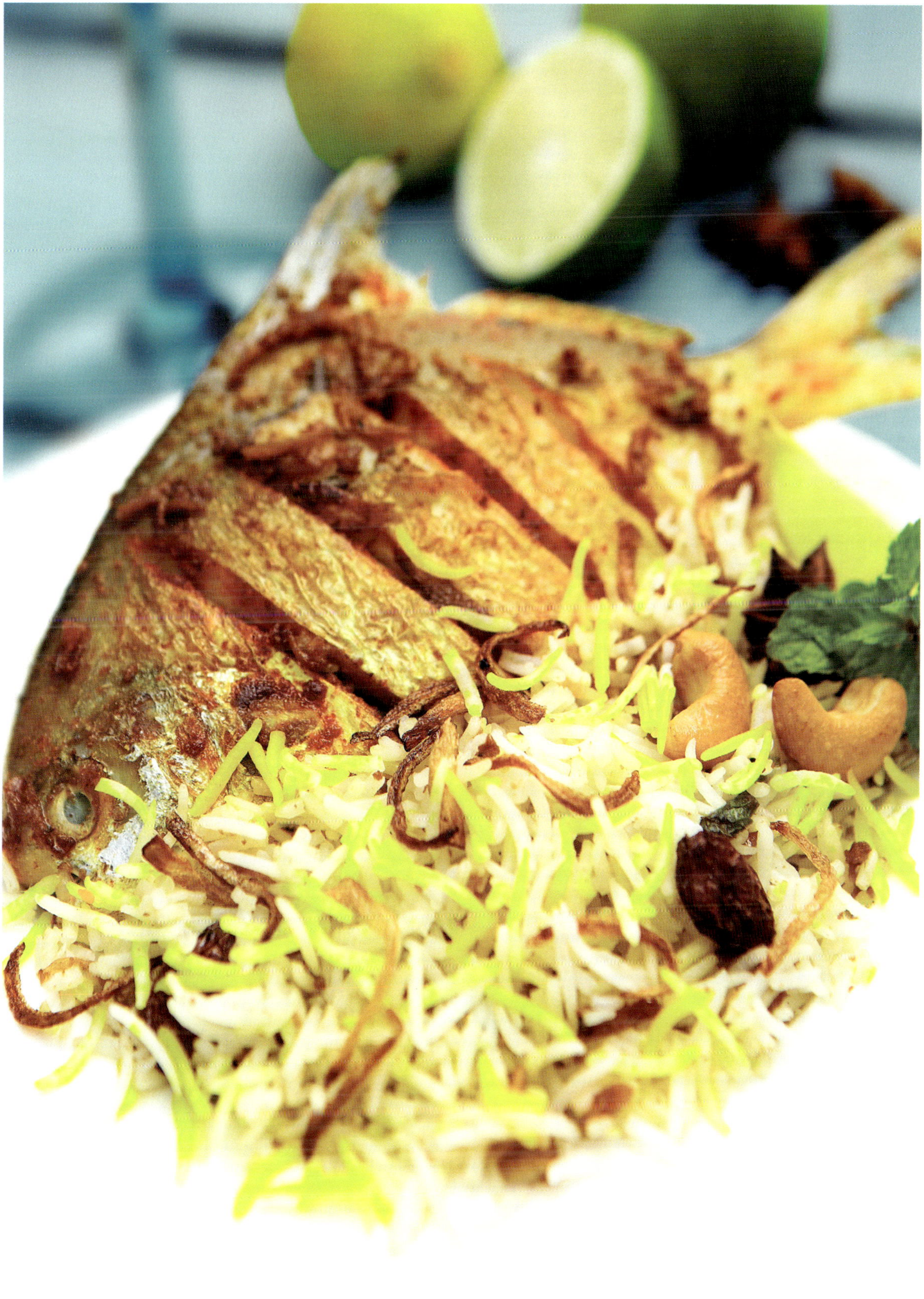

50	gm cashew nuts
30	gm raisins
3	medium onions, sliced
3–4	green cardamoms
1	1 inch cinnamon stick
5–6	cloves
1	tsp garam masala
	Juice of 1 lime
60	gm ghee–oil, mixed
	Oil to fry
	Salt

4. Prepare the rice: Heat ghee–oil. Fry the cashew nuts and then the raisins. Remove and reserve. Fry the onions till golden brown. Remove half and reserve. Add cardamom, cinnamon, and cloves and after a few seconds the rice. Fry for 2–3 minutes. Add a little salt and hot water to reach just about 1 inch over the surface of rice. Cover and cook, first on high flame for about 2 minutes and then on slow flame for about 8 minutes till the water is absorbed and the rice about 80 percent done.

5. Assemble: Take a heavy bottomed pan. Smear with oil. Spread half the rice. Place the fish with the masala over the rice. Spread the garam masala and juice of one lime over the fish. Cover with balance rice. Sprinkle a little water. Cover the pan with a tight fitting lid and cook first on medium flame for 1–2 minutes and then on dum for about 10 minutes till the dish starts to steam.

6. Garnish and serve: Carefully take out the fish biryani and serve hot, garnished with cashew, raisins, and fried onions.

Whole Fish Biryani
(Kerala)

Preparation time: 15 minutes
Cooking time: 45 minutes
Serves: 6–8

500	gms fish, whole and cleaned (pomfret or seer)
½	tsp turmeric powder
2	tsp red chilli powder
3	medium sized onions, finely sliced
2	inch ginger piece ⎫ *coarsely*
7–8	garlic cloves ⎬ *pounded*
6	green chillies ⎭
1	tsp coriander powder
1	tsp poppy seeds (khus khus), finely ground
½	cup yoghurt, whisked
	A few mint leaves, coarsely chopped
	A few sprigs of fresh green coriander, chopped
	Juice of 1–2 limes
400	gm (kaima) rice or long grain rice
½	cup ghee–oil, mixed, for frying
2	medium sized onions, finely sliced
10–15	cashew nuts, broken
15–20	sultanas

This is a whole fish biryani from Kerala, richly flavoured with star anise and rose water. Not only does it taste delicious, but it also looks alluring with the whole fish on top of the rice. It is a great recipe for parties, tantalizing all the senses.

1. Fry the pomfret: Take a cleaned whole seer fish or pomfret. Apply salt, turmeric, and red chilli powder. Heat oil in a pan, fry the fish, and remove.

2. Cook the fish: Keep 60 gm oil from the same oil in which the fish was fried and remove the rest. Heat the oil. Fry the onions till they become soft and pink. Add the pounded ginger, garlic and green chillies, and fry for a minute. Add coriander powder, poppy seeds, and yoghurt and fry well. Add salt, chopped mint, and fresh green coriander and ½ cup water and cook well. Add the fried fish and mix gently with the fried masala without breaking the fish. Squeeze the juice of lime.

3. Soak the rice: Wash rice and soak in water for 20 minutes. Drain and set aside.

4. Prepare the rice: Heat ghee–oil mix. Fry the onions till brown. Keep aside. Fry the cashew nuts till golden. Remove. Fry the sultanas. They will swell up in a few seconds. Remove and set aside. In the same ghee–oil, add star anise followed in a few seconds by rice and fry for 2–3 minutes. Add hot water, almost double the quantity of rice, a little salt and cook on slow flame for about 8 minutes till the rice absorbs the water and is almost done.

2	star anise
1	tsp garam masala
2–3	tbs rose water
	A few drops edible yellow colour, mixed with a little water
½	cup ghee–oil, mixed for frying
	Salt

5. **Assemble and serve:** Take a heavy bottomed pan and smear it with oil. Spread half of the rice in it, then place the masala coated fish over the rice. Sprinkle half of the garam masala and rose water and cover with the balance rice. Sprinkle the balance garam masala, rose water, and yellow colour, and sprinkle a little water. Close with a tight fitting lid. Cook on dum for about 15–20 minutes till the rice is done with each grain still separate. To serve, carefully take out the whole fish with rice. Garnish with fried onions, cashew nuts, and sultanas.

Thalassery Chicken Biryani (Kerala)

The biryanis of Kerala have a strong individuality, despite the Arabic and the Muslim influences. The rice used, be it kaima rice or jeerakashala rice, adds a distinctive taste of its own. Another distinguishing feature of this biryani is the use of star anise.

Preparation time: 10 minutes
Marination time: 1 hour
Cooking time: 50 minutes
Serves: 8

1	chicken, cut into 10–12 pieces
½	tsp turmeric powder
1	cup hung yoghurt
400	gms long grain rice
	Juice of ½ a lime

A:
2	bay leaves
2	star anise
1	tsp peppercorns
1	1 inch cinnamon stick
6	cloves
4	green cardamoms

1	tbs ginger, crushed
1	tbs garlic, crushed
8–10	green chillies, crushed
4–5	medium sized onions, sliced
3–4	tomatoes, sliced
2–3	tbs rose water
	A few sprigs of fresh green coriander, chopped
60	gm ghee–oil, mixed
	Salt

1. Marinate the chicken: Mix the chicken with salt, turmeric powder, and hung yoghurt for about 1 hour.

2. Prepare the rice: Wash and soak the rice for about 20 minutes, then drain. Boil about 2 litres of water. Add salt, juice of half a lime followed by the rice, and cook till it is two thirds done. Drain and transfer the rice to a flattish pan.

3. Cook the chicken: Heat the ghee–oil mixture. Add the whole spices at A. In a few seconds, add the crushed ginger, garlic, and the green chillies. Fry for 1–2 minutes, add the sliced onions and fry till they become translucent. Add the tomatoes and salt; fry for a couple of minutes, then add the marinated chicken. Cook till the water dries up and the oil starts to surface. Add a little water and cook the chicken for about 20 minutes till tender. When done, the dish should have about 1 cup gravy left.

4. Assemble and serve: Smear a heavy bottomed pan with ghee and put two thirds of the par-boiled rice in it. Place the chicken over the rice. Sprinkle half of the rose water and coriander. Cover with the balance rice. Sprinkle a little water, the balance of rose water, and coriander. Cover with a tight fitting lid and cook for 1–2 minutes on medium–high flame for the dish to get hot and then on low flame for about 15–20 minutes till it is steaming hot and the rice done. Take out gently in chunks from the side and serve hot.

Northern Malabar Kozhi Biryani (Kerala)

Preparation time: 20 minutes
Marination time: 2 hours
Cooking time: 40 minutes
Serves: 8

1	chicken cut into 10–12 pieces
500	gm kaima rice or long grain rice
1	fresh coconut
3	tsp ginger paste
1	tsp garlic paste
8–10	green chillies, ground
4	medium onions, finely sliced
2	sprigs curry leaves
1	tsp peppercorns
½	tsp turmeric powder
1	tsp red chilli powder
1	tsp coriander powder
6–8	cashew nuts
8–10	raisins
½	cup ghee–oil, mixed
2	tbs ghee
	Salt

A wedding speciality, this biryani is made with the famous small-grained kaima rice of Kerala. If kaima rice is not available, you may use basmati in its place. What is striking about this biryani is its rich taste of ginger and ghee.

1. Wash the chicken: Wash the chicken pieces and drain the water out.

2. Soak the rice: Soak rice in liberal quantity of water for about 20 minutes. Drain and keep for about 15 minutes.

3. Prepare the coconut milk: Grate the coconut, add about 1 glass of water, and churn it in a mixer. Squeeze to extract thick coconut milk. Set aside.

4. Marinate the chicken: Marinate the chicken in half the quantity of ginger, garlic, and green chilli paste for 2 hours.

5. Cook the chicken: Heat half a cup ghee–oil and fry the onions till golden brown. Add the balance of ginger, garlic, and green chilli paste. Fry for a few seconds, add the marinated chicken and fry a little. Then add the curry leaves, peppercorns, turmeric powder, chilli powder, coriander powder, and salt. Mix and tumble the chicken. Add a little water and cook covered till the chicken is a

little more than half done. Then add a little more water again and mix. Sprinkle the rice over the chicken in a layer without mixing with the chicken. Pour the thick coconut milk over the rice. The liquids should come 1¼ inch over the surface of rice. Cover and cook first on medium–high flame for about 2 minutes and then on low flame for about 15–20 minutes.

6. Garnish and serve: Heat 2 tbs ghee and fry the cashews till golden. Remove and set aside. Add raisins to the ghee and fry for a few seconds. When they swell up, remove and place with the cashews. When the rice has absorbed the water and when chicken and rice are cooked, sprinkle the cashew nuts and raisins and the ghee in which they were fried over the rice. When done, the chicken and rice should have been cooked and each grain of rice should be separate. Gently take out the rice and chicken from the side without mixing so that they come out in different layers and serve hot in a large platter.

Tellichery Biryani (Kerala)

Tellichery is an anglicized name for Thalassery, a district in Kerala. The original name of Thalassery has been restored post-Independence. Although both refer to the same place, the Tellichery Biryani is different from the Thalassery Biryani. As compared to the Thalassery Biryani, this one is simpler and is cooked without star anise and rose water.

Preparation time: 15 minutes
Cooking time: 50 minutes
Serves: 6

350	gm long grain rice
3–4	medium sized onions, finely sliced
1½	tsp ginger, crushed
1½	tsp garlic, crushed
6–8	green chillies, crushed
500	gm mutton, cut into medium pieces
1	tsp garam masala
250	gm yoghurt, whisked
2	large tomatoes, sliced round, of medium thickness
⅓	cup milk
2	tbs ghee
½	cup oil
1	tsb oil
	Salt

1. Prepare the rice: Wash and soak the rice for about 20 minutes then drain it out. Boil about 1½ litres of water with a little salt and 1 tsp oil. When the water starts boiling, add the rice, and cook for 7–8 minutes till two thirds done. Drain the water and transfer the rice to a flattish pan. Set aside.

2. Prepare the mutton: Heat oil and add the sliced onions. Fry till golden brown. Add ginger, garlic, and green chillies and fry for a minute. Now add mutton with garam masala and salt and fry on medium flame for 5–6 minutes. Add yoghurt and keep stirring till it comes to a boil. Cook for 4–5 minutes. Add a little water, just enough to cover the meat, and cook for about 20 minutes till the meat is tender. The meat should have a thickish gravy, when done.

3. Assemble and serve: Take a heavy bottomed pan, smear it with ghee and add the cooked mutton. Place the sliced tomatoes over the meat and cover with the par boiled rice. Sprinkle the milk and dot with ghee. Cover with a tight fitting lid and seal with dough or place a heavy stone on the lid to prevent the steam from escaping. Cook for the first 1–2 minutes on high flame to heat up the dish and then on low flame for about 10 minutes till the dish starts to steam and rice is done. Serve steaming hot.

Zafraan Pilaf (Hyderabad)

Preparation time: 10 minutes
Cooking time: 20 minutes
Serves: 4

250	gm long grain rice
½	tsp saffron, lightly roasted, crushed and dissolved in ½ cup warm milk
10–15	almonds, blanched, skin peeled and slivered
25	gm sultanas (black raisins, about 15–20)
6	cloves
3	tbs ghee
	Salt

Hyderabadi cuisine loves to use saffron or zafraan in its dishes. This particular biryani is quick and easy to make, as compared to most. It is suitable for all seasons and all occasions.

1. Prepare the rice: Wash and soak the rice for about 20 minutes. Drain. Place the rice in a heavy bottomed pan and add water 1 inch above the surface of rice. Add salt, ghee and saffron, dissolved in milk. Cover with a tight fitting lid. Cook first on high flame for about 2 minutes, then on low flame for about 8–10 minutes till the water is absorbed and rice cooked.

2. Garnish and serve: Heat the ghee. Fry the almonds till it turns light golden. Add and fry the sultanas for a few seconds followed by the cloves. Pour them over the saffron rice with the ghee. Serve steaming hot.

Qabooli (Hyderabad)

Preparation time: 20 minutes
Cooking time: 45 minutes
Serves: 6–8

500	gm long grain rice
250	gm yellow split gram lentils
	A pinch of turmeric
3	onions, finely sliced
1	tsp ginger paste
1	tsp garlic paste
1/3	tsp turmeric powder
1	tsp red chilli powder
1	cup yoghurt, whisked
1/2	inch piece cinnamon ⎫
2–3	cardamoms ⎬ ground
1/2	tsp caraway seeds ⎪
1/2	tsp peppercorns ⎭
1/2	cup fresh green coriander, chopped
1/4	cup mint leaves, chopped
4	green chillies, chopped
	Juice of 2–3 limes
1/3	cup milk
2	tbs ghee
2/3	cup oil
	Salt

A delicious vegetarian biryani, this recipe has come down from the Mughals, and is made with rice and split gram lentils. In Hyderabad, it is a celebration dish.

1. Prepare the rice: Wash and soak rice in water for 20 minutes, then drain. Boil about 2½ litres of water with a little salt. When the water starts to boil, add rice, and cook for about 6 minutes till two thirds done. Drain the water and transfer the rice to a flat dish and set aside.

2. Prepare the lentils: Wash and soak the yellow split lentils for 20 minutes. Boil in just enough water (2–3 cups) with a little salt and turmeric for about 15 minutes till 90 percent done. Drain any excess water. Set aside.

3. Cook the lentils: Heat oil. Fry the onions till golden brown. Remove half and set aside. Add ginger and garlic and fry till golden. Add turmeric and red chilli powder followed by yoghurt. Stir briskly till the contents come to a boil and the oil starts to surface. Add the lentils, fry for 2 minutes, and set aside.

4. Assemble and serve: Take a heavy bottomed pan and smear with oil. Place half of the par-boiled rice. Spread the lentils over the rice. Sprinkle half of the ground spices. Also spread half of the coriander, mint and green chillies, and lime juice. Cover with balance rice. Sprinkle milk, ghee, the balance powdered spices, fried onions and the balance coriander, mint, and green chillies. Cover with a tight fitting lid and cook for the first 1–2 minutes on high flame and then on slow flame for about 10 minutes till the rice starts to steam. Serve steaming hot.

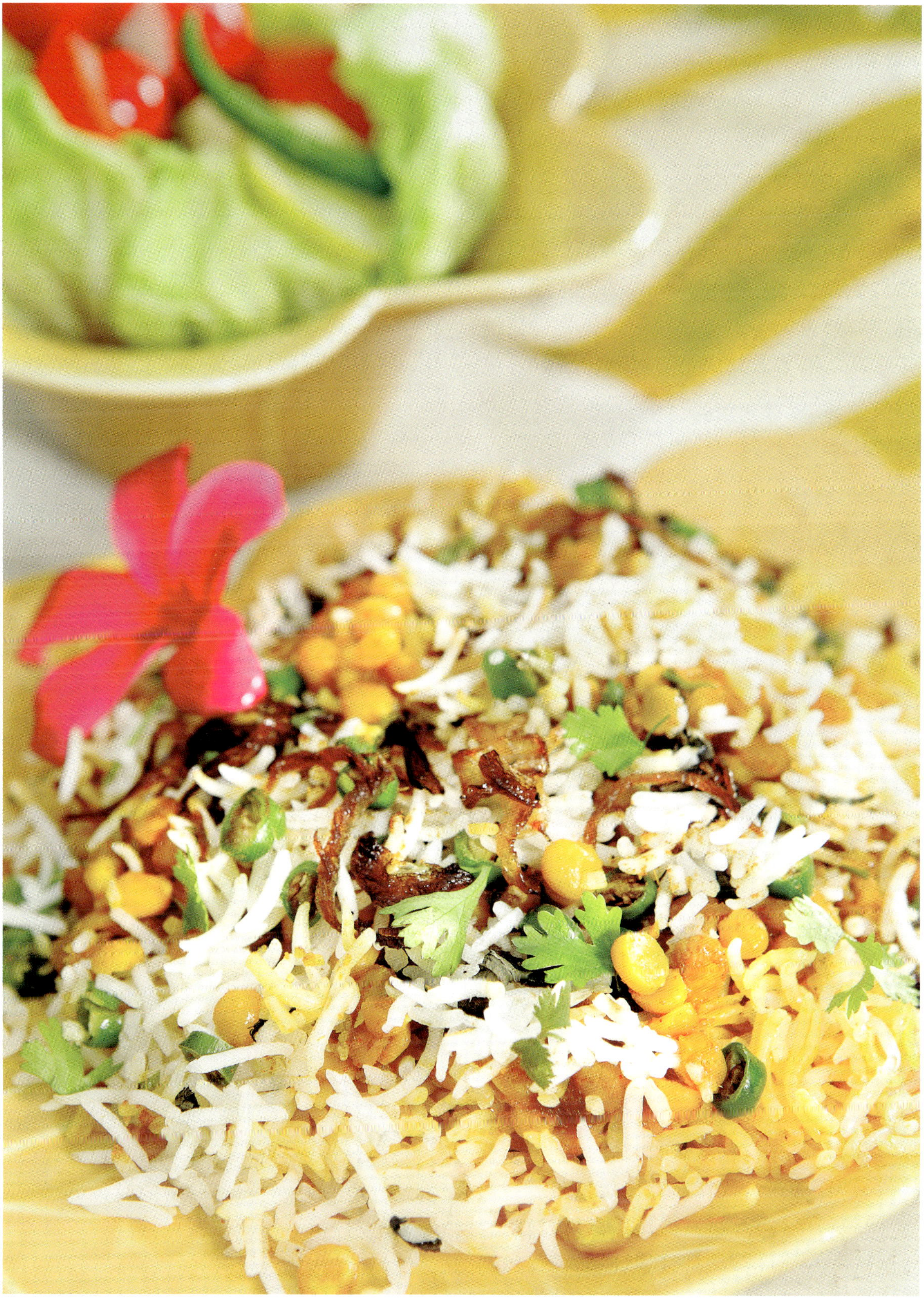

Udupi Vegetable Biryani (Karnataka)

Preparation time: 25–30 minutes
Cooking time: 50 minutes
Serves: 8–10

800	gm long grain rice
200	gm carrots, cut into 1 inch sized pieces
200	gm beans, cut into 1 inch sized pieces
200	cauliflower, cut into medium sized florets
200	gm knol kol, cut into medium sized pieces
3–4	medium sized onions

A — ground to a fine paste:

1	1 inch cinnamon stick
2	star anise
⅓	cup fresh green coriander, chopped
¼	cup mint leaves
8–10	green chillies, chopped
1	tsp cumin seeds
1	tbs fennel seeds
1½	inch piece ginger
10	garlic cloves
½	grated coconut

2–3	tomatoes, chopped
1	cup yoghurt, whisked
800	gm long grain rice
	Croutons from 4 slices of bread, each cut into 12 pieces and fried golden brown
150	gm oil
	Salt

Udupi, a temple town, is celebrated for its idlis, dosas and vadas as well as for its vegetarian food. This is a special vegetable biryani made with cauliflower and knol kol (kohlrabi).

1. Soak the rice: Wash and soak the rice in water for 15–20 minutes.

2. Cook the vegetables: Wash all the vegetables and put them in a colander for the water to drain. Heat the oil and add the onions and fry till golden brown. Then add the ground paste and fry for about 5–6 minutes. Add the chopped tomatoes, and mix and fry till it blends with the paste. Add the yoghurt and stir continuously till the contents come to a boil. Thereafter cook it for another minute. Add the vegetables and salt, and mix and cook on medium flame for about 5 minutes. Set it aside.

3. Assemble and serve: Take a heavy bottomed pan. Place the previously soaked rice in it and add hot water till it reaches just about 1 inch above the surface of rice. Add salt and cook for about 5 minutes till it is half done. Add the vegetables to it and mix. Cook covered on slow flame for about 6–7 minutes till the rice and vegetables are done. Add half of the croutons and mix gently with the rice. Serve hot, garnished with the remaining croutons.

Jackfruit Biryani–I (Andhra Pradesh)

Preparation time: 20 minutes
Cooking time: 50 minutes
Serves: 6–8

½	kg jackfruit (after removing the skin and the pith), cut into about 2 inch x 1 inch pieces
1	fresh coconut
2	onions, finely sliced, fried to a golden brown and crushed when cool
1	tbs ginger juice
1	tsp cumin powder
1	tbs green chillies, ground
350	gm long grain rice
2	onions, finely sliced
1	black cardamom, opened at the top end ⎫
2	green cardamoms ⎬ A
6	cloves ⎪
1	1 inch cinnamon stick ⎭
4	green chillies, chopped
	Juice of 1–2 limes
½	tsp saffron, dissolved in ⅓ cup warm milk
60	gm oil
3	tbs oil
1	tbs ghee
	Salt

This is a rare biryani from the Andhra region. Unlike the jackfruit biryani from Kerala, this one uses only saffron, and no screwpine or rose water. Fresh coconut lends a smooth creamy flavour to the dish.

1. Boil the jackfruit: Boil the jackfruit in about 3–4 glasses of water with salt for about 6–8 minutes till half done. Drain the water and set the jackfruit aside.

2. Prepare coconut milk: Grate the coconut, add 2–3 cups of warm water and churn it in a blender. Squeeze it to extract 2 cups coconut milk. Set it aside.

3. Cook the jackfruit: Mix the jackfruit with crushed onions, ginger juice, cumin powder, and ground green chillies. Heat 3 tbs oil and lightly fry the jackfruit. Sprinkle a little water and cook it covered for 5–6 minutes.

4. Prepare the rice: Soak the rice for about 20 minutes, then drain. Heat 60 gm of oil and fry the onions till they turn golden. Add the whole spices at A and after a few seconds, add the rice. Fry it for 2–3 minutes, then mix hot water to the coconut milk and pour into the rice so that water comes about 1 inch above the rice. Also add salt. Cook first on high flame for 2 minutes and then on medium low flame for about 6–7 minutes till the rice is about two thirds done.

5. Assemble: Take a heavy bottomed pan smeared with oil and place half of the rice in it. Spread the cooked jackfruit and cover with the balance rice. Dot with ghee, sprinkle the chopped green chillies and add lime juice. Also sprinkle saffron milk. Cook for 2 minutes on medium-high flame and then on low flame for about 10–15 minutes till the dish is steaming hot.

Masoor Dal Biryani–Vegetarian Version (Tamil Nadu)

Preparation time: 15–20 minutes
Cooking time: 50 minutes
Serves: 6–8

250	gm long grain rice
2	bay leaves
1	tsp oil
150	gm red lentils (masoor dal skinned)
1/3	tsp turmeric powder
5	onions, sliced

2	inch ginger piece	
4–5	cloves garlic	
5–6	green chillies	*ground to a fine paste*
4	dry red chillies	
1/2	tsp peppercorns	
2	tbs coriander seeds	
1	tsp cumin seeds	
1	1 inch cinnamon stick	

2–3	tomatoes, chopped
1½	tbs ghee
5–6	cloves
1/3	cup milk
1/2	cup oil
	Salt

This is a fine vegetarian biryani made with red lentils and spiced with chillies, both red and green, as well as peppercorns. Not for the faint-hearted, this one is really spicy.

1. Prepare the rice: Wash and soak the rice in water for 20 minutes, then drain. Boil about 2 litres of water with bay leaves, 1 tsp oil, and salt. Once the water starts to boil add rice and cook for about 8 minutes till 80 percent done. Drain the excess water and transfer the rice to a wide pan.

2. Prepare the dal: Boil the masoor dal with turmeric and salt in just enough water for about 7–8 minutes so that it is about 80 percent cooked. Drain any excess water.

3. Cook the dal: Heat the oil. Add the onions and fry till golden brown. Remove and reserve half. Add the ground paste to the remaining onions and fry for about 2 minutes. Add the chopped tomatoes and fry for 2–3 minutes. Add about ½ cup water and fry till the oil starts to surface. Add the masoor dal and mix and cook covered for about 2 minutes.

4. Assemble and serve: Take a heavy bottomed pan and grease it with oil. Spread half the quantity of rice and then the lentils over the rice. Cover this with the balance rice. Heat ghee and add cloves. In a few seconds, when the cloves turn brown, pour the ghee and cloves over the rice. Sprinkle milk. Cover with a tight fitting lid. Cook for the first 1–2 minutes on medium–high flame to heat up the dish and then cook on slow flame for about 10 minutes till the dish starts to steam. Serve hot garnished with fried onions.

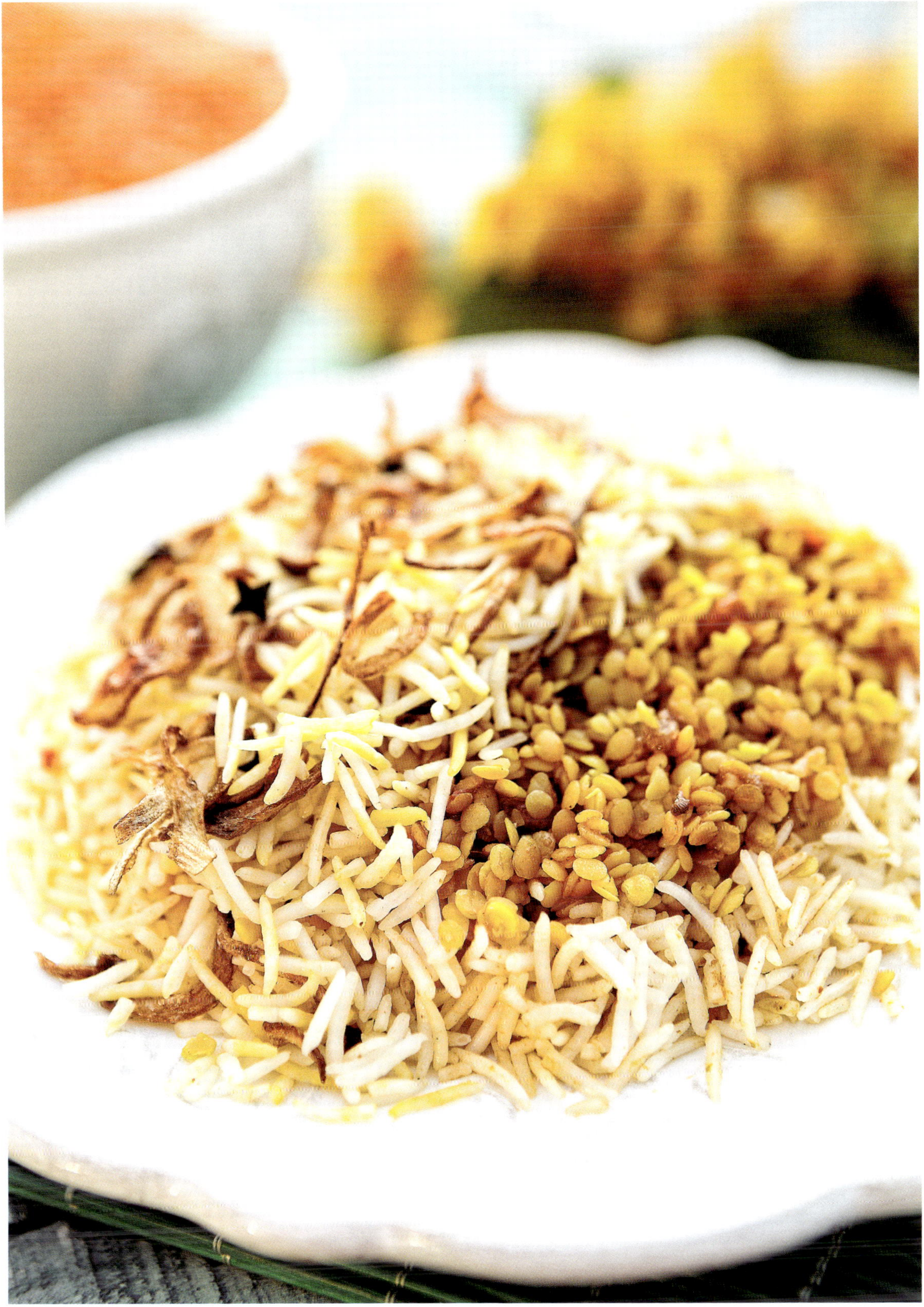

Coconut Pulao (Tamil Nadu)

Preparation time: 20 minutes
Cooking time: 20 minutes
Serves: 6

350	gm long grain rice
1	fresh coconut
1	inch piece of cinnamon
3–4	green cardamoms
1	bay leaf
2–3	cloves
2	medium onions, finely sliced
1½	inch piece of ginger, chopped
3–4	garlic cloves, crushed
1	tbs pepper, crushed
8	cloves
2	tbs ghee
50	gm oil
	Salt

Being a coastal state laden with coconut, this is a vegetarian coconut rice dish, flavoured with all the local spices.

1. Wash and soak the rice for about 20 minutes. Drain and set it aside.

2. Prepare the coconut milk: Grate the coconut. Add 1 glass of water and churn it in a mixer. Strain to extract thick coconut milk. Add another glass of water to the coconut, mix and strain to extract the second coconut milk, which will be lighter. Keep both these aside.

3. Cook the rice: Heat the oil. Add cinnamon, cardamom, bay leaf, and cloves and in a few seconds add the onions. When the onions begin to get pink, add ginger and garlic, and fry for just about one minute. Then add the previously soaked rice and fry for about 2 minutes. Now first add the thick coconut milk, followed by the thin coconut milk. The liquid should come 1 inch over the surface of rice. Adjust the level by adding water accordingly. Add salt and pepper. Cover and cook on high flame and bring the dish to a boil. Reduce the heat and cook on medium flame and then on very low flame for about 8–10 minutes till the liquids are absorbed and the rice is done.

4. Garnish and serve: Heat the ghee. Add the cloves and in a few seconds pour the ghee with the cloves over the rice. Serve hot.

Jackfruit Biryani–II (Kerala)

Preparation time: 15 minutes
Cooking time: 50 minutes
Serves: 8

400	gm long grain rice
750	gm baby jackfruit, skinned and cut into about 50 gm pieces with the hard inner core removed.

1	tsp ginger paste	
1	tsp garlic paste	
1	medium onion, ground	
8–10	green chillies, ground into paste	A
1	tsp cumin powder	
½	tsp garam masala powder	
1	tsp crushed pepper	
½	tsp red chilli powder	
⅓	tsp turmeric powder	

2	green cardamoms
6	cloves
3	medium onions, finely sliced
¾	cup yoghurt, whisked
½	tsp saffron, lightly roasted and dissolved in ⅓ cup warm milk
2	tbs rose water (gulab jal)
2	tbs screwpine water (kewra)
2	inch ginger piece, sliced
3	green chillies, slit
1	tsp ghee
	Oil to fry
	Salt

This is a vegetarian biryani made with jackfruit, which adds to its unique taste. Here jackfruit is mixed with saffron, screwpine water and rose water.

1. Prepare the rice: Wash and soak rice in water for 20 minutes, then drain. Boil about 2 litres of water with a little salt and 1 tsp oil. When the water starts to boil, add rice and cook for 6–7 minutes till two thirds done. Drain the water and transfer the rice to a flattish pan. Set aside.

2. Prepare the jackfruit: Add all the ingredients at A to the jackfruit and marinate for about 15 minutes. Heat oil and deep-fry lightly. Set aside. Take about 60 gm oil from the same oil in which the jackfruit was fried and heat it. Add cardamom and cloves and fry for a few seconds. Now add the sliced onions and fry till golden brown. Add yoghurt and stir constantly till it comes to a boil. Add the fried jackfruit, mix, and sprinkle a little water. Cover and cook for about 10–12 minutes till the jackfruit is tender.

3. Assemble and serve: Take a heavy bottomed pan and smear it with ghee. Place the jackfruit with the gravy coating it in the pan and cover with the par-boiled rice. Sprinkle saffron milk, rose and screwpine water and if need be, a little water. Also sprinkle ginger and green chillies. Cover with a tight fitting lid and cook for about 10 minutes on medium-slow flame till the rice steams and is done. Serve hot.

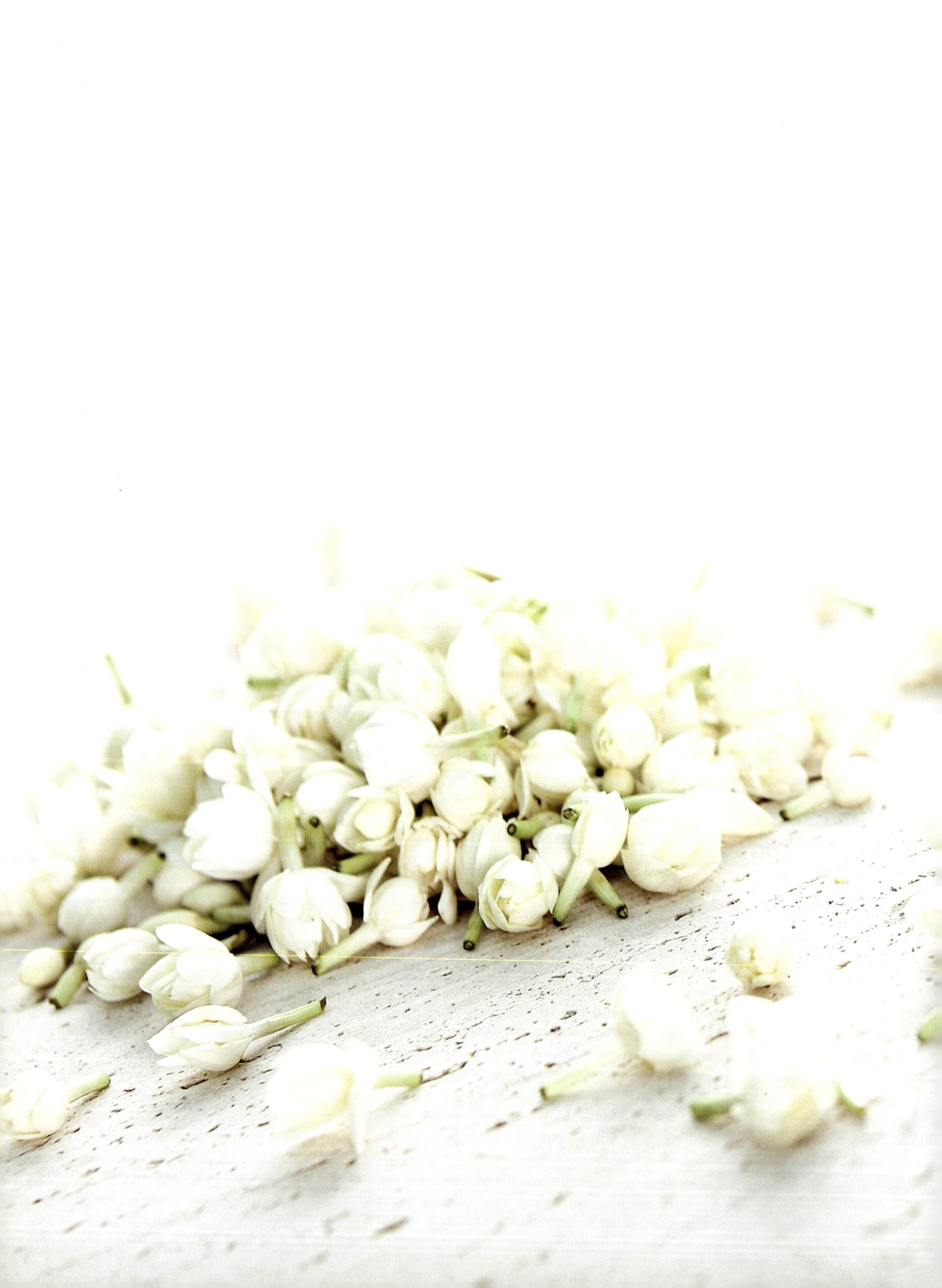

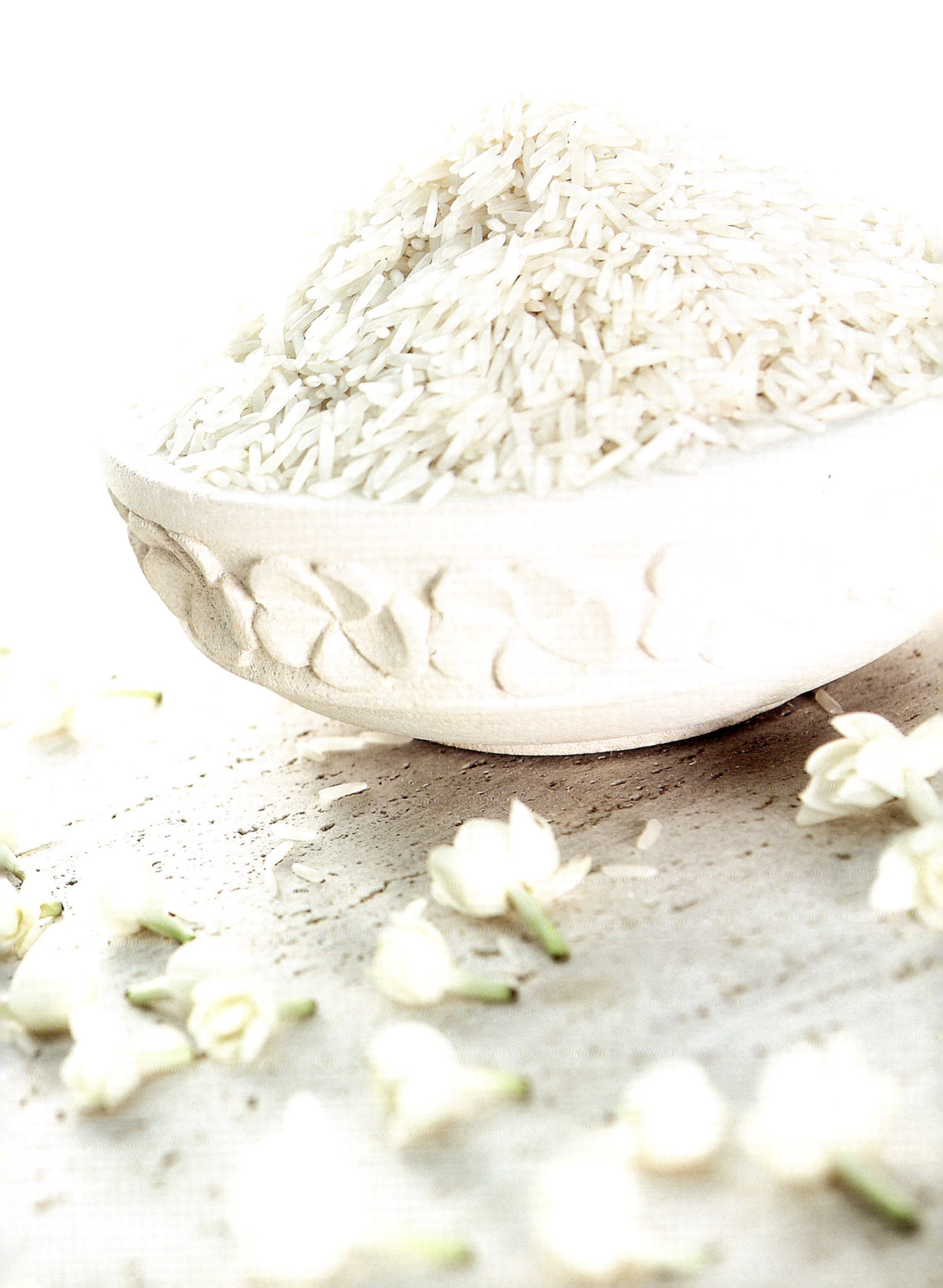

East

East India has a rich culinary history, particularly in Bengal. Apart from its own rich cuisine, Bengal has also seen the flowering of royal Muslim cuisine such as the inimitable bakhar khani roti, gifted to us by Bakhar Khan, the governor of Bengal. As the Mughal empire in Delhi started tottering, Bengal witnessed the flowering of the satrap courts at Dacca and Murshidabad. After the state of Murshidabad collapsed, the Nawab took refuge in Kolkata. Similarly, after Tipu Sultan of Mysore was killed in battle, his family relocated to Kolkata. Last but not least, when the British deposed the Awadh ruler, Wajid Ali Shah, he too was exiled to Kolkata. These royal families brought with them their own range of pulaos and biryanis, the kormas and kaliyas and various other dishes that had evolved in Mughal and Awadh courts. In due course, several of the biryanis underwent Bengali orientation, acquiring their own special flavour with the use of fish and mustard seeds.

Bihar seems to lack a biryani repertoire and I could locate just one chicken and mutton recipe. Assam, too, lacks a wide range although we have from the state, the famous Kampuri biryani, native to the town of Kampur. The seven north–eastern states, even the erstwhile princely states of Manipur and Tripura, do not seem to have any tradition of biryanis.

Fish Biryani with Aloo Bukhara
(West Bengal)

Preparation time: 15 minutes
Marination time: 15 minutes
Cooking time: 50 minutes
Serves: 8

750	gm sea bass or king fish, cut across into 1½ inch thick pieces
6	green chillies
2	inch ginger piece } ground
10	garlic cloves
⅓	tsp turmeric powder
1½	tsp red chilli powder
½	tsp mustard seeds
½	tsp cumin seeds
1	large onion, finely sliced
1	tomato, coarsely chopped
	Juice of ½ a lime
400	gm rice
10–12	dried plums, deseeded
½	cup milk
	A few mint leaves
1	tbs ghee or butter
½	cup oil
	Salt

India boasts of several fish biryanis but what makes this one special is that it is made with dried plums, commonly called Aloo Bukhara, which adds a mildly sweet flavour to the dish. The unusual blend of fish and dried plums with mustard seeds makes this truly exotic.

1. Marinate the fish: Wash and drain fish of all the water. Mix the ground green chillies, ginger, and garlic with turmeric, red chilli powder, and salt and apply this paste to the fish. Marinate for about 10 minutes.

2. Cook the fish: Heat the oil and add the mustard seeds followed by cumin seeds. When the mustard starts to splutter add the sliced onions and fry till golden brown. Add the chopped tomato and stir and cook. Sprinkle a little water and cook till the oil starts to surface. Add the marinated fish and fry for 3–4 minutes, turning the fish so that it is fried on both sides. Sprinkle a little water and cook on low flame for about 10 minutes till the fish is ready.

3. Prepare the rice: Wash and soak the rice for about 10 minutes. Drain. Bring about 2 litres of water to a boil with salt and the juice of half a lime. Add the rice and cook for about 6–7 minutes till it is two thirds done. Drain the water and transfer the rice to a flat pan.

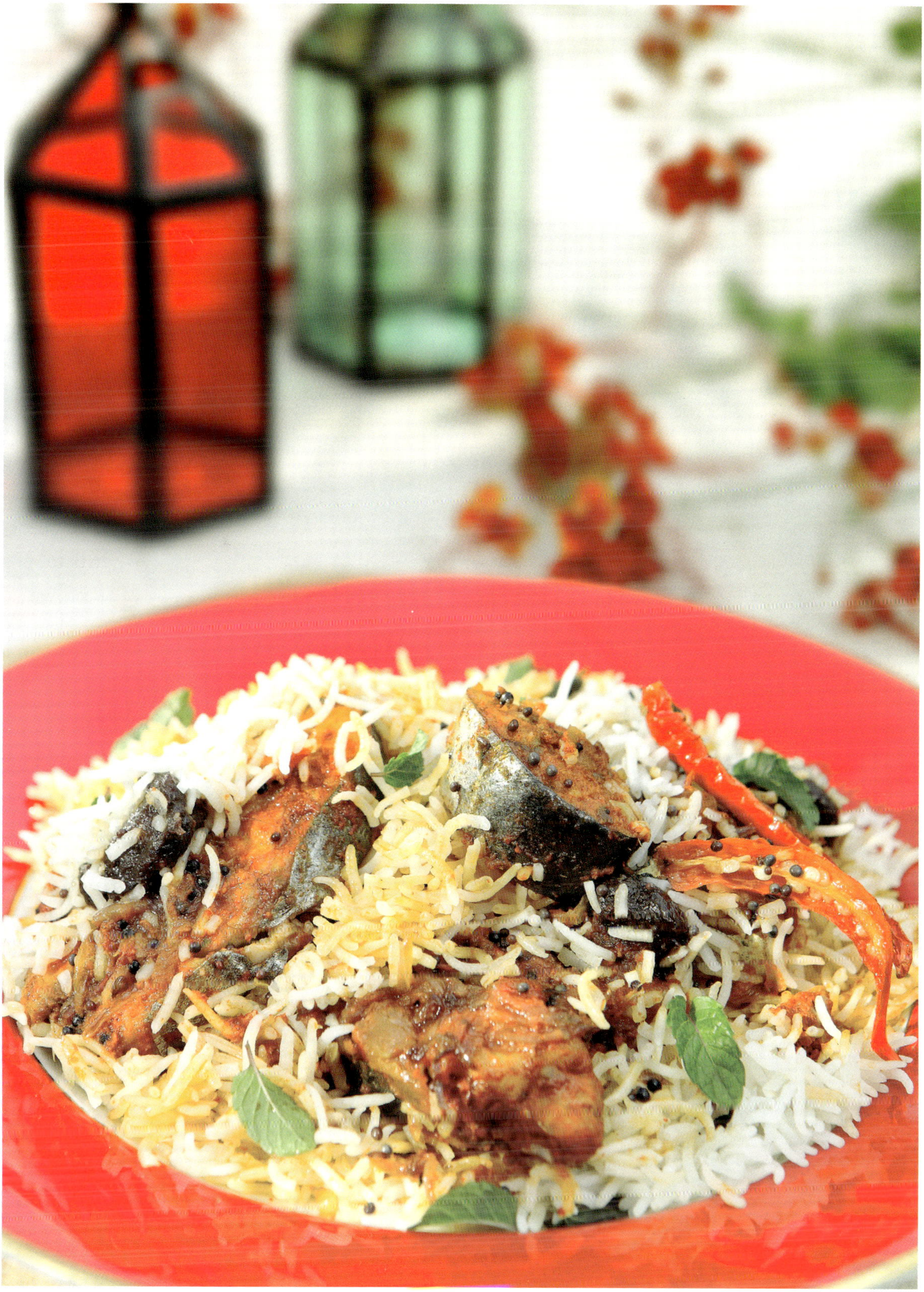

4. Assemble and serve: Take a large heavy base pan and smear it with oil. Put two thirds of the par-boiled rice in the pan and gently spread the fish with the masala over the rice. Place the plums over the fish and cover with the balance rice. Sprinkle half a cup of milk over the rice and mint. Dot the rice with 1 tbs ghee or butter. Now cover with a tight fitting lid. Cook for the first 1–2 minutes on high flame to heat up the dish. Then cook on slow flame for about 10–15 minutes till the rice is done and steaming hot. When done, each grain of rice should be separate. Gently take out the fish and rice and serve hot.

Chicken and Apricot Biryani (West Bengal)

Preparation time: 10 minutes
Cooking time: 50 minutes
Serves: 6

500	gm boneless chicken, cut into 1½ inch pieces
350	gm long grain rice
12	apricots, soaked in water for ½ an hour
4	medium sized onions, finely sliced
1½	cups chicken stock
2	tbs ginger, finely chopped
6	green chillies, chopped
1½	tsp pepper powder
3	tbs thick cream
1	tbs ghee
	Oil to fry
	Salt

Apricot Biryani, as the name suggests, is made with soaked apricots. It is a biryani of boneless chicken unusually flavoured with apricot puree, and cooked in chicken stock. The apricot puree adds its own special flavour to the biryani.

1. Wash the meat: Wash and place the chicken in a colander for the water to drain.

2. Prepare the rice: Wash and soak the rice in water for about 20 minutes, then drain out the water. Boil 1½ litres of water with a little salt and 1 tsp oil. Cook for about 7–8 minutes till the rice is two thirds done. Drain the rice, and transfer it to a wide dish. Set aside.

3. Prepare the apricots: Cut each apricot into 6 pieces. Break and remove the kernel from the stone. Soak the kernels in warm water for a few minutes, peel the skin, and set aside.

4. Make the apricot puree: Heat the ghee. Add half of the apricots and fry for a few seconds. Set it aside. In a heavy base pan, large enough to take the chicken and the rice, heat the oil and fry the onions till golden brown. Remove and allow to cool, then add the balance apricots and 1 cup of chicken stock. Put it all in a blender and churn to make puree. Set it aside.

5. Cook the chicken: Leave about 60 gm oil in the pan in which the onions were fried and remove the rest. Heat the oil. Add the chopped ginger and green chillies and after a few seconds add the chicken. Stir and fry the chicken till somewhat brown. Add salt and pepper and fry for about a minute. Then add the onion and apricot puree and fry for another 2 minutes. Add a little water and cook on medium slow fire, covered, for about 15 minutes till the chicken is tender. When done, the chicken should have around one cup gravy left.

6. Assemble and serve: Place the par–boiled rice over the chicken. Pour the balance chicken stock over it and spread the previously fried apricot, with ghee over the rice. Dot the rice with cream and cover with a tight fitting lid. Cook for the first 2 minutes on medium–high flame and once the dish is heated up reduce flame to low and cook for about 10–15 minutes till the dish is steaming hot and rice done. Serve hot garnished with apricot kernels.

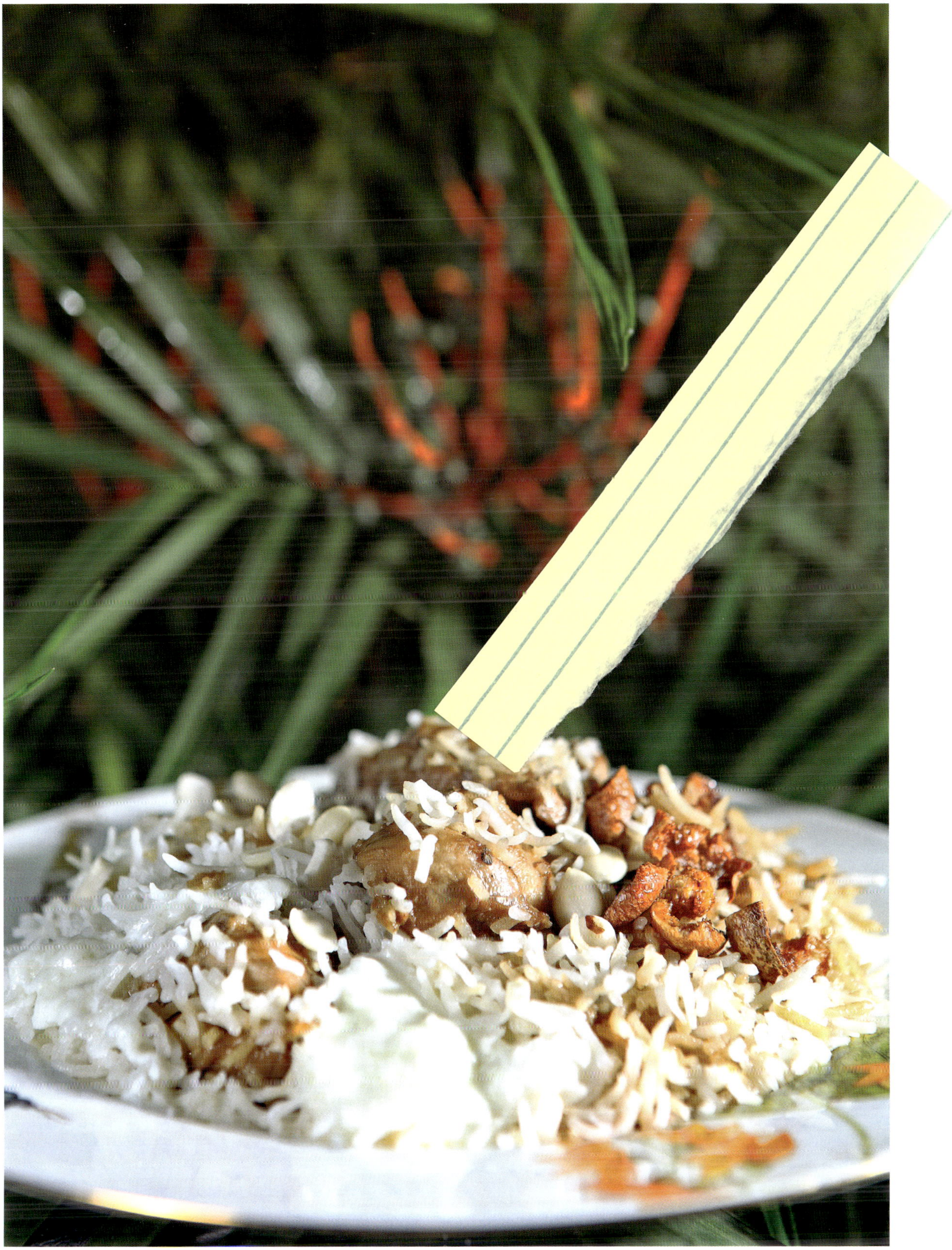

Kolkata Mutton Biryani (West Bengal)

Preparation time: 20 minutes
Cooking time: 1 hour
Serves: 8

1	kg mutton, cut into medium sized pieces
4–5	onions, finely sliced horizontally into rings

1	bay leaf	
6	cloves	
1	tsp peppercorns	A
½	tsp caraway seeds	
2	1 inch cinnamon sticks	

1	tbs ginger and garlic paste
8–10	dried plums, deseeded
2	tsp yellow chilli powder
3	tomatoes, chopped
1	cup yoghurt, whisked
4	potatoes, peeled and cut into medium sized pieces
500	gm long grain rice
1½	tsp saffron
1	tsp ghee
1	bay leaf
½	tsp caraway seeds
	A few mint leaves
	Lemon wedges
100	gm oil
	Salt

This is a lightly flavoured mutton biryani from Bengal, a treat for all seasons, especially summers. It is cooked with potatoes and yoghurt, and delicately flavoured with saffron.

1. Wash and fry the mutton: Wash the mutton and drain the water completely. Heat oil and add the onions. Fry till they turn translucent. Add the whole spices at A and salt followed by the ginger and garlic paste. In a few seconds add the mutton, dried plums, salt, and yellow chilli powder and fry for 5 minutes. Add the chopped tomatoes and cook for about 3–4 minutes till they turn soft. Add the yoghurt and stir continuously till the contents come to a boil and the oil starts to surface. Keep stirring on medium flame for 1 minute thereafter. Add a little water and cook tightly covered till the meat is three fourths done. At this stage, add the potatoes and cook further till the meat and potatoes are done. There should be 1½ cups of gravy left when the meat and potatoes are done.

2. Prepare the rice: Meanwhile, wash and soak the rice for about 20 minutes, then drain the water. Place rice in a heavy bottomed pan with salt, saffron, and 1 tsp ghee. Add water so as to come just about 1 inch above the surface of rice. Boil rice for about 8–10 minutes till all the water is absorbed and the rice is two thirds cooked.

3. Assemble and serve: Now take a large heavy bottomed pan and grease it with oil. Place 1 bay leaf in the centre and sprinkle the caraway seeds. Place the par-boiled rice over the bay leaf and caraway seeds. Arrange the cooked meat with the gravy over the rice. Cover with a tight fitting lid and cook on slow flame for about 10 minutes till the rice is done. Carefully take it out in large chunks without mixing. Garnish with mint leaves and lemon wedges. Serve hot.

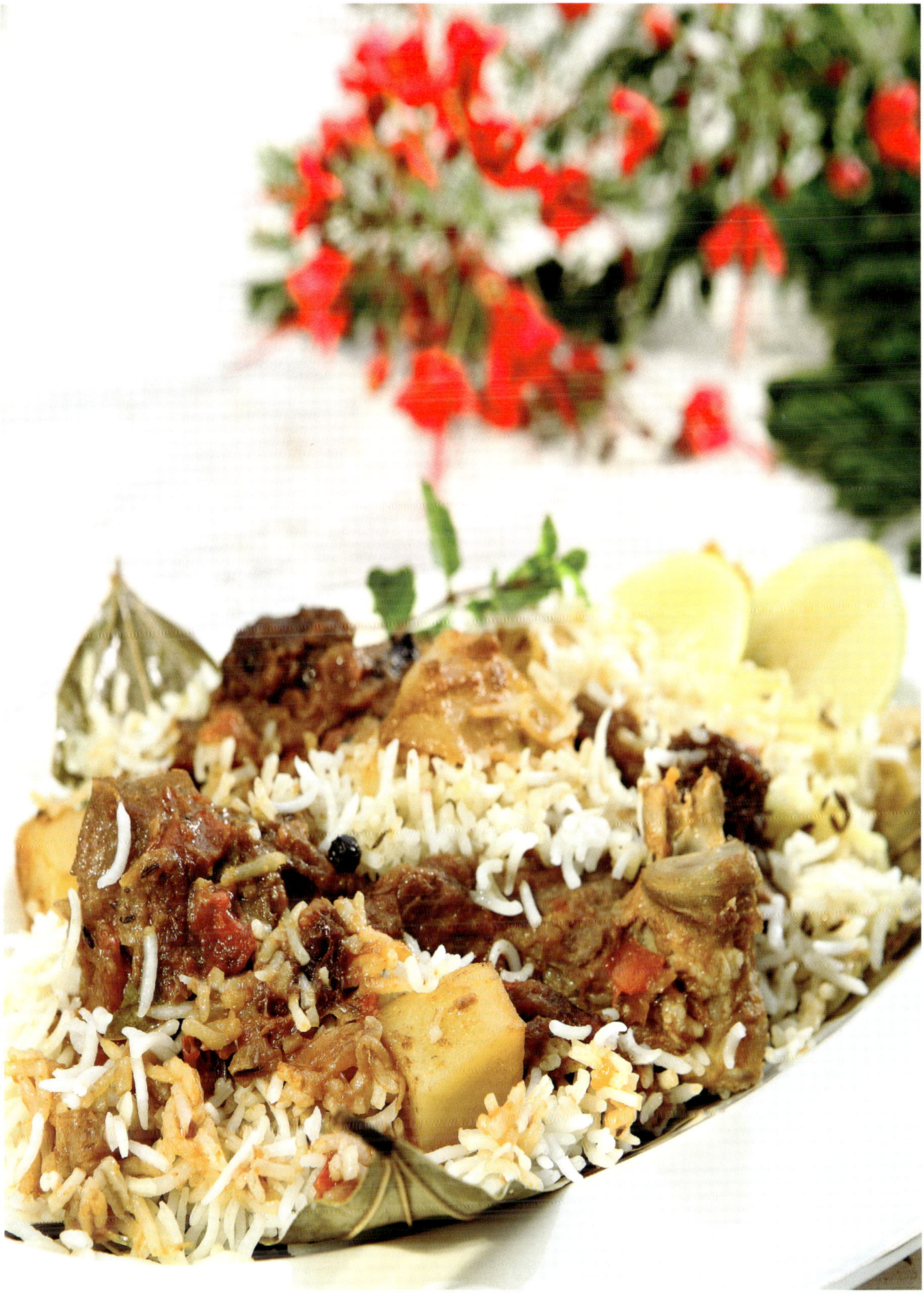

Easy Fish Biryani (West Bengal)

Preparation time: 10 minutes
Cooking time: 40 minutes
Serves: 6–8

500	gm fish
½	tsp turmeric
2	tsp red chilli powder
4–5	dry red chillies, broken
1	tsp garam masala
	A few sprigs of fresh green coriander, chopped
	Juice of 1–2 limes
300	gm long grain rice
1	tsp caraway seeds
2	tbs melted ghee
60	gm oil
	Salt

An uncomplicated dish, this is made with boneless fresh fish. It is gently spiced with garam masala and caraway seeds and uses minimal ingredients. This is perfect for making on short notice, when you don't want to run around searching for ingredients.

1. Marinate the fish: Take any good fish such as sea bass or sole and cut into 2½ inch sized boneless pieces. Apply salt, turmeric powder, and red chilli powder. Set it aside for 10 minutes.

2. Fry the fish: Heat oil in a heavy base pan. Add the whole red chillies. As soon as they turn colour, add the fish pieces, and fry them well on both sides. Sprinkle garam masala, coriander leaves, and the lime juice.

3. Prepare the rice: Wash and soak the rice for 20 minutes, then drain out the water. Boil about 6 glasses of water with ghee, caraway seeds, and a little salt. Once the water comes to a boil, add the rice, and cook for about 10 minutes till it is 80 percent done. Drain excess water.

4. Assemble and serve: Take a heavy bottomed pan and smear it with oil. Place half the rice in the pan. Carefully take out and place the fish over the rice. Cover it with balance rice. Sprinkle the melted ghee and a little water and cover tightly. Cook for the first 1–2 minutes on medium–high flame and then on low flame for about 10 minutes till the dish steams. Carefully take out the biryani in a flattish serving dish. Serve steaming hot.

Ramzan Biryani (East Bengal–now Bangladesh)

Preparation time: 15 minutes
Cooking time: 1 hour
Serves: 6–8

750	gm mutton, a mix of medium sized pieces from the shoulder, a few chops and a few pieces cut from the puth (backbone)
500	gm long grain rice
	Juice of half a lime
2	onions, sliced
2	tbs ginger juliennes
1	tbs garlic paste
1	bay leaf
1	1 inch cinnamon stick
4	green cardamoms
5	cloves
1–2	mace flakes
4	greenish tomatoes, chopped
1	tsp coarsely ground red chilli powder
½	cup fresh green mint leaves
½	cup yoghurt, whisked
4–5	green chillies, slit
½	tsp saffron lightly roasted, crushed and soaked in ½ cup warm milk
2	tbs melted ghee
50	gm oil
1	tsp oil
	Salt

This mutton biryani has a rich history behind it and as the name suggests, was made during the holy month of Ramzan (or Ramadan). A distinguishing feature of this biryani is the use of green tomatoes and mint leaves.

1. Wash the mutton: Wash the mutton and put it in a colander for the water to drain.

2. Prepare the rice: Wash and soak rice in water for about 20 minutes. Drain. Boil about 3 litres of water. When the water starts boiling, add rice, salt, 1 tsp oil, and juice of half a lime. Boil for about 6–7 minutes till the rice is two thirds done. Drain the water and transfer the rice to a flat dish. Run a fork through to open up the rice.

3. Cook the mutton: Heat oil in a heavy base pan. Add onions and fry for 1–2 minutes till translucent. Add ginger juliennes, garlic paste, and the whole spices. After just about a minute, add tomatoes and fry for 2–3 minutes. Then add salt, 1 tsp coarsely ground red chilli powder, and meat and fry for 6–7 minutes. Add mint leaves and fry for a minute. Add yoghurt, mix well and fry for another 2 minutes. Add a little water and cook the meat till tender. When done, the meat should have about 1 cup gravy left.

4. Assemble and serve: Now take a heavy bottomed pan and smear with oil. Place half of the par-boiled rice. Arrange the meat with the gravy over the rice. Place the green chillies over the meat. Cover with the balance rice. Sprinkle the saffron milk and ghee over the rice. Cover with a tight fitting lid. Cook for the first 2 minutes on high flame and reduce the flame to low and cook on dum for about 15 minutes till the rice is done. Serve hot.

Mutton Biryani (Bihar)

While the ingredients in this biryani from Bihar are not uncommon, a distinguishing feature is the use of curry leaves. Raw papaya and yoghurt are both used to tenderize the mutton. This biryani is relatively light and is perfect for all seasons.

Preparation time: 20 minutes
Marination time: 2 hours
Cooking time: 45 minutes
Serves: 10

1	kg mutton, from the goat's shoulder, cut into medium sized pieces

A (ground to a fine paste)
1	small bunch fresh green coriander
50	gm green chillies
1	tbs green papaya paste (pulp and skin ground together)
1	pod garlic
½	cup curry leaves
⅓	tsp turmeric powder

1	cup yoghurt, beaten
	Juice of 1 lime
500	gm long grain rice

B
2	bay leaves
2	black cardamoms
4	green cardamoms
2	1 inch cinnamon sticks
4–6	cloves
1	tsp peppercorns

2	large onions, finely sliced
1	tbs ghee
100	gm oil
	Salt

1. Marinate the mutton: Wash the mutton and drain out the water completely. Mix it with all the ingredients at A, salt, yoghurt, and juice of a lime. Marinate it for 2 hours.

2. Soak the rice: Wash and soak the rice in water for about 20 minutes.

3. Cook the mutton: Heat the oil and add the whole spices at B. After a few seconds add the onions and fry till golden. Then add the marinated mutton and fry, stirring continuously till the contents come to a boil. Continue cooking on medium flame for about 10–12 minutes till the meat is well fried and browned.

4. Assemble and serve: Add the previously soaked rice to the mutton and fry for 2–3 minutes. Add water so as to come 1¼ inches above the surface of the meat and rice. Also add 1 tbs ghee. Once the water starts to boil, cover, and cook on dum for about 20 minutes till the meat is tender and the rice is done. Serve hot.

Chicken Biryani (Bihar)

This biryani dish is an offering from the eastern state of Bihar. What makes it special is the use of ground poppy seeds commonly called khus–khus, which is widely popular in eastern India. The rich blend of khus–khus, yoghurt, and chicken lends it a fine creamy flavour.

Preparation time: 25 minutes
Marination time: 1 hour
Cooking time: 30 minutes
Serves: 8

1	chicken, cut into 10–12 pieces
1½	tsp ginger paste
1½	tsp garlic paste
⅓	cup green chilli paste
4–5	onions, ground
⅓	cup poppy seeds (khus khus), finely ground
1	cup yoghurt, whisked
1	tsp pepper powder

(A)

500	gm long grain rice
4	green cardamoms
2	1 inch cinnamon sticks
6	cloves
2	bay leaves
1	tsp cumin seeds

(B)

1	tbs ghee
75	gm oil
	Salt

1. Marinate the chicken: Marinate the chicken with all the ingredients at A together with salt for an hour.

2. Soak the rice: Wash and soak rice in water for about 20 minutes. Drain and set aside.

3. Assemble and serve: Heat the oil in a heavy bottomed pan. Add all the spices at B, salt, and in just a few seconds add the marinated chicken. Keep stirring till the contents come to a boil. Cook further till the oil starts to surface and the chicken turns golden brown. Add the previously soaked rice to the chicken and fry for 2–3 minutes. Add water to come 1 inch above the rice and chicken. Also add 1 tbs ghee. Once the dish starts to boil, lower flame, and cook covered for about 15–20 minutes till the chicken and rice are done. Serve hot.

Kampuri Biryani (Assam)

Preparation time: 20 minutes
Marination time: ½ an hour
Cooking time: 45 minutes
Serves: 8

500	gm boneless chicken, cut into 1½ inch sized pieces
1	yellow bell pepper } ground
5–6	green chillies
2	inch ginger piece, chopped
1	tbs crushed garlic
500	gm long grain rice
4	medium onions, chopped
4	cloves
2	green cardamoms
¼	tsp grated nutmeg
100	gm shelled green peas
100	gm carrots, diced
100	gm beans, cut into 1 inch pieces
150	gm potatoes, diced
¼	cup fresh green coriander stems, chopped
50	gm garlic, chopped and fried golden brown
1	tsp butter
1	tbs oil
½	cup oil
	Salt

Kampur is a town in Assam with a large Muslim population. The Kampuri Biryani fuses local flavours with boneless chicken. Here chicken and rice are cooked with yellow bell peppers, peas, carrots, beans and potatoes, and flavoured with cardamom and nutmeg.

1. Marinate the chicken: Marinate the chicken with ground bell pepper, green chillies, ginger, garlic, and 1 tbs oil for half an hour.

2. Soak the rice: Wash and soak rice in water for 20 minutes, then drain it out.

3. Assemble and serve: Heat the oil, then add the onions and fry till they turn golden. Add the cloves, cardamom, nutmeg, salt, and the marinated chicken, and fry for about 10 minutes till the chicken is somewhat browned. Now add the rice, the vegetables, and the chopped coriander stems. Fry for 2–3 minutes, then add water about 1¼ inch over the surface of rice. Once the water starts to boil, cover and cook on low flame for about 15–20 minutes till the rice and vegetables are done. Dot with 1 tsp butter. Serve hot garnished with fried garlic.

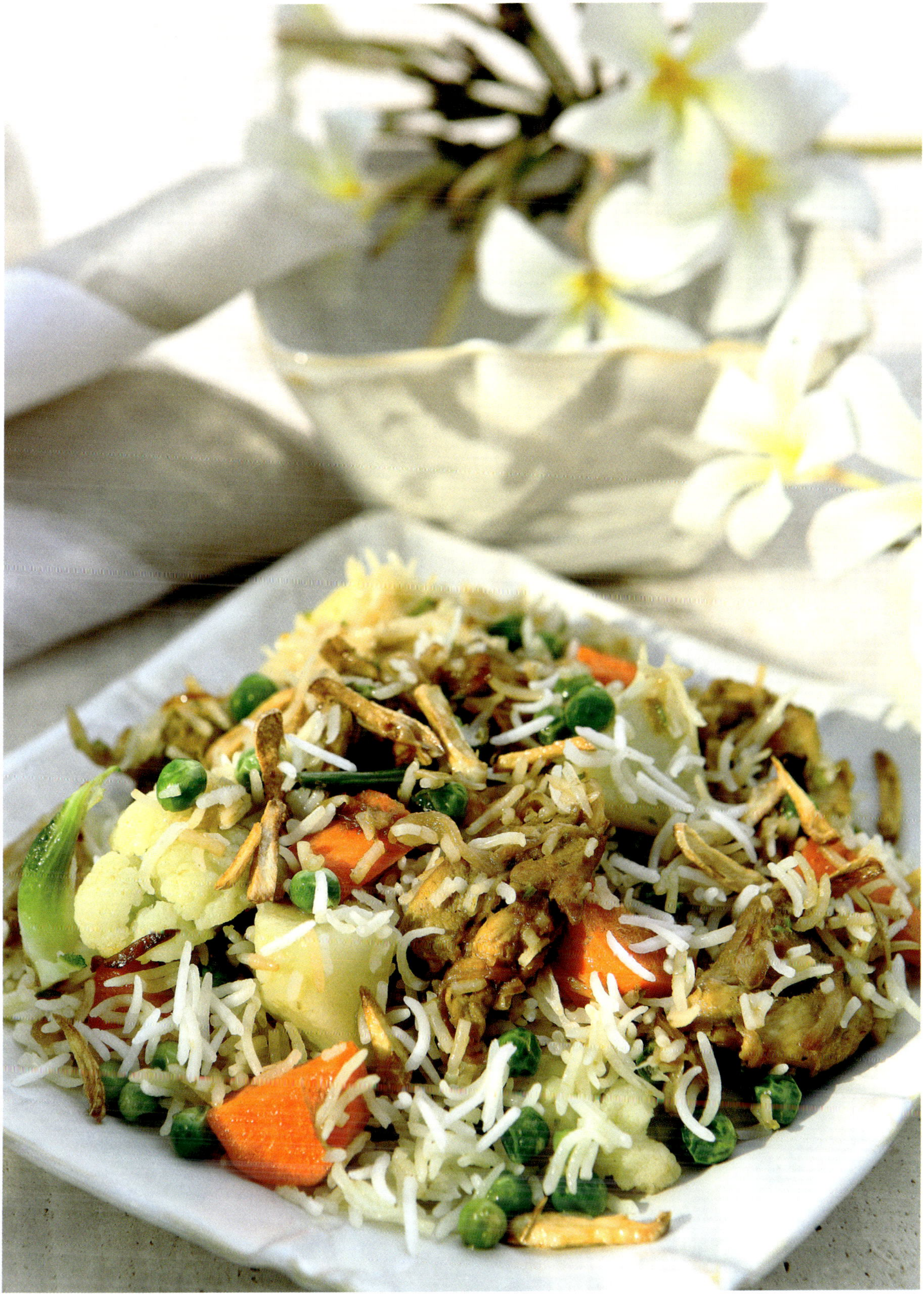

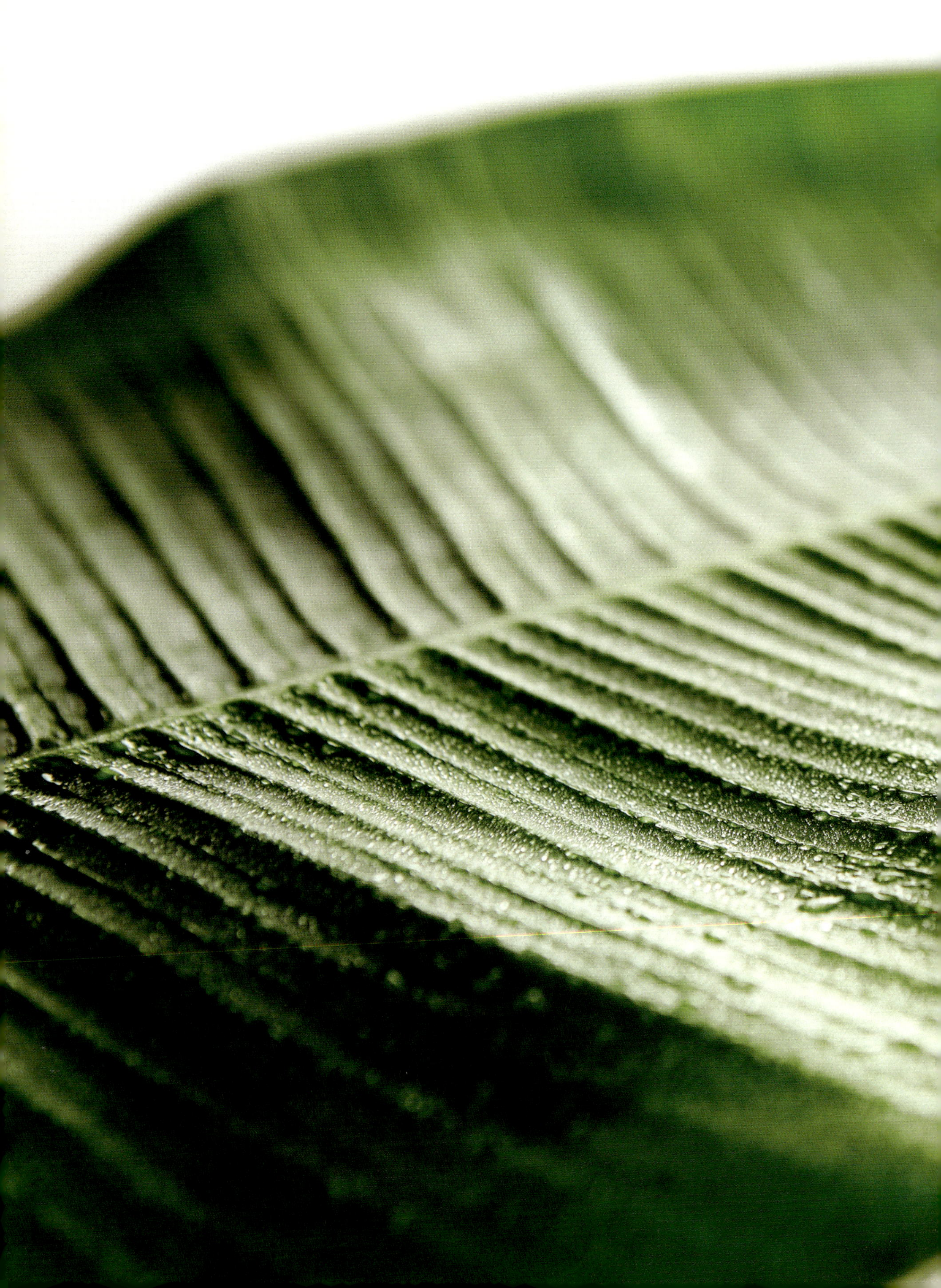

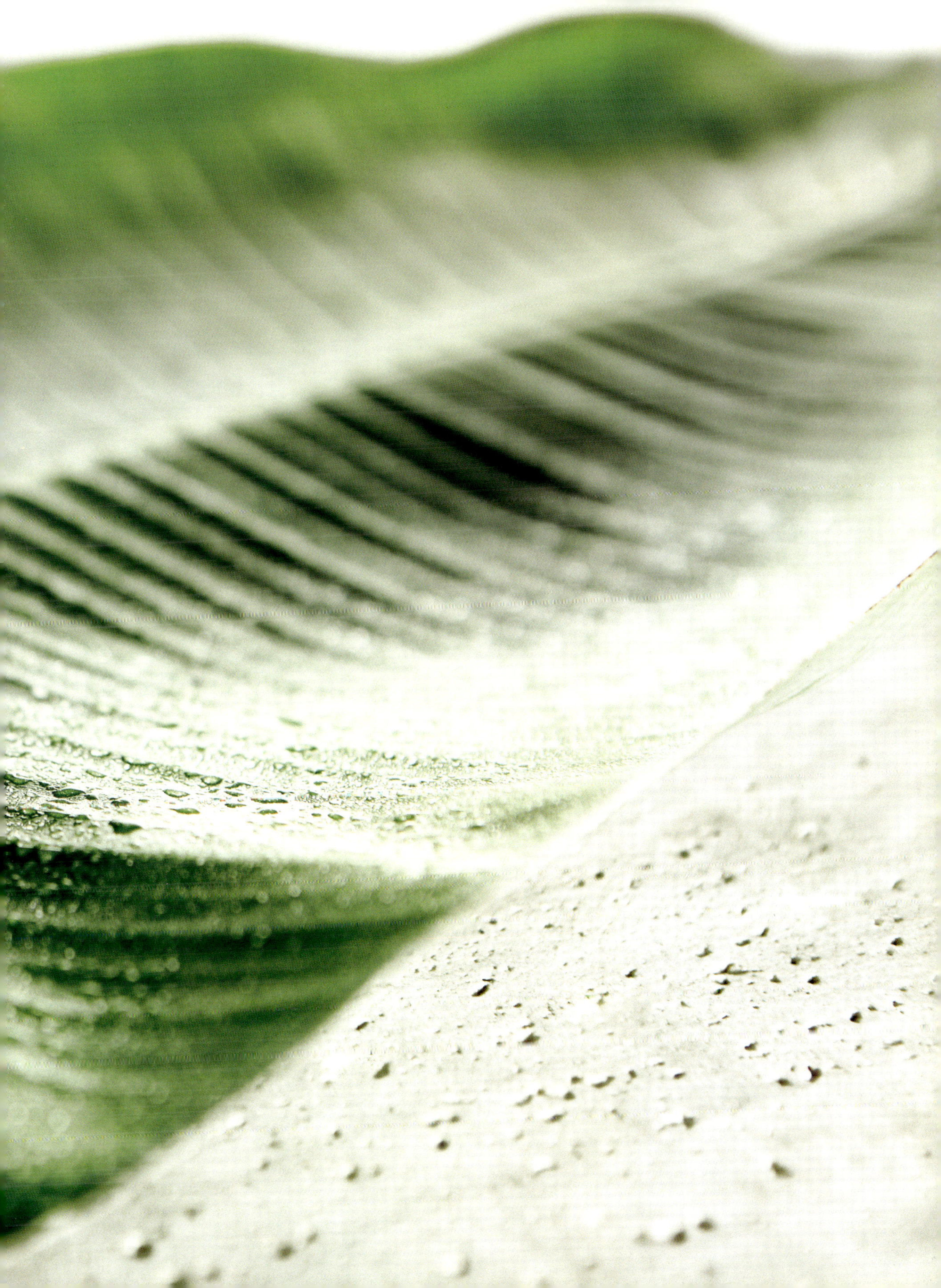

West

The culinary history of western India is markedly more vegetarian than other parts of India. Though Gujarat has a considerable Muslim presence, it has always been dominated by Hindu vegetarianism. In fact, it is very difficult to get non-vegetarian food in the restaurants of most Gujarat towns, except in five star hotels or in the Muslim areas. Gujarat does have seafood, mutton and chicken dishes, but these come from the princely houses of the state, the Muslim community and the business communities of the Khojas and Bohris, and the Parsis. Thus, most of the biryani recipes come from them as well.

Maharashtra is no different, though some Hindu sub-castes and Hindu princely families have contributed greatly to Maharashtra's non-vegetarian culture. Mumbai is a very cosmopolitan city and it too boasts of excellent Parsi, Khoja, Bohri, and Sindhi cuisine. Its biryani is characterized by its use of potatoes and tomatoes and its street biryani, called the Tawa Biryani, is much sought after. Most of the Khoja, Bohri and Parsi dishes included in this section come from Mumbai rather than Gujarat.

Goa possesses its own magnetic culinary personality with its strong Portuguese and Konkanese influences. It too has its own biryanis but, like much of South India, hardly any pulaos. Goa is also one of the few states where dishes are spiced with vinegar.

It is only in princely Rajasthan that one finds traces of the classic northern style biryanis with its usage of screwpine, rosewater, saffron, and cream. The region is known for its use of game, hard to find these days.

Kolhapuri Biryani (Maharashtra)

Preparation time: 20–25 minutes
Marination time: 6 hours
Cooking time: 1 hour 45 minutes
Serves: 10

1	kg chicken, cut in to 10–12 pieces
1	tbs ginger paste
1	tbs garlic paste

A — *lightly dry roasted and ground fine.*

½	tsp coriander seeds
½	tsp cumin seeds
½	tsp aniseeds
2–3	dry red whole chillies
½	tsp peppercorns
	A small piece desiccated coconut
2–3	cloves
½	inch piece cinnamon
¼	tsp turmeric powder
1	tbs red chilli powder
1	cup yoghurt, whisked

750	gm long grain rice

B

2	green cardamoms
3–4	cloves
1	1 inch cinnamon stick
1	bay leaf

5–6	medium sized potatoes
4–5	onions, finely sliced

The cuisine in certain places in India, such Andhra Pradesh, Chettinad and southern Maharashtra, is known for being extremely spicy. This red-hot dish is from Kolhapur, a one-time princely state in southern Maharashtra.

1. Marinate the chicken: Wash the chicken and put it in a colander for the water to drain completely. Marinate the chicken with half of the ginger and garlic paste and all the ingredients at A for 5–6 hours in the refrigerator.

2. Prepare the rice: Wash and soak rice in liberal quantity of water for 20 minutes, then drain. Boil 3½ litres of water with salt. When the water starts boiling, add rice, and cook for about 5 minutes till half done. Drain the water and transfer the rice to wide flat dish. Heat 1 tbs of ghee. Add all the ingredients at B and after a few seconds add the rice, mix and fry for 1–2 minutes. Set it aside.

3. Prepare the potatoes: Boil the potatoes for about 10 minutes till ¾ done. Peel and slice them into half inch to three fourth inch round pieces, then set aside.

4. Prepare the masala paste: Heat 1½ cup oil. Fry the sliced onions till golden. Remove and set aside. Fry the cashew nuts to a rich gold and light brown colour. Remove and set aside. Add the chopped onions to the same oil. When the onions turn pink, add the remaining ginger paste, and all the ingredients at C and fry for about a minute. Remove it from the flame. When slightly cool, grind to a paste.

8–10	cashew nuts, broken
3–4	onions, chopped

3–4	cloves	
1	1 inch cinnamon piece	
½	tsp cumin seeds	
1	tbs coriander seeds	C
3–4	dry whole red chillies	
5–6	cashew nuts	
5–6	almonds	
10–12	raisins	

½	tsp saffron, crushed and soaked in ⅓ cup milk
3	tbs ghee
	Oil
	Salt

5. Cook the chicken: Heat 50 gm of oil. Add the ground masala paste and fry for 2–3 minutes. Then add the marinated chicken and salt and cook, stirring frequently for about 7–8 minutes. Cook further, covered, for about 6–7 minutes till the chicken is two thirds done with about 1 cup of gravy left.

6. Assemble and serve: Take a heavy bottomed pan and smear it with oil. Arrange the potato pieces as the first layer. Sprinkle a handful of rice and then place half the chicken over it. Cover it with half of the rice. Sprinkle the fried onions and cashew nuts over the rice and place the balance chicken over the rice. Cover with the balance rice. Make 3–4 holes with a wooden spoon and pour the saffron milk into the holes. Cover the holes with rice and smoothen the surface. Pour 2 tbs of ghee over the rice. Now cover the biryani vessel with a tight fitting lid. Place on a pre-heated griddle (tawa). Cook on dum for about half an hour till the chicken and rice are done. Take out in large chunks from the sides and serve hot.

Jhinga Biryani (Mumbai)

Preparation time: 20 minutes
Marination time: 15 minutes
Cooking time: 1 hour
Serves: 8

1	kg medium sized prawns, cleaned and deveined
½	tsp turmeric powder
½	tsp red chilli powder
½	tsp ginger paste
½	tsp garlic paste
	Juice of 1 lime
4–5	onions, finely sliced
4	green cardamoms
4–5	mace flakes
2	tbs ginger paste
1	tbs garlic paste
¾	tsp turmeric powder
2	tsp yellow chilli powder
1	tbs coriander powder
4	tomatoes, chopped
1	cup yoghurt, well beaten
600	gm long grain rice
1	bay leaf
3–4	cloves
1	1 inch cinnamon stick
½	tsp mace powder
½	tsp green cardamom powder

(Items with turmeric, red chilli, ginger paste, garlic paste, and lime juice are grouped as A.)

This jhinga or prawn biryani seems to fuse northern and coastal flavours, cooked as it is with whole spices and saffron.

1. Marinate the prawns: Wash the prawns well and put them in a colander for the water to drain completely. Mix the prawns with all the ingredients at A and marinate for 15 minutes.

2. Cook the prawns: Heat the oil and fry the onions till golden brown. Remove half and set aside. Then add the green cardamoms, mace flakes followed by ginger and garlic paste. In just about a minute, add turmeric powder, yellow chilli powder and coriander powder. Add the chopped tomatoes and fry, stirring now and then till the tomatoes are soft and somewhat cooked. Add the well–beaten yoghurt and stir continuously till the whole mixture starts to boil and thereafter keep stirring for 1 more minute. Cook for about 2 minutes more on medium flame till the oil starts to surface. Now add the marinated prawns, mix gently and simmer on medium flame for about 6–7 minutes. When done, the prawns should have about 1 cup gravy left.

3. Prepare the rice: Meanwhile, wash and soak rice in water for about 15 minutes. Bring 2½ litres of water to a boil along with the bay leaf, cloves, cinnamon, and salt. Once the water starts boiling, add rice and cook for about 7–8 minutes till it is two thirds done. Drain the water.

1	tsp saffron, lightly roasted and soaked in ½ cup warm milk
4	tbs thick cream
	A few mint leaves
¾	cup oil
	Salt

4. Assemble and serve: Take a heavy bottomed pan and smear it with oil. Place half of the par–boiled rice in it followed by the cooked prawns over it. Sprinkle half of the mace powder, green cardamoms, and saffron milk over the prawn. Also sprinkle half of the reserved fried onions and cover with the balance rice. Sprinkle the remaining mace, cardamom powder, and saffron milk. Dot the rice with thick fresh cream and sprinkle the balance fried onions and mint leaves. Now cover with a tight fitting lid and cook for the first 1–2 minutes on high flame and then on low flame for about 15 minutes till the rice is done. Take out the biryani in large chunks from the side and serve steaming hot.

Pork Biryani (Mumbai)

Preparation time: 10 minutes
Cooking time: 1 hour
Serves: 8

500	gm pork, cut into medium sized pieces

1	tsp poppy seeds (khus–khus)	
12	cashew nuts	**A**
6	cloves	*ground to a fine paste*
8	dry whole red chillies	
1	tsp cumin seeds	
1	tsp coriander seeds	
½	tsp turmeric powder	

500	gm long grain rice
1	tsp butter
50	gm oil
	Salt

An unusual Parsi innovation, this is made with pork, poppy seeds, and cashew nuts.

1. Prepare the pork: Wash and put the pork in a colander for the water to drain. Heat oil in a heavy bottomed pan large enough to take both meat and rice. Add the ground spices and fry for 2 minutes. Add pork and fry further for about 5 minutes. Add salt and water, and cook the pork till tender. When done, the pork should have about 1 cup gravy left.

2. Prepare the rice: Meanwhile, wash and soak the rice for about 10–15 minutes. Boil about 2½ litres of salted water. Add rice and cook for about 7–8 minutes till 90 percent done. Strain the excess water through a sieve.

3. Assemble and serve: Now place the rice over the pork. Dot with butter. Cover with a tight fitting lid and cook on dum for about 10 minutes till the rice is done and steaming. Serve hot.

Parsi Prawn Pulao (Mumbai)

Preparation time: 10 minutes
Cooking time: 25 minutes
Serves: 8

400	gm long grain rice
500	gm medium sized prawns, cleaned and deveined
	Juice of 1 lime
4–5	tomatoes (about 350 gms)
1	tsp ginger paste
1	tsp garlic paste
½	tsp nutmeg, powdered
2	tsp red chilli powder
1	tbs coriander powder
1	tbs cumin powder

} A

2–3	sprigs of curry leaves
3	small capsicums, sliced vertically in 4–5 pieces each
½	tsp saffron, dissolved in juice of 2 limes
50	gm oil
	Salt

A Parsi recipe from Mumbai, this is a tomato-based pulao. Both the tomato and the saffron-dipped lime impart a gentle sourness to the dish.

1. Wash the rice: Wash and soak rice in water for about 20 minutes. Drain.

2. Marinate the prawns: Wash and drain the prawns. Mix with a little salt and juice of 1 lime and let it stay for 8–10 minutes.

3. Prepare tomato puree: Roughly chop and boil the tomatoes in ½ cup of water for a few minutes. Strain to get tomato puree. Add all the ingredients at A to the tomato puree.

4. Assemble and serve: Heat the oil and add the curry leaves followed by the prawns. Fry for 1–2 minutes. Add rice and fry for 2–3 minutes, then add the tomato puree. Add a little water so that the liquid comes 1 inch above the surface of the rice. Cook covered, first on high flame till the liquid comes to a boil and then on low flame for about 15 minutes. When the rice is 90 percent ready, add the capsicum and sprinkle saffron with lemon juice. Simmer covered for a few minutes till the rice is done and each grain separate. Serve hot.

Machhi Jo Pulao (Sindh)

India has a substantial Sindhi population, which migrated to India during the Partition and settled primarily in western India, especially Mumbai and other parts of Maharashtra. They brought with them their language, their lifestyle, and their cuisine. Sindhi food has its own irresistible personality. It is, therefore, a matter of concern that today only a few restaurants in western India offer Sindhi food although mercifully, it is still made in Sindhi homes. Though Sindh is a coastal state, this pulao is made from river fish, showing the range of the Sindhi palate.

Preparation time: 10 minutes
Cooking time: 50 minutes
Serves: 8–10

1	kg river fish, Seer or Rahu with skin but scales removed and cut straight across into 1½ inch thick slices
600	gm long grain rice
3	onions, finely sliced
1	cup yoghurt, whisked
2	tomatoes, finely chopped

A:
- 2 bay leaves
- 1 tsp crushed ginger
- 1 clove garlic, crushed
- ½ tsp red chilli powder
- ½ tsp turmeric powder
- 1 tsp coriander powder
- ½ tsp garam masala powder
- 4 green chillies, slit

½ cup oil
Salt

1. Prepare the fish: Wash the fish slices and put them in a colander for the water to drain completely.

2. Prepare the rice: Soak rice in water for about ½ an hour.

3. Cook the fish: Heat oil in a large frying pan. Add the onions and fry till golden brown. Add yoghurt and fry stirring continuously till the gravy starts to boil and the oil surfaces. Add the chopped tomatoes and fry for about 2 minutes. Then add the spices at A. Cook till you get a thick gravy. Add the fish and simmer it on one side for 5 minutes. Delicately turn over the fish and let it simmer for another 5 minutes. Remove the fish. Place the slices in a flat dish.

4. Cook the rice: Drain the previously soaked rice and add to the fish masala. Fry for 2–3 minutes. Add hot water almost double the quantity of rice and cook rice first on medium flame for 2–3 minutes and then on low flame for 7–8 minutes till almost done with each grain separate.

5. Assemble and serve: Now place the fish over the rice, cover tightly and cook on dum for about 10 minutes. Take out gently and serve hot on a large platter.

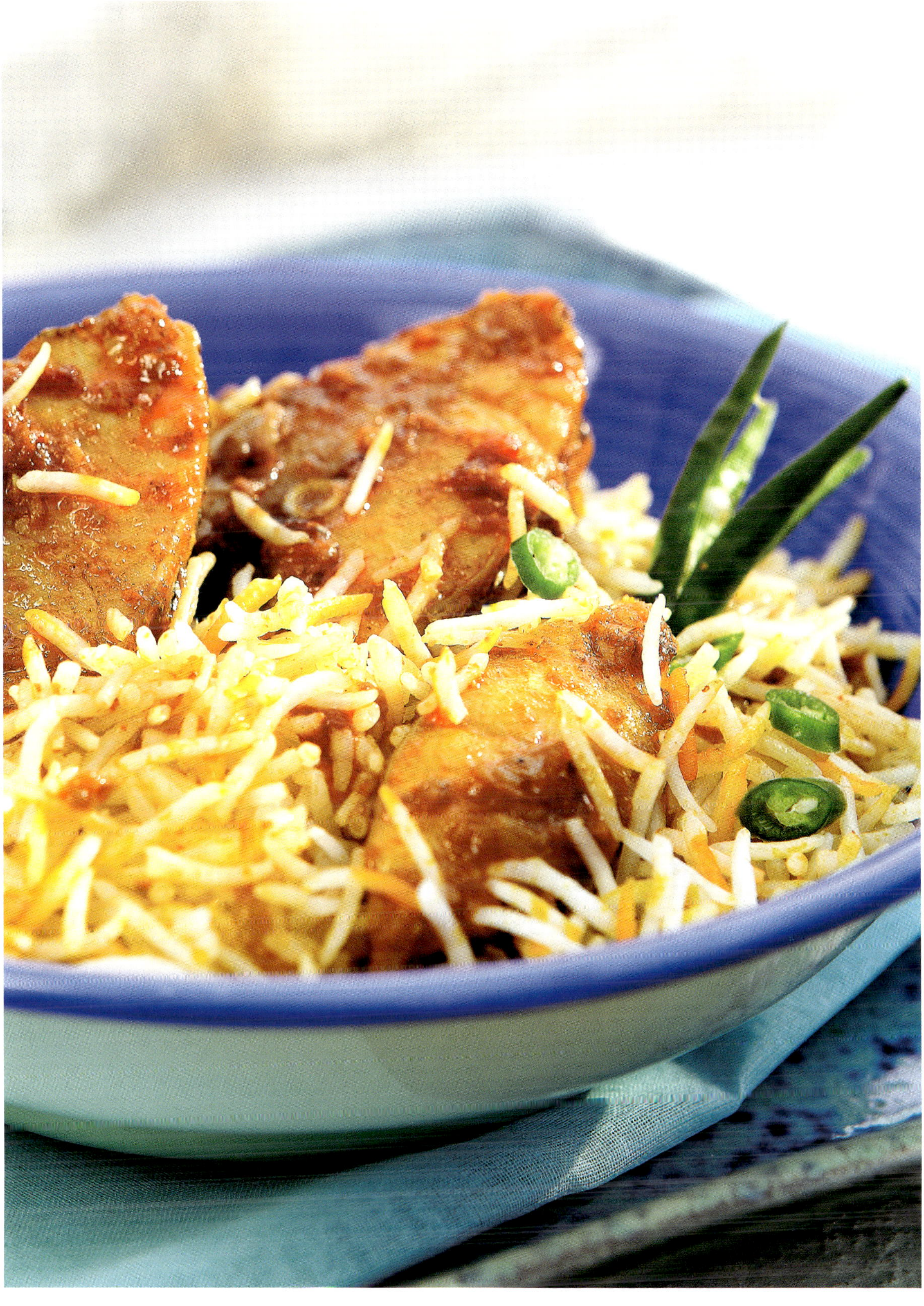

Choozon ka Pulao (Mumbai)

A 'chooza' is a tender young bird. Here, it is stuffed with boiled eggs and minced mutton in the typical west Asian style and placed on a bed of saffron flavoured rice.

Preparation time: 10 minutes
Marination time: 1 hour
Cooking time: 1 hour
Serves: 8

4	whole spring chickens with skin, cleaned and weighing about 250–300 gms each
2	tsp red chilli powder
	Juice of 1 lime
1	onion, finely chopped
1	tbs ginger paste
1	tsp black cardamom seeds and cloves, ground ⎫
½	tsp pepper powder ⎬ A
1	tsp red chilli powder ⎭
250	gm keema (mutton mince)
4	hard-boiled eggs
500	gm long grain rice
½	tsp saffron, crushed
½	tsp caraway seeds (shahzeera)
10–12	cloves
4	tbs ghee–oil, mixed in the ratio of 1:1
½	cup oil
2	tbs ghee
	Salt

1. Marinate the chicken: Wash the chicken and set aside in a colander for 5 minutes to allow the water to drain off. Apply salt, red chilli powder, and juice of 1 lime and marinate for an hour.

2. Cook the keema: Heat the ghee–oil mixture and add the chopped onion. When the onion turns pink, add the ginger paste and after a few seconds, add all the ingredients at A together with salt. In a few seconds, add the keema and fry for 5 minutes. Add a little water. Cover and cook till tender.

3. Cook the chicken: Stuff each chicken with one hard–boiled egg and keema. Stitch up the open end with thread and needle. Heat ½ cup oil in a wide and deep pan. Fry the chicken till it turns golden. Add a little water and cover. Cook for about 20 minutes till the chicken is tender.

4. Prepare the rice: Wash and drain the rice. Add saffron, caraway seeds, salt followed by water almost 1 inch above the surface of rice. Cook covered first on high flame till the water comes to a boil and then on low flame for about 15 minutes till the rice is done.

5. Garnish and serve: Untie the strings on the chicken and place the hot chicken in the centre of a large and flattish serving dish. Add steaming rice around it. Any balance keema can be placed close to the chicken over the rice. Heat ghee and add cloves and fry for a few seconds till they turn brown. Pour the ghee and cloves over the dish.

Mumbai Tawa Biryani (Mumbai)

This is Mumbai's trademark street biryani. Available at street corners and railway stations, it is truly a common man's meal-by-itself. The tawa (a flat pan) gives it an inviting look even as the sizzling hot biryani is made right in front of the customer.

Preparation time: 15 minutes
Cooking time: 1 hour
Serves: 10–12

1	kg mutton, cut into medium sized pieces
1	bay leaf
4–5	cardamoms
6	cloves
2	1 inch cinnamon sticks
4–5	onions, chopped
1½	tbs ginger paste
1	tbs garlic paste
3	tomatoes, chopped
1	tsp red chilli powder
1	tsp coriander powder
1	tsp cumin powder
3–4	medium sized potatoes, cut into chunky pieces
1	kg rice
½	tsp turmeric powder
	Juice of half a lime
100	gm oil
	Salt

1. Cook the meat: Wash the meat and put it in a colander for all the water to drain. Heat the oil in a heavy bottomed pan. Add the whole spices, followed in a few seconds by the chopped onions. When the onions turn brown, add the ginger and garlic paste, and in a few seconds add the tomatoes. When the tomatoes get soft and somewhat cooked, after 4–5 minutes, add salt, red chilli, coriander and cumin powder followed by the meat. Mix and cook, stirring now and then till the spices become homogeneous and the oil starts to surface. Add a little water, cover tightly, and cook for about 30 minutes till the meat is three fourths done. At this stage, add the potatoes and cook further for another 10–15 minutes till the potatoes and the meat are done, leaving about 1½ cups of gravy.

2. Prepare the rice: When the meat is cooking, boil 4–5 litres of water. Add salt, turmeric, and the juice of half a lime. When the water starts boiling, add the rice and cook for about 9–10 minutes till it is done. Drain the water.

3. Assemble and serve: Now place the meat in the middle of a flat pan (tawa), simmering on slow flame. Place the cooked rice around the meat. Take small portions of meat and rice, mix and serve hot accompanied by sliced onions and lemon wedges. The extra meat can be served on the side with the biryani.

Aloo Bukhara Biryani (Mumbai)

Biryanis of Mumbai are often made with potatoes and dry fruit, such as Aloo Bukhara (dried plums). Another special feature of this biryani is the use of cassia buds or kabab chini for flavouring.

Preparation time: 15 minutes
Marination time: 30 minutes
Cooking time: 1 hour
Serves: 8

750	gm mutton, cut into medium pieces
1	cup yoghurt, well beaten
1	tsp ginger paste
1	tsp garlic paste
1½	tsp red chilli powder, coarsely ground
1	tsp cassia buds (kabab chini)
12	dried aloo bukhara (plums), deseeded
400	gm long grain rice
2	bay leaves
6	cloves
½	tsp seeds of black cardamom
4	onions, finely sliced
2	potatoes, cut into medium sized pieces
2	tbs ghee
	Oil to fry
	Salt

Ingredients from yoghurt through dried aloo bukhara are marked A. Bay leaves, cloves, and black cardamom seeds are marked B.

1. Marinate the meat: Wash and drain the meat completely of all water. Mix it well with all the ingredients at A and salt. Marinate for half an hour.

2. Prepare the rice: Wash and soak the rice in water for 20 minutes, then drain out the water. Boil 2 litres of water with all the ingredients at B together with 1 tsp of oil and salt. When the water starts to boil, add rice. After about 7–8 minutes when the rice is two thirds done, drain the water and transfer the rice to a flat dish.

3. Prepare the meat: Heat oil in a heavy bottomed pan large enough to take the meat and rice. Fry the onions till golden brown. Remove and set aside and crush when cool. In the same oil, fry the potatoes till they turn golden. Remove and set aside. Keep about 50 gm oil from the same oil in which the onions and potatoes were fried and remove the rest. Add the marinated meat with the marinade and fry and cook till the oil starts to surface. Add a little water, cover and cook for 15–20 minutes till the meat is three fourths done. At this stage, add the crushed onions and the fried potatoes. Add a little water, if necessary and cook covered till the meat is tender. When done the meat should have about one cup gravy left.

4. Assemble and serve: Cover the meat with the par-boiled rice. Sprinkle a little water, dot with ghee, and cover with a tight fitting lid. Cook for the first 1–2 minutes on moderate-high flame, then cook further on low flame for about 10 minutes till the rice is done. Serve steaming hot.

Subzi Gosht Biryani (Mumbai)

Preparation time: 25–30 minutes
Cooking time: 1 hour
Serves: 8–10

1	kg mutton, cut into medium sized pieces
5	onions, finely sliced
1½	tsp ginger paste
1	tbs garlic paste
⅓	tsp turmeric powder
1½	tsp red chilli powder
2	medium tomatoes, chopped
2–3	potatoes, cut into medium-large sized pieces
150	gm french beans, cut into 1¼ inch sized pieces
150	gm dil (soya), chopped
150	gm fresh fenugreek, chopped

(Items marked A)

⅓	cup fresh coconut, grated
650	gm long grain rice
	A few sprigs of fresh green coriander, chopped
	Juice of 2 limes
150	gm oil
	Salt

This is an unusual dish created by Sanjay Khan and his wife Zarine, India's famed Bollywood couple. It is made with mutton and several vegetables, and the use of grated coconut shows a clear coastal influence.

1. Cook the mutton: Wash the mutton and put it in a colander for the water to drain. Heat oil in a large heavy bottomed pan. Fry the onions till golden brown. Remove half and reserve. Add the ginger and garlic paste to the onions and fry for about 1 minute. Add turmeric and red chilli powder and sprinkle a little water. Add mutton and salt, mix and fry on medium-slow flame for about 20–25 minutes till the meat is almost done. Then add the chopped tomatoes and fry together till the tomatoes blend well with the other ingredients. Now add all the vegetables at A and fry on medium flame for about 5 minutes. Add 1 cup of water and cook further on medium-slow flame for about 5–10 minutes till the meat is tender and vegetables done. Add the grated coconut and mix and keep it on dum.

2. Prepare the rice: Meanwhile, soak the rice in water for 20 minutes. Boil 3½ litres of water with salt. Once the water starts to boil, add rice and cook for 6–7 minutes till it is two thirds done. Drain the water.

3. Assemble and serve: Place the rice over the cooked meat, which is simmering on dum. Sprinkle the reserved onions and the chopped coriander. Also squeeze the juice of lime. Cover tightly and cook on dum for about 10 minutes till the rice is done and steaming. Serve hot.

Parsi Pasanda Biryani (Mumbai)

The Parsis came to India from Persia over a thousand years ago to escape persecution in their country. Very soon, they became part of India's plural culture. They adapted to local food and customs to which they gave their own distinct personality. The Parsi community is known for its culinary innovations. This biryani is made with pasanda and flavoured with red lentils, baby potatoes and tomatoes.

Preparation time: 30 minutes
Marination time: 4 hours
Cooking time: 1 hour 45 minutes
Serves: 10–12

1	kg boneless mutton from the leg of a goat, cut into ½ inch thick and 2 inch long pieces called pasandas
5	onions, finely sliced
250	gm baby potatoes, peeled
1	tbs ginger paste
1	tbs garlic paste
1	tbs raw green papaya (skin & pulp) paste
1	tsp cumin seeds } *powdered*
2–3	green cardamoms
4	cloves
1	1 inch cinnamon stick
1½	tsp red chilli powder
5–6	green chillies, ground
2	tomatoes, chopped fine
1	cup hung yoghurt
½	tsp saffron, soaked in juice of 2 limes

1. Prepare the mutton: Wash the meat and put it in a colander for the water to drain.

2. Fry the onions and the potatoes: Heat the oil and fry the onions till golden brown. Remove and set aside. When cool, crush half of the onions. Reserve the remaining half. Fry the potatoes till golden. Remove and set aside.

3. Marinate the meat: Apply ginger, garlic, and the green papaya paste to the meat, and leave for 10–15 minutes. Then with the help of a mallet or the thick end of a knife, beat them for 10–15 minutes. Add the powdered spices, salt, red chilli powder, green chilli paste, tomatoes, hung yoghurt, crushed onions, and half of the saffron soaked in lemon juice. Leave to marinate for 3–4 hours.

4. Prepare the rice: Wash the rice well. Boil about 3½ litres of water with salt and cloves, cinnamon, and cardamoms. When the water starts boiling add rice and cook for about 5 minutes till 40–50 percent done. Strain the water and transfer the rice to a flat dish.

750	gm rice
3–4	cloves
1	1 inch cinnamon stick
3–4	whole green cardamoms
350	gm red lentils (masoor dal)
3	green chillies, slit
2	tbs melted ghee
4	hard–boiled eggs, each cut into half
1½	cup oil
	Salt

5. Prepare the lentils: Boil the lentils in salted water till half done. Strain excess water and transfer the lentils to another pan. Set aside.

6. Assemble and serve: Take a heavy bottomed pan and put in the oil left over from frying the onions and the potatoes. Add the marinated meat and spread the red lentils over the meat. Arrange the potatoes over the lentils. Spread the rice over the potatoes. Sprinkle the balance fried onions and the green chillies over the rice. Pour the melted ghee and the balance saffron soaked in lemon juice. Also sprinkle half a glass of water. Now cover with a tight fitting lid and cook on high flame for about 5 minutes and then on medium flame for another 10–15 minutes. Thereafter, reduce flame to low and cook for another 30 minutes till the meat and rice are done. Remove in large chunks from the sides so that the arrangement of the dish is not disturbed. Serve garnished with hard–boiled eggs.

Bohri Biryani (Mumbai)

Bohris are an affluent business community concentrated in and around Mumbai. Being Muslims, they have a rich repertoire of delicious non-vegetarian fare, this biryani being one of them. It is cooked with mutton, whole spices and flavoured with screwpine water.

Preparation time: 10 minutes
Marination time: 6–8 hours
Cooking time: 1 hour
Serves: 10

1	kg mutton from the leg of a small goat, cut into medium pieces
500	gm yoghurt, whisked
30–40	gm ginger juliennes
1	tbs garlic, chopped
6–8	green chillies, slit
2	tbs coriander, chopped
1½	tbs mint leaves
1	tsp turmeric powder
1	tsp red chilli powder
1	tsp cardamom powder
750	gm long grain rice
2	bay leaves
1	1 inch cinnamon stick
2	mace flakes
	Juice of half a lime
1	tbs screwpine water
1	tbs ghee
½	cup ghee–oil, mixed
	Salt

(Ingredients from yoghurt to cardamom powder marked as A)

1. Marinate the meat: Wash and drain the mutton of all the water. Mix it with all the ingredients at A and leave to marinate for 6–8 hours.

2. Prepare the rice: Wash and soak the rice in water for about 20 minutes. Boil 4–5 litres of water. Add bay leaves, cinnamon, mace flakes, 1 tbs ghee, salt, and juice of half a lime. Drain and add rice to the boiling water. When the rice is 50 percent done, after 6–7 minutes, drain the water.

3. Assemble and serve: Take a heavy bottomed pan, large enough to take meat and rice. Heat the ghee–oil mixture. Add the meat and salt and mix. Spread the rice over the meat. Also sprinkle kewra water. Cover with a tight fitting lid and cook first for about 10 minutes on high flame and then on dum (low flame) for about 20 minutes till the meat and rice are done. Let the biryani rest covered for 8–10 minutes. Serve hot with onions, green chillies, and yoghurt relish or just plain yoghurt.

Sindhi Mutton Biryani (Sindh/Mumbai)

This biryani is a Sindhi offering. It is made with mutton, tomatoes and garam masala, but what is special is its use of dried plums.

Preparation time: 20 minutes
Cooking time: 1 hour 10 minutes
Serves: 8

1	kg mutton, cut into medium pieces, preferably from the shoulder

A:
- 4–5 garlic cloves
- 1 bay leaf
- 1 tbs coriander seeds
- 1 black cardamom
- 1 tbs pepper
- 1 tsp fennel seeds
- 1 onion, quartered

500	gm rice
4	onions, finely sliced
5–6	whole dried red chillies
1	tsp fennel seeds

ground:
- A small piece of ginger
- 4–5 garlic cloves
- 6–8 green chillies
- 1/3 cup fresh green coriander, chopped
- 1/4 cup fresh mint leaves

1/2	tsp garam masala powder
10–12	dried plums, deseeded
4	tomatoes, chopped
100	gm oil
	Salt

1. Prepare mutton stock: Wash mutton and pressure cook with all the ingredients at A and salt in about 4–5 glasses of water first on high flame and then low, for 10–15 minutes till it is 90 percent done. Strain to get about 3 glasses of clear mutton stock. Pick and set aside the mutton pieces.

2. Soak the rice: Wash and soak rice in water for about 20 minutes. Drain and set aside.

3. Cook the mutton: Heat oil in a heavy base pan. Add the sliced onions along with the dry whole red chillies and the fennel seeds. Fry till the onions are golden. Add the ground paste and fry for about 2 minutes. At this stage add the mutton pieces and the garam masala, and fry for 4–5 minutes. Then add the plums and the tomatoes and fry till the tomatoes are soft and the oil separates.

4. Assemble and cook on dum: Add rice, mutton stock, and a little salt. The stock should be 1 inch above the surface of the meat and the rice, so adjust stock/water accordingly. Cover it and cook for the first 1–2 minutes on high flame and then on slow flame till the rice is done and each grain is still separate. Serve hot.

Khoja Biryani (Mumbai)

The Khojas are a business community centred around Mumbai and other parts of western India. They are the followers of the famed Agha Khan, who, it is said, is a descendant of the Prophet. Though essentially non–vegetarian, Khoja cuisine has a predominant Gujarati influence. Here fully cooked meat is layered with almost cooked rice and then cooked together for just a short while on dum. This biryani uses chilli abundantly.

Preparation time: 15 minutes
Marination time: 10 minutes
Cooking time: 1 hour 10 minutes
Serves: 8

1	kg mutton, from the raan (leg of a small goat), cut into medium sized pieces
½	tsp turmeric powder
750	long grain rice
100	gm red chilli paste of whole dried chillies
1	tsp cumin seeds
2	1 inch cinnamon sticks
3–4	green cardamoms, cracked open
2	black cardamoms, cracked open
6–8	cloves
4	onions, finely sliced

1. Marinate the mutton: Wash the mutton and put it in a colander for the water to drain. Add ½ tsp turmeric powder, mix, and marinate for 10 minutes.

2. Prepare the rice: Wash and soak the rice in water for 20 minutes. Boil about 3½ litres of water. Once the water starts to boil, add the rice, and salt. Cook for 7–8 minutes, till the rice is three fourth done. Drain the water and set the rice aside.

3. Prepare the chilli paste: Soak the chillies without seeds overnight. The next morning, drain the water. Boil the chillies in 1 tbs vinegar and a little water, just enough to cover the chillies. Give just one boil. When cool, grind to a fine paste. Set aside.

1	tbs ginger paste
1	tbs garlic paste
3	tomatoes, chopped, pureed and strained
1	tsp turmeric powder
1	tsp red chilli powder
1	tsp coriander powder
½	cup yoghurt, whisked
2	tbs ginger juliennes
1	tbs rose water
½	cup ghee–oil, mixed
	Salt

4. Cook the mutton: Take a heavy bottomed pan and heat the ghee–oil mixture. Add cumin seeds. Once they change colour to light brown, add the whole spices. In a few seconds, add the onions and fry till golden brown. Add the ginger, garlic paste and after about half a minute add the tomato puree, salt, turmeric, red chilli powder, and coriander powder and cook for about 2 minutes. Add the meat and fry for 5–6 minutes. Add 1 tbs chilli paste, mix and fry for about 1 minute. Add a little water and cook the meat covered till tender. Towards the end, add yoghurt, mix well and cook for another 1–2 minutes. When done, the meat should have about 1½ cups gravy left.

5. Assemble and serve: Now take a heavy bottomed pan and smear it with oil. Arrange the meat and rice in 4 layers starting with the meat. Sprinkle ginger juliennes over the first 3 layers and rose water over the final layer of the rice. Also sprinkle a little water. Cook for the first 3–4 minutes on high flame to heat up the dish and then for about 5 minutes on low flame till the dish is steaming hot and the rice done. Take out the meat and rice in large chunks from the sides without disturbing the layers. Serve hot.

Teevan Jo Pulao (Sindh)

Sindh has a rich non-vegetarian repertoire, and quails, partridges, and organs of the goat like brain, liver and kidney are very much a part of their cuisine. It has hardly any biryanis but many pulaos. This one has liver and kidneys too. The word teevan means mutton in Sindhi.

Preparation time: 15 minutes
Marination time: 30 minutes
Cooking time: 1 hour
Serves: 10

500	gm mutton from the leg of a small goat, cut into small pieces
250	gm single mutton chops
250	gm kidneys and liver, from the goat, cut into small pieces
1	cup yoghurt, whisked
4	onions, sliced finely
4	tomatoes, chopped finely
1	tsp garam masala powder
4	bay leaves
2–3	green cardamoms
½	tsp cumin seeds
6	dry whole red chillies
½	tsp pepper powder
1	tbs ginger juliennes
500	gm rice
1	tbs fresh green coriander, chopped
3–4	green chillies, chopped
¾	cup oil
	Salt

(Items from garam masala powder through ginger juliennes are grouped as A)

1. Marinate the mutton: Wash the meat and drain the water completely. Mix it with yoghurt and marinate the meat for half an hour.

2. Cook the mutton: Heat oil in heavy base pan, large enough to take both the meat and rice. Add and fry the onions till golden brown. Add mutton and fry, stirring continuously. Cook further for about 10–12 minutes till the meat is well browned. Add the chopped tomatoes followed in 2–3 minutes by all the ingredients at A and salt. Fry for about 4–5 minutes. Add a little water and cook covered till the meat is tender and about 2 cups gravy are left.

3. Soak the rice: Wash and soak the rice for about half an hour. Drain.

4. Assemble and serve: When the meat is done, add rice, a little salt and also some boiling water so that the level of water reaches about 1 inch over the surface of meat and rice. Cook covered first on medium and then slow flame for about 8 minutes till the rice is done without getting soggy and each grain is separate. Serve hot, garnished with fresh green coriander and green chillies.

Kutch Khoja Biryani (Gujarat)

Preparation time: 20 minutes
Marination time: 6 hours
Cooking time: 1 hour 30 minutes
Serves: 8–10

1	kg mutton, cut into medium pieces
1½	cup yoghurt, whisked
2	tomatoes, chopped
1	tsp garam masala
1	tbs red chilli powder

A — ground to a fine paste:
¾	cup fresh green coriander
2	inch ginger piece
10–15	garlic cloves
6–8	green chillies
2	inch raw papaya piece (pulp and skin)

	Juice of 2 limes
4	onions, sliced
2	potatoes, peeled and cut into medium sized pieces
650	gm long grain rice

B:
2-3	black cardamoms
2	star anise
1	tsp peppercorns
2	1 inch cinnamon sticks
1	tsp caraway seeds

10–12	dried apricots, deseeded and chopped
½	tsp saffron, lightly dry roasted and crushed
150	gm oil
2	tbs oil
2	tbs ghee
	Salt

This is a delicious biryani from the Kutch region of Gujarat. It is made with mutton, (tenderized with raw papaya and yoghurt), apricots and flavoured with saffron.

1. Marinate the mutton: Wash the mutton and put it in a colander for the water to drain. Put the mutton in a pan and add yoghurt, tomatoes, garam masala, red chilli powder, and salt. Also add the ground paste at A and squeeze the juice of lime. Mix nicely and leave to marinate for 6 hours.

2. Prepare the mutton: Take a heavy bottomed pan and heat oil. Fry the onions till golden. Remove with a slotted spoon and set aside. Apply a little salt to the potatoes and fry till golden. Remove and set aside. Add the marinated meat and fry on medium flame stirring continuously till the contents come to a boil. Cover and cook further on medium–slow flame for 10 more minutes.

3. Prepare the rice: Wash the rice well. Heat 2 tbs oil and add the whole spices at B, followed in a few seconds by rice and salt. Mix and fry for 2 minutes.

4. Assemble and serve: Now transfer half of the rice and place it over the meat. Put the fried potatoes over the layer of rice. Sprinkle the fried onions and the apricots over the potatoes and cover with balance rice. Pour 2 tbs ghee over the rice and also sprinkle the crushed saffron. Add hot water to reach 1 inch above the surface of rice. Do not mix. Cover with a tight fitting lid and put a heavy stone on the lid. Now place the biryani pan on a pre–heated griddle and cook on medium–low flame for 10 minutes and then cook further on low flame for about 30 minutes till the meat and rice are done. Let the biryani rest for 5 minutes after it is done. Remove in large chunks from the sides without disturbing the layers and serve hot.

Goan Special (Goa)

Goan special is a typically Goan rice dish, akin to a biryani in process but entirely unique in taste. It is cooked in the somewhat pungent Bancal sauce, a local ingredient. Bancal sauce is made with chilli, ginger, garlic, vinegar, tamarind, sugar, salt, and some other local spices. Since it is hardly available outside Goa, Worcestershire sauce is a good substitute.

Preparation time: 15 minutes
Marination time: 1 hour
Cooking time: 1 hour
Serves: 8

1	chicken, cut into 12 pieces
1	tbs ginger paste
1	tbs garlic paste
½	tsp turmeric powder
500	gm long grain rice

6	cloves	
1	1 inch cinnamon stick	
4	green cardamoms	A
1	tsp peppercorns	
2	bay leaves	

5–6	onions, finely sliced
2	tomatoes, roughly chopped
1	heaped tsp pepper powder
1	tsp garam masala
3	medium–large potatoes, cut into medium sized pieces
3	tbs bancal sauce or Worcestershire sauce
	A few sprigs of fresh green coriander, chopped

1. Marinate the chicken: Add ginger, garlic, turmeric, and a little salt to the chicken and marinate for one hour.

2. Prepare the rice: Wash and soak rice for about 15–20 minutes. Drain. Bring about 1½ litres (about 6–7 glasses) of water to a boil. Add the rice together with all the ingredients at A, and salt and cook it for about 7 minutes till it is about 70 percent done. Strain the rice through a sieve and drain the water. Set the rice aside in a flattish pan.

3. Cook the chicken and potatoes: Heat the oil and fry the onions till they turn golden brown. Remove three fourth and set aside. To the balance onions, add the tomatoes and fry it for 3–4 minutes. Add salt, pepper, garam masala, and add chicken pieces. Fry for 10 minutes, first 5 minutes open and then covered. Add a little water and cook further. When the chicken is more than half done, add the potatoes and cook covered till both the chicken and the potatoes are done. When chicken is almost done, add Bancal sauce and cook for another 5 minutes. Sprinkle chopped coriander.

5	hard–boiled eggs, grated
1	tbs ghee
¾	cup oil
1	tbs oil
	Salt

4. Assemble and serve: Brush a heavy bottomed pan with oil. Spread half the rice on it. Add the chicken on top of it. Sprinkle some fried onions over the chicken and a layer of grated eggs. Cover with the balance rice. Sprinkle the balance onions and dot with ghee. Sprinkle a little water and cover with a tight fitting lid. Cook for the first 2 minutes on medium–high flame to allow the initial steam to form, then reduce the flame to low and cook on dum for about 15–20 minutes so that rice is done and steaming. Serve hot.

Arroz Con Pollo (Goa)

'Arroz' means rice and 'pollo' means chicken in Portuguese. A Goan pulao of shredded chicken, this reflects the Portuguese–Spanish influence on this beautiful coastal region. This biryani is made with chicken breasts, whole spices and olives.

Preparation time: 10 minutes
Cooking time: 40 minutes
Serves: 6–8

400	gm chicken, preferably chicken breast
300	gm long grain rice
6	cloves
2	1 inch cinnamon sticks
3	green cardamoms
1	black cardamom
3	medium onions, finely sliced
2	inch piece ginger, crushed
6–8	cloves of garlic, crushed
1	tomato, roughly chopped
1/3	tsp turmeric powder
	Chicken stock
	Juice of 1 lime
	A few olives
60	gm ghee–oil, mixed
	Salt

1. Prepare the chicken: Boil the chicken with a little salt. Shred it with your fingers and keep it aside.

2. Soak the rice: Wash and soak rice in water for about 15 minutes, then drain and set aside.

3. Assemble and serve: Heat the ghee–oil mixture. Add the whole spices and in a few seconds, the sliced onions. When the onions turn golden brown, add ginger, and garlic and fry for 1 minute. Then add the tomatoes and fry for another 2 minutes. Add the rice and turmeric powder and sauté for 5 minutes. Add the chicken stock till 1 inch above the surface of rice followed by lime juice and salt. Cook covered first on high flame and then low till the stock is absorbed and rice is light and fluffy. Serve the rice hot, garnished with shredded chicken and olives.

Chicken Biryani (Goa)

Preparation time: 10 minutes
Cooking time: 50 minutes
Serves: 8

1	chicken, cut into 10–12 pieces
1½	tsp crushed pepper
1	tbs ginger paste
1½	cup yoghurt, beaten
150	gm cream
⅓	tsp turmeric powder
500	gm long grain rice
2	bay leaves
6	cloves
3	green cardamoms
1	star anise

⎫ A

1	tsp oil
½	tsp saffron, crushed
½	cup milk
1	tsp sugar
100	gm oil
	Salt

A Goan biryani with a lone star anise flavouring it.

1. Marinate the chicken: Mix the chicken well with pepper, ginger paste, and salt and leave it for an hour.

2. Prepare the chicken: Mix together the yoghurt, cream, and turmeric powder. Heat the oil. Add the marinated chicken and cook for 3–4 minutes, followed by the yoghurt and cream mixture. Bring it to a boil, stirring all the time. Once the liquids come to a boil, reduce the heat and cook on slow fire for about 15–20 minutes till the chicken is tender and the gravy almost dry.

3. Prepare the rice: Simultaneously, wash and soak the rice in water for 20 minutes. Drain. Boil 2 litres of water with all the ingredients at A and salt. Once the water starts to boil, add the rice and cook it for 7–8 minutes till three fourth done. Drain the rice of excess water and collect the water in a pan. Transfer the rice to a wide pan. Run a fork through the rice to separate the grains.

4. Assemble and serve: Mix saffron with warm milk and sugar and set it aside. Take a heavy bottomed pan and smear it with oil. Spread half of the rice in it. Over the rice, spread the chicken. Scrape the bottom of the pan in which chicken was cooked and spread the scraping over the chicken. Cover it with the balance rice. Make four holes into the rice with the back of a wooden spoon and pour the saffron milk into them. Now cover the holes with rice. Sprinkle a little water saved from the rice. Cook first on medium–high flame for about 2 minutes till the dish is heated and then simmer on a low flame for about 10 minutes till the dish is steaming hot. Carefully take out the dish from the sides in chunks and serve hot.

Mutton Biryani Upside Down (Goa)

This biryani is so named because it has to be emptied from the pan upside down so that the rice is down and the meat is up. Notice the influence of north India, in its usage of pine nuts and raisins. This is a unique dish cooked with mutton, aubergines and olive oil.

Preparation time: 15 minutes
Marination time: 15 minutes
Cooking time: 50 minutes
Serves: 8

750	gm boneless mutton, cut into small pieces
1	tbs coarsely ground pepper
1	large aubergine (the round variety)
400	gm long grain rice
	A dash of cinnamon powder
3	onions, finely sliced
1	pod garlic, crushed
50	gm pine nuts
20	gm raisins
⅓	tsp turmeric powder
4–5	cups meat stock
3	tbs oil for frying the aubergine
50	gm olive oil
	Salt

1. Marinate the meat: Wash the mutton. Drain out the water. Apply salt, pepper and marinate for 15 minutes.

2. Prepare the aubergine: Cut the aubergine into ½ inch round slices. Apply salt and shallow fry in a non–stick pan till golden brown. Set aside.

3. Prepare the rice: Soak the rice in water for about 20 minutes, then drain. Boil about 2 litres of water. Add rice, a dash of cinnamon powder, and salt and cook for about 5–6 minutes till it is half done. Drain out the excess water. Transfer the rice to a flattish pan and fork through to separate the grains. Set it aside.

4. Cook the meat: Heat oil in a heavy bottomed pan. Add the onions and fry till golden. Add the crushed garlic and fry for about 1 minute till it turns pale gold. Add the pine nuts, raisins, and turmeric followed by the marinated meat. Cook till the water dries up. Add 4–5 cups meat stock and cook for about 25–30 minutes till the meat is done and about 1 cup of gravy left.

5. Assemble and serve: Place the fried aubergine slices over the meat and spread the rice over it. Sprinkle about ½ cup meat stock and cover with a tight fitting lid. Cook, first on medium–high flame for 1–2 minutes and then on low flame for about 10 minutes till the rice is done. When ready, place a large serving platter over the pan and flip the dish so that the rice is down and meat up. Serve hot.

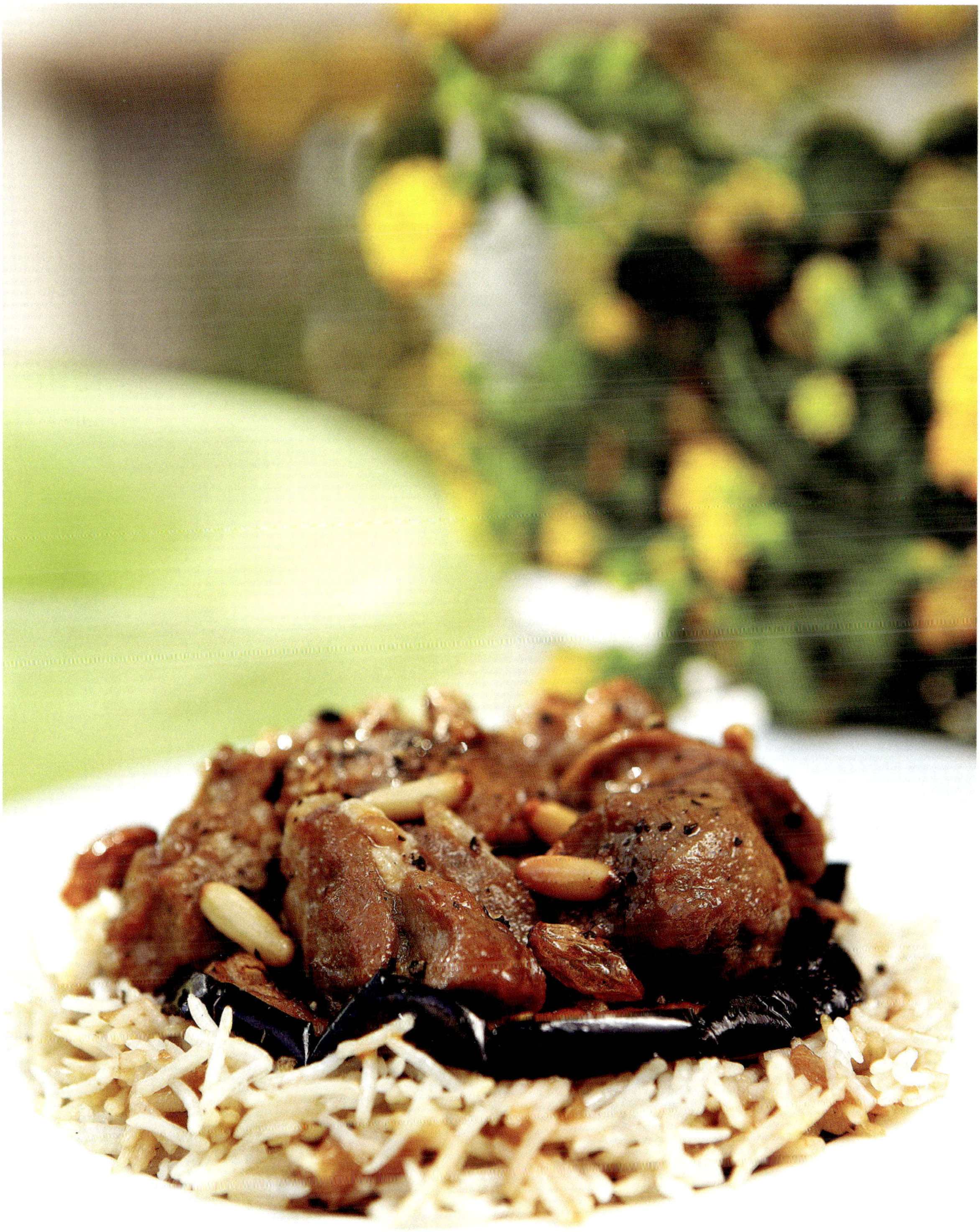

Malai ki Biryani (Rajasthan)

Preparation time: 10 minutes
Cooking time: 1 hour
Serves: 8–10

1½	kg milk
1	kg meat, cut into pasandas (flattened pieces of boneless mutton)
1	cup yoghurt, whisked
2	tbs thick cream

1	tsp red chilli powder	
1	tbs ginger paste	
1	tsp dry red chillies, coarsely ground	A
1	tsp garam masala	
25	gm raisins, ground	
1	tbs vinegar	

500	gm long grain rice
1	glass milk
2	tbs screwpine water (kewra)
3–4	silver leaves (chandi ke varq)
50	gm ghee

This biryani is made with the pasanda, a chunky boneless meat much in the fashion of a steak. A classy biryani, it is scented with screwpine water and dressed with real silver leaf.

1. Make rabri: Boil 1½ kg of full cream milk, stirring every now and then for about 45 minutes. You will get about 1½ cups of thick milk rabri. Set it aside.

2. Prepare the pasandas: To make pasandas, cut boneless meat into 2 inch wide and 2 inch long pieces of ¼ inch thickness and beat each piece with a mallet or the sharp end of a knife without breaking the pieces. Any good butcher can also do it for you.

3. Cook the pasandas: Wash the pasandas. Put them in a colander and drain the water. Mix pasandas with all the ingredients at A, 50 gm oil and salt in a heavy bottomed pan. Cook it first on a high flame, stirring continuously till the dish comes to a boil, then on low flame, covered, stirring now and then. Sprinkle a little water, as may be required. Cook for about 25 minutes till the meat is tender. When done, the meat should have some thick gravy coating it.

2	tbs ghee
1	tsp oil
	Salt

4. Prepare the rice: Meanwhile, wash and soak the rice for 20 minutes, then drain the water. Bring about 2¼ litres of water to a boil and add rice, a little salt, and one tsp oil. Cook for about 7–8 minutes till the rice is two thirds done. Put it in a colander and let the water drain. Transfer the rice to a wide dish. Stir with a fork to separate the grains.

5. Assemble: Take a heavy bottomed pan, large enough to take the meat and the rice. Grease it with ghee. Place half the rice in it and sprinkle half glass of milk over it. Spread the meat over the rice and cover it with the balance rice. Sprinkle the remaining milk, screwpine water, and ghee over the rice. Cover with a tight fitting lid. Cook for the first 1–2 minutes on medium–high flame to allow the steam to form and then on dum for about 20 minutes till the dish steams and the rice is done.

6. Garnish and serve: Transfer to a nice serving dish. Spread the rabri over the biryani and decorate with silver leaves. Serve hot.

Pasande ki Biryani (Rajasthan)

Preparation time: 10–15 minutes
Marination time: 2 hours
Cooking time: 40–45 minutes
Serves: 10

1	kg boneless mutton, from raan i.e. the leg of a goat
1	tbs raw green papaya paste (pulp and skin ground together)
1	heaped tbs ginger paste
1	large onion, ground
500	gm long grain rice

1	1½ inch cinnamon stick	
1	tbs peppercorns	
1	tbs caraway seeds	A
¼	tsp nutmeg	*finely powdered*
2	tbs coriander seeds	
	Seeds of 2 black cardamoms	

1½	cups yoghurt, whisked
10–12	cloves
½	tsp saffron
1	tbs ghee
½	cup ghee–oil, mixed
	Salt

This is an irresistible dish, ideal for parties and celebrations.

1. Prepare the meat: Prepare pasandas (i.e. flat boneless mutton pieces) of 2 inch x 2 inch size and ¼ inch thickness. Beat them lightly with a mallet or the sharp end of a thick knife or when you buy the meat, the butcher can do it for you. The thing about the pasanda is that the process of beating it breaks the fibre in the meat making it non-rubbery and yet nicely chewy. It also helps absorption of spices. Wash the pasandas and put them in a colander to let the water drain out completely. Mix the meat with papaya, ginger paste, ground onion, and salt and rub them well into the meat. Marinate for 2 hours.

2. Prepare the rice: Wash and soak the rice in liberal quantity of water with 1 tsp salt for 10–15 minutes. Drain out the water and set aside.

3. Assemble and serve: Mix the powdered spices at A with yoghurt, add it to the meat, and mix well. Take a heavy bottomed pan and spread the meat on it. Separately heat the ghee–oil mix and add cloves to it. When the cloves turn dark brown, pour the ghee–oil with the cloves, over the meat evenly. Now spread the rice over the meat. Do not mix the rice with the meat. Add water and allow it to come 1¼ inch over the surface of the rice. Add a little salt, saffron, and 1 tbs of ghee. Cook for the first 2–3 minutes on high flame for the contents to come to a boil. Then reduce heat, cover tightly with a heavy lid, or seal the pan with dough and cook on dum for about 40 minutes till the meat and rice are done with each grain of rice separate. Serve hot.

Seviyon ki Biryani (Rajasthan)

Preparation time: 10–15 minutes
Cooking time: 1 hour
Serves: 6–8

750	gm mutton, cut into medium sized pieces

2	bay leaves	
1	tsp aniseed	
1	tsp coriander seeds	
1	tsp peppercorns	
1	inch cinnamon stick	A
1	black cardamom, crushed	
1	onion, quartered	
4	garlic cloves	
5	cloves	

2	onions, finely sliced
250	gm vermicelli
1	tbs ginger juice
1½	tsp red chilli powder
1	tsp coriander powder
½	cup milk
2	tbs rose water
1	tsp ghee
1	cup ghee–oil, mixed
	Salt

A Rajasthani seviyon ki biryani. It not only tastes different but also looks enticing because of the golden thread-like vermicelli mixed with mutton.

1. Prepare the mutton stock: Boil the meat in about 3–4 glasses of water with all the ingredients at A first on high flame till the contents come to a boil and then on low flame, for about 25 minutes till the meat is tender. Remove the meat pieces and set aside. Strain and squeeze out the liquids through a muslin cloth. You should get about 3 cups of meat stock (yakhni). Heat 1 tsp of ghee and add cloves to it. In a few seconds when the cloves turn brown, add the ghee and the cloves to the meat stock.

2. Fry the vermicelli: In a heavy bottomed pan, large enough to take the vermicelli and meat, heat the ghee–oil mixture. Fry the onions till they turn golden brown. Remove and reserve. Next add vermicelli to the ghee–oil and lightly fry carefully (to prevent burning it), on medium-low flame, in two lots till golden. Remove and set aside.

3. Prepare the mutton: In the same ghee, add the meat pieces. Also add ginger juice, red chilli powder, coriander powder, and a little salt. Fry the meat till it turns brown. Spread the vermicelli over the meat. Heat the meat stock and pour it over the vermicelli. Also sprinkle half a cup milk, rose water, and the fried onions.

4. Assemble and serve: Cover the pan with a tight fitting lid and cook for 2 minutes on medium-high flame to heat up the dish. Then place a griddle under the pan over high flame. After 1–2 minutes, reduce the heat to medium low and cook till the vermicelli has absorbed all the liquids and is cooked with each strand separate. Serve hot.

Soola Biryani (Rajasthan)

Soola in Rajasthani means small morsels of mutton, in particular from the spare ribs of the wild boar. With the ban on hunting, mutton is now widely substituted for the preparation of the soola dishes. Here, pasandas are cooked in mutton stock and flavoured with rose water.

Preparation time: 15 minutes
Marination time: 1 hour
Cooking time: 1 hour and 10 minutes
Serves: 6–8

750	gm boneless mutton, from the leg made into pasandas of 2 inch x 2 ½ inch size and ¼ inch thickness
3	onions, finely sliced
1	tsp garlic paste ⎫
1	tsp red chilli powder ⎬ A
1	tbs raw green papaya paste (pulp and skin ground together) ⎭
400	gm long grain rice
4	glasses yakhni (mutton stock)
2	tbs ghee
6	cloves
½	cup milk
3	tbs rose water
50	gm ghee
	Oil for frying
	Salt

1. Marinate the pasandas: Get pasandas (flat pieces of boneless mutton) made from a butcher 2 inch x 2½ inch in size and ¼ inch in thickness. Get them lightly beaten with the sharp end of a knife as it will help absorption of spices and will also cook more easily. Heat oil. Fry the onions till golden. Remove and crush when cool. Mix all the ingredients at A, including salt and the crushed onions with the pasandas. Marinate for an hour.

2. Barbeque the pasandas: Pass a skewer through the centre of each piece of pasanda and secure it tightly. Barbeque on the live charcoal, rotating it in between so that the pasandas are evenly cooked. Barbeque for about 10–15 minutes till they turn tender and brown. Remove the pasandas from the skewers and reserve.

3. Prepare the rice: Wash and soak the rice in water for about 15–20 minutes. Drain out the water and set aside. Heat the yakhni in a heavy bottomed pan. When the yakhni starts to boil add the rice, ghee, and salt. The level of yakhni should be 1 inch above the surface of rice. Cook first on medium–high flame for about 2–3 minutes and then on low flame for about 7–8 minutes, covered till the rice is about two thirds done and has absorbed all the liquid.

4. Assemble and serve: Smear a heavy bottomed pan with a little oil. Spread two thirds of the rice on it and place the pasanda over the rice. Cover it with the balance rice. Heat ghee and add the cloves. When they turn brown, sprinkle the ghee and cloves over the rice. Also sprinkle the milk mixed with rose water and cover with a tight fitting lid, cooking first on high flame for about 1–2 minutes to heat the dish and then on dum for about 15–20 minutes till the rice is done. Serve hot.

Masala Bhat (Maharashtra)

Masala bhat is a spicy vegetarian rice dish from Maharashtra, which is cooked in the same way as a biryani. Here cauliflower is cooked with rice and coconut, and flavoured with asafoetida.

Preparation time: 15–20 minutes
Marination time: 1 hour
Cooking time: 30 minutes
Serves: 6

2	cauliflowers, weighing about 600 gms, cut into large sized florets
1	tsp cumin seeds *powdered* ⎫
1	tsp peppercorns ⎬ A
1	tsp ginger paste ⎪
2	tbs yoghurt ⎭
350	gm rice
1	1 inch cinnamon stick
4–5	green cardamoms
2	bay leaves
1	onion, roughly chopped
	A pinch of asafoetida
2–3	garlic cloves
½	cup grated fresh coconut
½	tsp turmeric powder
1	tsp yellow chilli powder
1	tsp coriander powder
	Juice of 1 lime
¾	tsp sugar
4–5	cloves
½	tsp saffron, crushed and mixed with 2 tbs water
10–15	cashew nuts ⎫ *fried*
10–15	raisins ⎭
3	tbs oil
1	tbs ghee
	Salt

1. Marinate the cauliflower: Wash the cauliflower florets well and put them in a colander for the water to drain. Mix together the ingredients at A and apply them to the cauliflower florets. Refrigerate and marinate for 1 hour.

2. Prepare the rice: Wash and soak rice in water for about half an hour. Drain the rice. Heat 1 tbs of ghee. Add the whole spices followed in a few seconds by the rice. Fry for 2 minutes and set aside.

3. Prepare the coconut paste: Heat 3 tbs oil. Add onion followed by garlic. Also add asafoetida. After a minute also add coconut, turmeric powder, yellow chilli powder, and coriander powder. When the onion becomes translucent, remove from flame. Add salt, lime juice, and sugar. Grind to a paste.

4. Assemble and serve: Now, take a heavy bottomed pan. Heat 1½ tbs of oil and add the ground masala and then the marinated cauliflower. Mix and cook for 2 minutes. Add rice and a little salt. Add water to reach three fourth inch above the surface of the rice. Cook on high flame. When the water starts boiling reduce flame to medium–low and after 1–2 minutes to low. Cook, with the pan tightly covered, on low flame for about 10 minutes. When the rice is almost done, remove the cover, make 3–4 holes in the dish with say a wooden spoon and put saffron water in these holes. Cover and cook on low flame till the rice is done. Switch off the flame and let the rice rest for about 5 minutes. Serve hot garnished with cashew nuts and raisins.

Mixed Dal Vada Biryani (Maharashtra)

Preparation time: 5–10 minutes
Soaking time: 3–4 hours
Cooking time: 50 minutes
Serves: 8

300	gm split gram lentils (channa dal)
100	gm red gram lentils (arhar ki dal)
100	gm white lentils (urad ki dhuli dal)
50	gm yellow lentils (moong ki dhuli dal)
½	tsp fenugreek seeds
4–5	green chillies, chopped
½	cup fresh green coriander, chopped
2	ginger pieces, grated
½	tsp thymol seeds (ajwain)
⅓	tsp turmeric powder
1	tsp crushed red chilli powder
	} A
500	gm long grain rice
1	tsp black mustard seeds
1½	tsp cumin seeds
8–10	dry whole red chillies
	A pinch of asafoetida
	Oil for frying
1	tsp oil
1	tbs oil
	Salt

An unusual vegetarian biryani from Maharashtra, this is made with lentil balls, commonly known as vadas.

1. Soak the lentils: Wash and soak all the lentils together with fenugreek seeds for 3–4 hours. Drain the water and coarsely grind the lentils.

2. Make the vadas: Mix the lentils with all the ingredients at A and salt. Take 1 tbs of the lentils and form a ball (vada). Press lightly to flatten it a little. Repeat the process for the remaining lentils. Now heat the oil. Fry the lentil vadas, a few at a time, to a rich golden colour. Set aside.

3. Prepare the rice: Wash and soak rice for about 15–20 minutes. Boil about 3 litres of water. When the water starts boiling, add 1 tsp oil, and salt. Drain the rice and add to boiling water. Cook for about 6–7 minutes till the rice is three fourths done. Drain and transfer to a flat pan.

4. Prepare the baghar: Heat 3 tbs oil. Add mustard seeds followed in a few seconds by cumin seeds. When mustard starts to crackle, add the whole red chillies, and in a few seconds remove from flame. Do not over-brown the red chillies. After 5 seconds, add asafoetida.

5. Assemble and serve: Take 7–8 vadas and crush them coarsely. Mix the crushed vadas and half of the baghar (cumin, mustard seeds and red chillies seasoning) with the rice. Take a heavy bottomed pan smeared with oil and place half of the par-boiled rice in it. Spread the vadas over the rice and cover with the balance rice. Sprinkle a little water and cover it with a tight fitting lid. Cook for the first 1–2 minutes on high flame, then on dum for about 10 minutes till the rice is steaming hot and done. Serve hot garnished with the remaining baghar (seasoning).

Ravan Bhat (Maharashtra)

Ravan was the legendary Sri Lankan king who kidnapped Sita, the wife of Lord Ram. A scorching contribution from Kolhapur, it is made with whole red chillies, raw green mangoes and peanuts, and flavoured with asafoetida. As the name suggests, this is a fiery biryani, so try it at your own risk.

Preparation time: 15–20 minutes
Soaking time: 20 minutes
Cooking time: 40 minutes
Serves: 8

500	gm long grain rice
	Juice of ½ lime
3	green cardamoms
4–5	cloves
2	1 inch cinnamon sticks
2	bay leaves
1	tbs mustard seeds
1	tsp cumin seeds
⅓	cup curry leaves
	A large pinch of asafoetida
150	gm raw peanuts
100	gm split gram lentils (washed and soaked in water for 1 hour)
½	desiccated coconut, cut into thin long slices
8	whole red chillies
50	gm raw green mangoes, grated
5–6	dry whole red chillies for garnish
⅓	cup fresh green coriander, chopped
	Oil
	Salt

1. Prepare the rice: Wash and soak the rice in water for 20 minutes. Boil about 3 litres of water. Add 1 tsp oil, juice of half a lime, salt, and the drained rice. Cook for about 6–7 minutes till it is three fourths done. Drain the water and transfer the rice to a flat pan.

2. Fry the rice: Heat 2 tbs oil. Add the whole spices and in a few seconds, add the rice. Mix and in just about a minute, remove from flame. Set it aside.

3. Cook the lentils: Heat 100 gm oil. Add mustard seeds followed in a few seconds by cumin seeds. When the mustard starts to splutter, add curry leaves, and asafoetida. Then add the raw peanuts and fry till golden brown. Next add the previously soaked lentils and fry for about 8–10 minutes on medium flame, sprinkling a little water now and then. Then add the desiccated coconut and the whole red chillies and fry for a minute. Add the grated mango and salt and cook for about 1 minute.

4. Assemble and serve: Now take a heavy bottomed pan and smear it with oil. Place half of the prepared rice. Arrange the fried lentils and peanuts mixture over the rice. Cover with the balance rice. Sprinkle about 1 cup water and cover with a tight fitting lid. Cook for the first 1–2 minutes on high flame and then low flame for about 10 minutes till the rice is done and steaming hot. Heat 1 tbs of oil. Add the whole red chillies till they turn a light red-brown. Serve steaming hot, garnished with fried chillies, and fresh green chopped coriander.

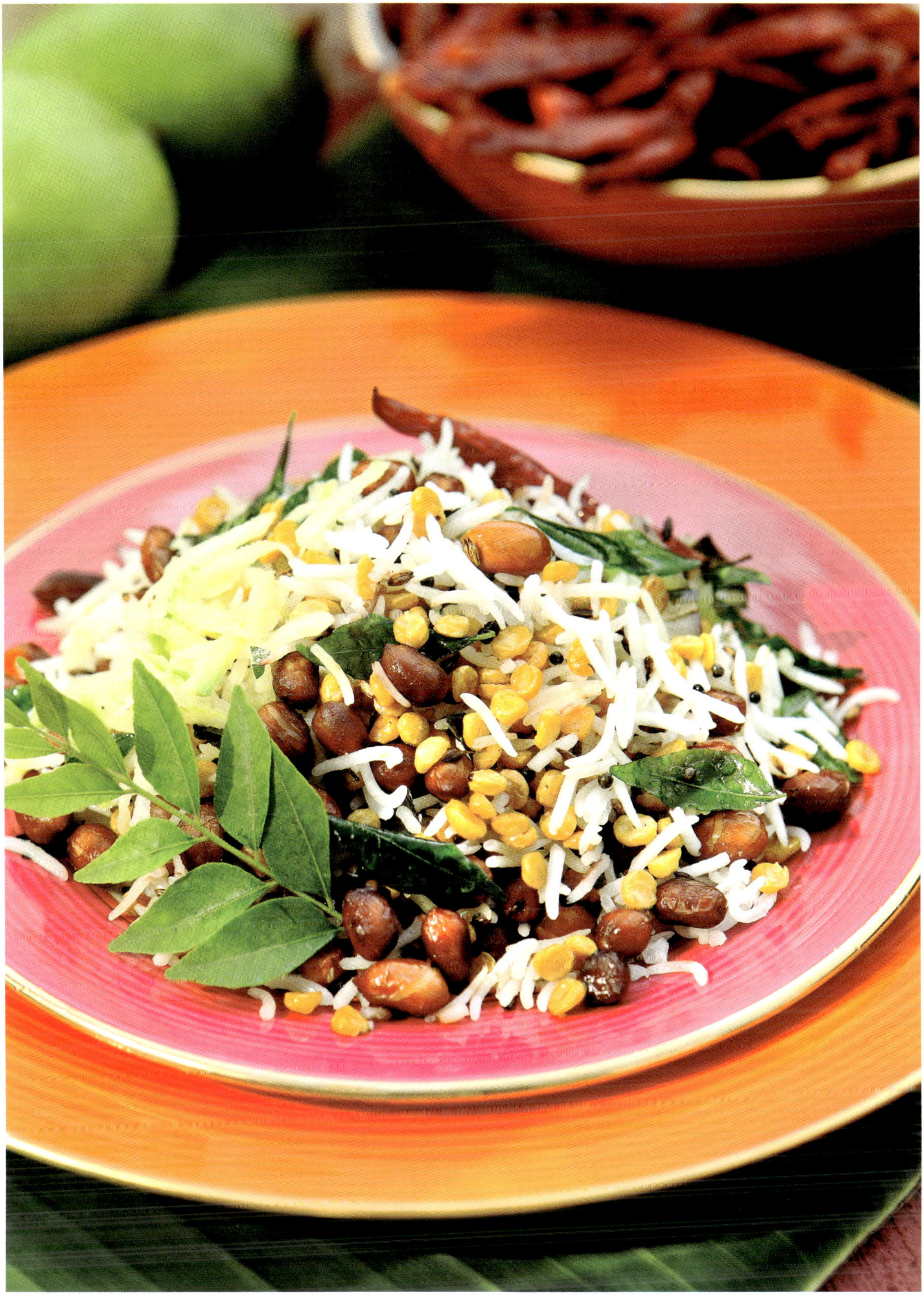

Relishes

The use of accompaniments is a matter of individual choice. Purists consider it sacrilegious to tamper with the biryani flavour with anything, even a dahi or raita. In fact, relishes, which include raitas, are preferred more with pulaos as they are generally drier. Hyderabadis prefer a raita of onions with yoghurt as the onions add a crunch to the biryani. In the south, they insist on pachidi, again a raita simply dressed with coriander and green chillies. Others like just chopped green chillies and chopped onions with their biryani while many like to add korma or mirchi ka saalan gravy to the dish.

Bengal Raita

This is a classic biryani accompaniment from Bengal. Interestingly, it uses both black mustard seeds or sarson, and brown mustard or rai and is mildly sweetened with sugar.

Preparation time: 10 minutes

250	gm hung yoghurt
¼	tsp fennel seeds
¼	tsp black mustard seeds (sarson)
¼	tsp brown mustard seeds (rai)
¼	tsp fenugreek seeds
¼	tsp nigella seeds
¾	tsp powdered sugar
	Salt

The fennel seeds, black mustard seeds (sarson), brown mustard seeds (rai), fenugreek seeds, and nigella seeds are grouped as A.

1. Prepare the yoghurt: Whisk the hung yoghurt well.

2. Assemble and serve: Grind together all the ingredients at A to a fine paste. Mix the paste, sugar, and salt with the yoghurt and keep refrigerated till you serve. Serve in an attractive glass bowl.

Mango Raita

Preparation: 10 minutes

500	gm yoghurt, whisked
¼	tsp coarsely ground red chilli powder
1	large ripe mango (alphonso or any other mango peeled and cut into small pieces)
½	tsp mustard seeds
10–15	curry leaves
2	tsp oil
	Salt

An excellent relish for the summer months, it fuses yoghurt with fresh mangoes and curry leaves.

1. Prepare the yoghurt: Whisk the yoghurt well. Add salt and red chilli powder and mix it further. Also add the chopped mango. Mix and transfer to a nice, glass serving bowl.

2. Season and serve: Heat the oil and add the mustard seeds. When the mustard starts to splutter, add the curry leaves and in a few seconds, remove from the flame and pour the baghar (seasoning) over the yoghurt. Serve chilled.

Aubergine Raita

Preparation time: 20 minutes

500	gm yoghurt
3–4	garlic cloves
3–4	green chillies
⅓	cup fresh green coriander, chopped
2	aubergines (round variety) weighing about 350 gm, cut into ¼ inch thick round slices
½	tsp roasted cumin powder
½	tsp red chilli powder, coarsely ground
½	tsp cumin seeds
3–4	dry whole red chillies
10–15	curry leaves
	Oil
	Salt

Here, fried aubergines are placed over yoghurt and seasoned with roasted cumin powder to produce this delectable relish.

1. Prepare the yoghurt: Whisk the yoghurt, then set it aside. Grind the garlic, green chillies, and coriander together to a fine paste. Mix this paste and a little salt with the yoghurt.

2. Fry the aubergines: Heat 50 gm of oil in a flat pan. Sprinkle a little salt over the aubergine on both sides. Fry the aubergine pieces to a rich golden brown. Set aside.

3. Assemble: Place the yoghurt in a slightly deep and wide serving dish. Arrange the fried aubergine over the yoghurt. If the pieces are too large they can be cut into 2. Sprinkle the roasted cumin powder and the red chilli powder over the aubergine.

4. Prepare the baghar: Heat 1 tbs of oil. To this, add cumin seeds followed in just about 5–10 seconds by the red chillies. As soon as the colour of the red chillies darkens a little, add the curry leaves and remove from flame in about 5–10 seconds. When slightly cool, pour the baghar over the aubergine relish. Keep refrigerated till it is served.

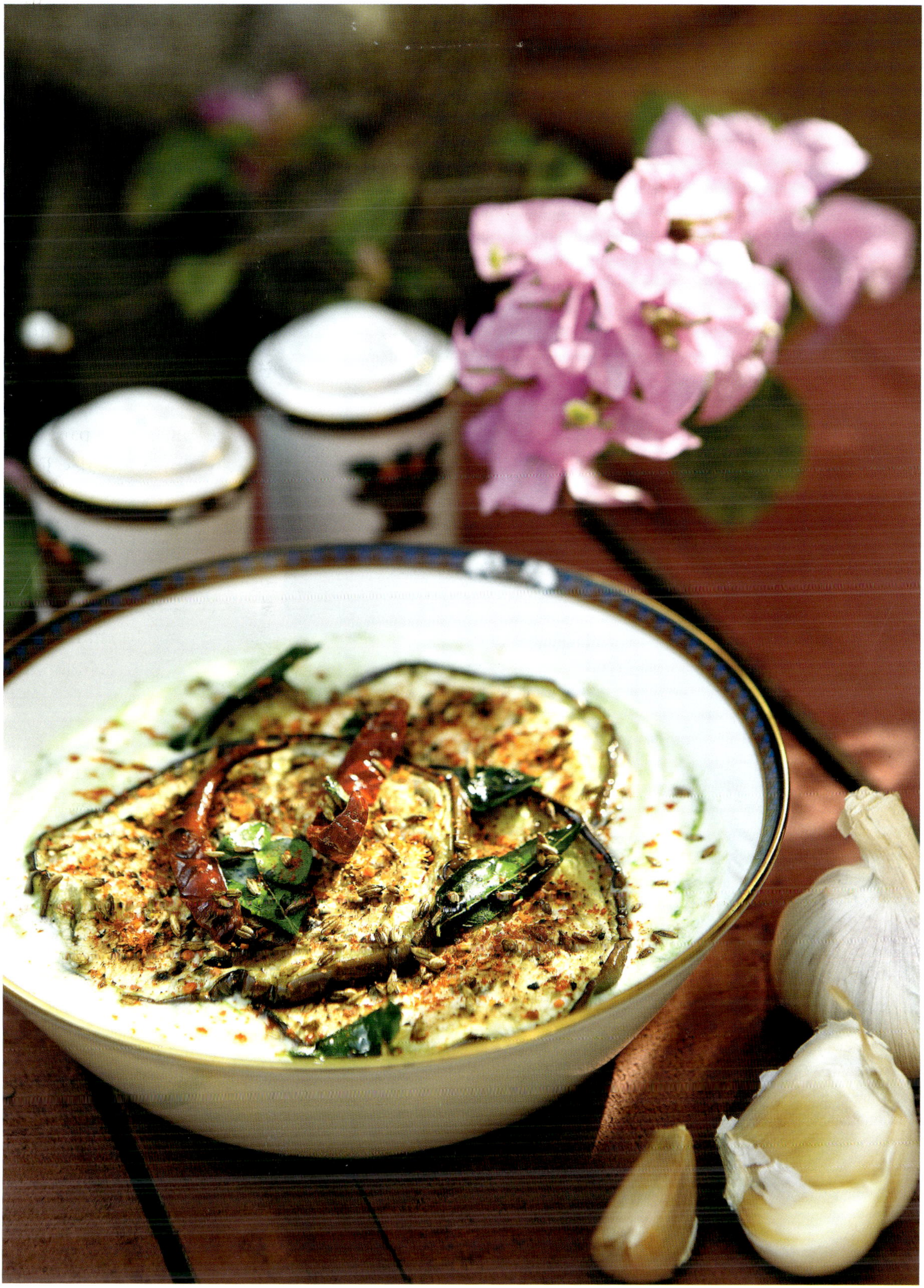

Smoked Onion and Tomato Raita

Preparation time: 15 minutes

500	gm yoghurt
1	large onion, chopped
1	large tomato, chopped
½	tsp peppercorns, crushed
3	cloves, crushed
	A piece of charcoal
	Salt

An unusual accompaniment for biryanis, this one uses charcoal to impart a smoky flavour to the dish.

1. Prepare the yoghurt: Whisk the yoghurt well. Add the chopped onion, tomato, pepper, cloves, salt, and mix.

2. Smoke it and serve: Heat a charcoal piece over the flame till it becomes flaming red in most parts. Place the charcoal in a steel or brass katori (a small bowl), put it in the centre of the yoghurt relish and cover for 5 minutes. Remove the cover. Transfer to a nice serving bowl and serve.

Okra Raita

A lovely accompaniment made with whisked yoghurt and fried okra, flavoured with asafoetida.

Preparation time: 15 minutes

500	gm yoghurt, whisked
½	tsp red chilli powder, coarsely ground
½	tsp fennel seeds, roasted and powdered
	A small pinch of asafoetida
2–3	green chillies, chopped
	A few sprigs of fresh green coriander, chopped
125	gm okra, washed and sliced thin
50	gm oil
	Salt

1. Prepare the yoghurt: Whisk the yoghurt. Add salt, red chilli powder, powdered fennel seeds, asafoetida, green chillies, and fresh green coriander. Transfer to a nice serving bowl.

2. Assemble and serve: Heat oil and fry the okra till golden brown. Remove with a slotted spoon and place on absorbent paper. Sprinkle over the yoghurt and serve.

Burrani

Burrani is a raita made with hung yoghurt, although in this recipe I have set it in a matka to impart a special flavour to it and thickened it with cream. It does not use any vegetables, not even onions, and is flavoured with ginger and garlic juice.

Preparation time: 5–10 minutes

500	gm yoghurt, set in an earthern pot (matka)
2	tbs cream
½	tsp roasted cumin powder
1	tbs ginger and garlic juice
½	tsp mustard seeds
2–3	whole red chillies
1	tbs mustard oil
	Salt

1. Set the yoghurt: Use a matka for setting the yoghurt, as it imparts a lovely earthy flavour. Add 2 tbs of cream, roasted cumin powder, ginger and garlic juice and salt. Mix and transfer to a nice, crystal serving bowl.

2. Season the yoghurt and serve: Heat oil to a smoking point. Add mustard seeds, followed in a few seconds by the whole red chillies. When they start to splutter and the colour of chillies darkens, pour the baghar over the yoghurt relish. Serve chilled.

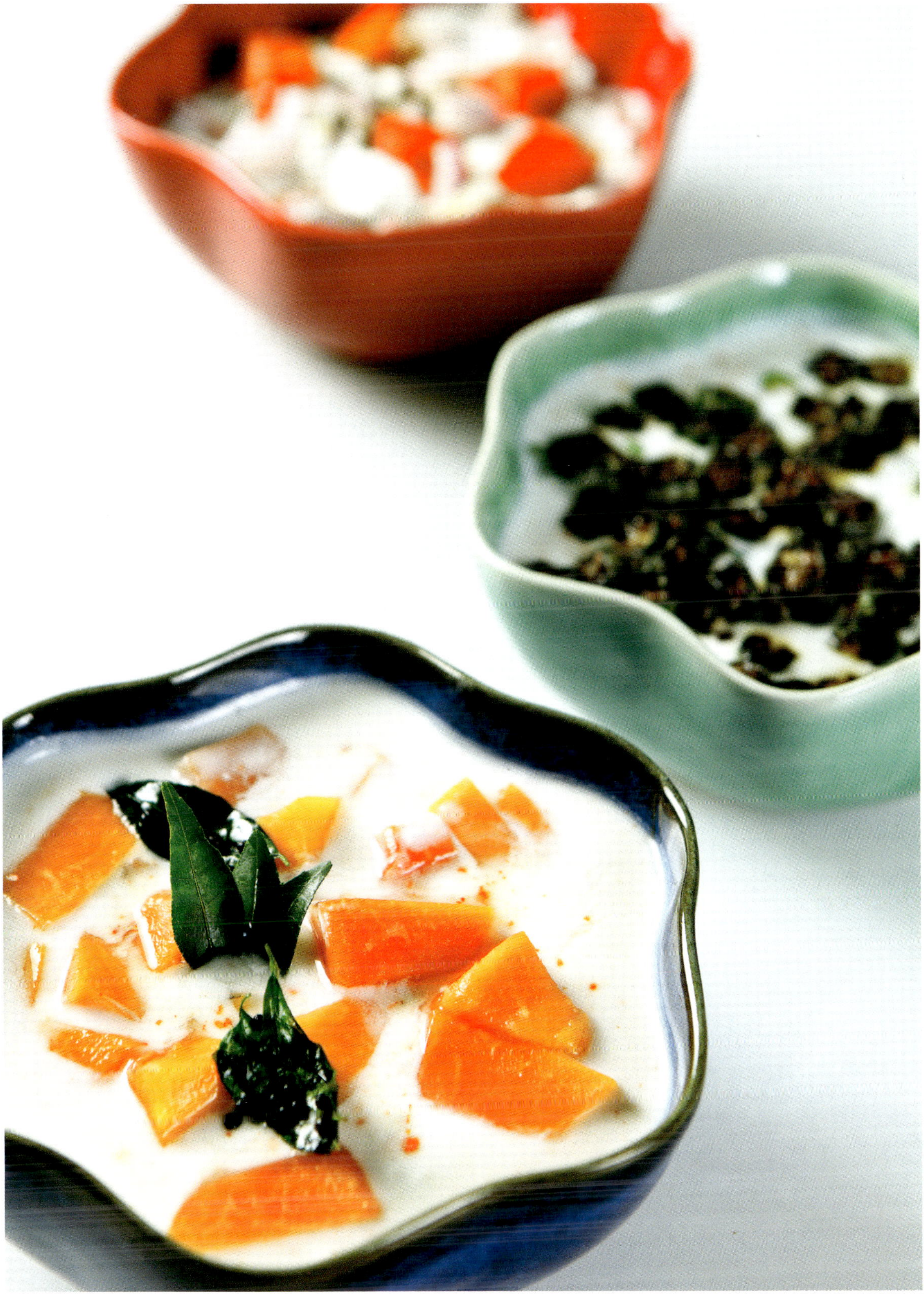

Pachidi/Churri

A simple yet refreshing raita, a pachidi, or churri as it is also called in some parts of the country, is made with yoghurt and the fresh green leaves of coriander and mint.

Preparation time: 5 minutes

250	gm yoghurt
1	small onion, chopped
	A few sprigs of fresh green coriander, chopped
	A few green mint leaves, chopped
2	green chillies, chopped
	Salt

1. Prepare the yoghurt: Whisk the yoghurt well. Set it aside.

2. Assemble and serve: Add all the ingredients to the yoghurt. Keep it refrigerated till you serve.

Onion Relish

This is the simplest of the relishes, made with just onion rings, chilli powder, and vinegar.

Preparation time: 5–10 minutes

2	medium sized onions, sliced round and with some of the rings opened up
¼	tsp red chilli powder
1	tbs vinegar
	Salt

1. Assemble and serve: Add red chilli powder, vinegar, and salt to the ringed onions, mix and serve.

Kachumber

Preparation time: 10 minutes

1	onion, chopped
1	tomato, chopped
½	capsicum, chopped
1	small white radish, chopped
¼	cucumber, chopped
	A few sprigs of fresh green coriander, chopped
2	green chillies, chopped
	Juice of 1 lime
	Salt

Kachumber is made without yoghurt. It uses fresh vegetables like onion, tomato, cucumber, capsicum, and radish.

1. Assemble and serve: Put together all the ingredients. Mix and serve.

Carrot and Cabbage Relish

This is a colourful relish made with sliced cabbage and carrots. The flavours are brought alive with vinegar, mustard and curry leaves.

Preparation time: 20 minutes

150	gm carrots, finely sliced
150	gm cabbage, finely sliced
1	tsp sugar, powdered
1	tbs vinegar
½	tsp mustard seeds
½	tsp cumin seeds
2–3	dry whole red chillies
10–15	curry leaves
	Oil
	Salt

1. Prepare the vegetables: Mix the carrots and cabbage with sugar, vinegar, and salt.

2. Make the baghar: Heat 1½ tbs of oil. Add mustard seeds, followed in a few seconds by the cumin seeds. When mustard starts to crackle, add the whole red chillies. In a few seconds, when the colour of the red chillies darkens a little, add the curry leaves. After 5 seconds, remove from flame.

3. Assemble and serve: Pour the baghar (seasoning) over the carrot and cabbage relish. Mix and serve.

List of Biryanis in the order of appearance

Gosht Biryani (Lucknow) 16
Ananas ki Biryani (Lucknow) 17
Rose Biryani (Lucknow).................................... 20
Motiye ki Biryani (Lucknow) 22
Dumpukht Biryani (Lucknow) 24
Purani Dilli ki Ande aur Sabzion ki
Biryani (Delhi) 25
Purani Dilli ki Gosht ki Biryani (Delhi) 26
Kofta Biryani (Delhi) 28
Mutton Biryani (Delhi)..................................... 29
Babu Shahi's Matka Peer Biryani (Delhi) 30
Santare ki Biryani–I (Delhi) 32
Santare ki Biryani–II (Delhi) 34
Kabab Biryani (Delhi) 35
Moti Pulao (Delhi)... 36
Muthanjan Pulao (Delhi) 38
Pork Chops Pulao (Delhi).................................. 40
Maya's Biryani (Delhi) 42
Mutton Pulao (Kashmir) 43
Mutton Biryani (Kashmir) 44
Vegetable Biryani (Lucknow)............................ 46
Aloo Aur Tamater Ka Pulao (Lucknow) 47
Mewa Pulao (Delhi)... 48
Guchchi Biryani (Delhi) 50
Gosht Biryani–I (Hyderabad) 56
Bater ki Biryani (Hyderabad) 57
Murgh ki Biryani (Hyderabad).......................... 60
Fenugreek and Chicken Biryani (Hyderabad)... 62
Gosht Biryan–II (Hyderabad) 64
Dumpokht Biryani (Hyderabad) 66
Masoor Dal Mutton Biryani (Hyderabad) 67
Doodh ki Biryani (Hyderabad) 68
Kairi ki Biryani (Hyderabad) 70
Korme ki Biryani (Hyderabad).......................... 72
Paye ka Pulao (Hyderabad) 75
Katchi Biryani (Hyderabad) 76
Seviyon ki Biryani (Hyderabad) 78
Bone Marrow Pulao (Hyderabad) 80
Keeme ki Khichri (Hyderabad) 81
Keeme ki Biryani (Hyderabad) 82
Karonde ki Biryani (Hyderabad) 84
Boote aur Keeme ki Biryani (Hyderabad) 86
Salem Biryani (Tamil Nadu) 88
Aambur Biryani (Tamil Nadu) 89

Egg Biryani (Tamil Nadu).................................. 90
Chettinad Mutton Biryani (Tamil Nadu)........... 92
Dindigul Biryani (Tamil Nadu) 93
Mangalore Fish Biryani (Kerala) 94
Karwar Prawn Biryani (Karnataka) 95
Coorg Mutton Biryani (Karnataka).................... 96
Belgaum Chicken Biryani (Karnataka).............. 97
South Canara Chicken Biryani (Karnataka)...... 98
Prawn Biryani with Curry leaves and
Aniseed (Kerala) 100
Mutton Biryani (Kerala)................................... 101
Chemeen Biryani (Kerala) 102
Meen Choru (Kerala) 104
Whole Fish Biryani (Kerala) 107
Thalassery Chicken Biryani (Kerala) 109
Northern Malabar Kozhi Biryani (Kerala) 110
Tellichery Biryani (Kerala) 112
Zafraan Pilaf (Hyderabad)................................ 113
Qabooli (Hyderabad).. 114
Udupi Vegetable Biryani (Karnataka).............. 116
Jackfruit Biryani I (Andhra Pradesh)............... 117
Masoor Dal Biryani–Vegetarian Version
(Tamil Nadu) 118
Coconut Pulao (Tamil Nadu) 120
Jackfruit Biryani II (Kerala).............................. 121
Fish Biryani with Aloo Bukhara (West Bengal)..... 126
Chicken and Apricot Biryani (West Bengal) 129
Kolkata Mutton Biryani (West Bengal) 132
Easy Fish Biryani (West Bengal) 134
Ramzan Biryani (East Bengal–now Bangladesh) ... 135
Mutton Biryani (Bihar).................................... 136
Chicken Biryani (Bihar)................................... 137
Kampuri Biryani (Assam)................................ 138
Kolhapuri Biryani (Maharashtra) 144
Jhinga Biryani (Mumbai) 146
Parsi Prawn Pulao (Mumbai) 148
Pork Biryani (Mumbai).................................... 149
Machhi Jo Pulao (Sindh).................................. 150
Choozon ka Pulao (Mumbai)........................... 152
Mumbai Tawa Biryani (Mumbai) 153
Aloo Bukhara Biryani (Mumbai) 154
Subzi Gosht Biryani (Mumbai)........................ 155
Parsi Pasanda Biryani (Mumbai) 156
Bohri Biryani (Mumbai) 158
Sindhi Mutton Biryani (Sindh/Mumbai)......... 159

Khoja Biryani (Mumbai) 160
Teevan Jo Pulao (Sindh) 162
Kutch Khoja Biryani (Gujarat) 163
Goan Special (Goa) 164
Arroz Con Pollo (Goa) 166
Chicken Biryani (Goa) 167
Mutton Biryani Upside Down (Goa) 168
Malai ki Biryani (Rajasthan) 170
Pasande ki Biryani (Rajasthan) 172
Seviyon ki Biryani (Rajasthan) 173
Soola Biryani (Rajasthan) 174
Masala Bhat (Maharashtra) 176
Mixed Dal Vada Biryani (Maharashtra) 177
Ravan Bhat (Maharashtra) 178

List of Biryanis by ingredients

Fruits, nuts and vegetables
Vegetable Biryani (Lucknow) 46
Aloo Aur Tamater Ka Pulao (Lucknow) 47
Mewa Pulao (Delhi) 48
Guchchi Biryani (Delhi) 50
Zafraan Pilaf (Hyderabad) 113
Qabooli (Hyderabad) 114
Udupi Vegetable Biryani (Karnataka) 116
Jackfruit Biryani I (Andhra Pradesh) 117
Masoor Dal Biryani–Vegetarian Version
(Tamil Nadu) 118
Coconut Pulao (Tamil Nadu) 120
Jackfruit Biryani II (Kerala) 121
Kolhapuri Biryani (Maharashtra) 144
Masala Bhat (Maharashtra) 176
Mixed Dal Vada Biryani (Maharashtra) 177
Ravan Bhat (Maharashtra) 178

Eggs
Purani Dilli ki Ande aur Sabzion ki
Biryani (Delhi) 25
Egg Biryani (Tamil Nadu) 90

Prawn
Karwar Prawn Biryani (Karnataka) 95
Prawn Biryani with Curry leaves and
Aniseed (Kerala) 100
Chemeen Biryani (Kerala) 102

Jhinga Biryani (Mumbai) 146
Parsi Prawn Pulao (Mumbai) 148

Fish
Mangalore Fish Biryani (Kerala) 94
Meen Choru (Kerala) 104
Whole Fish Biryani (Kerala) 107
Fish Biryani with Aloo Bukhara (West Bengal) 126
Easy Fish Biryani (West Bengal) 134
Machhi Jo Pulao (Sindh) 150

Chicken
Murgh Ki Biryani (Hyderabad) 60
Fenugreek and Chicken Biryani (Hyderabad) 62
Belgaum Chicken Biryani (Karnataka) 97
South Canara Chicken Biryani (Karnataka) 98
Northern Malabar Kozhi Biryani (Kerala) 110
Chicken and Apricot Biryani (West Bengal) 129
Chicken Biryani (Bihar) 137
Kampuri Biryani (Assam) 138
Kolhapuri Biryani (Maharashtra) 144
Choozon ka Pulao (Mumbai) 152
Goan Special (Goa) 164
Arroz Con Pollo (Goa) 166

Other poultry
Bater ki Biryani (Hyderabad) 57

Mutton
Gosht Biryani (Lucknow) 16
Ananas ki Biryani (Lucknow) 17
Rose Biryani (Lucknow) 20
Motiye ki Biryani (Lucknow) 22
Dumpukht Biryani (Lucknow) 24
Purani Dilli ki Gosht ki Biryani (Delhi) 26
Kofta Biryani (Delhi) 28
Mutton Biryani (Delhi) 29
Babu Shahi's Matka Peer Biryani (Delhi) 30
Santare ki Biryani I (Delhi) 32
Santare ki Biryani–II (Delhi) 34
Kabab Biryani (Delhi) 35
Moti Pulao (Delhi) 36
Muthanjan Pulao (Delhi) 38
Maya's Biryani (Delhi) 42
Mutton Pulao (Kashmir) 43

Mutton Biryani (Kashmir) 45
Gosht Biryani–I (Hyderabad) 56
Gosht Biryan–II (Hyderabad) 64
Dumpokht Biryani (Hyderabad) 66
Masoor Dal Mutton Biryani (Hyderabad) 67
Doodh ki Biryani (Hyderabad) 68
Kairi ki Biryani (Hyderabad) 70
Korme ki Biryani (Hyderabad) 72
Paye ka Pulao (Hyderabad) 75
Katchi Biryani (Hyderabad) 76
Seviyon ki Biryani (Hyderabad) 78
Bone Marrow Pulao (Hyderabad) 80
Salem Biryani (Tamil Nadu) 88
Aambur Biryani (Tamil Nadu) 89
Chettinad Mutton Biryani (Tamil Nadu) 92
Dindigul Biryani (Tamil Nadu) 93
Coorg Mutton Biryani (Karnataka) 96
Mutton Biryani (Kerala) 101
Tellichery Biryani (Kerala) 112
Kolkata Mutton Biryani (West Bengal) 132
Ramzan Biryani (East Bengal–now Bangladesh) ... 135
Mutton Biryani (Bihar) 136
Mumbai Tawa Biryani (Mumbai) 153
Aloo Bukhara Biryani (Mumbai) 154
Subzi Gosht Biryani (Mumbai) 155
Parsi Pasanda Biryani (Mumbai) 156
Bohri Biryani (Mumbai) 158
Sindhi Mutton Biryani (Sindh/Mumbai) 159
Khoja Biryani (Mumbai) 160
Teevan Jo Pulao (Sindh) 162
Kutch Khoja Biryani (Gujarat) 163
Mutton Biryani Upside Down (Goa) 168
Malai ki Biryani (Rajasthan) 170
Pasande ki Biryani (Rajasthan) 172
Seviyon ki Biryani (Rajasthan) 173
Soola Biryani (Rajasthan) 174

Keema

Keeme ki Khichri (Hyderabad) 81
Keeme ki Biryani (Hyderabad) 82
Karonde ki Biryani (Hyderabad) 84
Boote aur Keeme ki Biryani (Hyderabad) 86

Pork

Pork Chops Pulao (Delhi) 40
Pork Biryani (Mumbai) 149

List of Biryanis by places

Lucknow
Ananas ki Biryani 17
Rose Biryani 20
Motiye ki Biryani 22
Dumpukht Biryani 24
Vegetable Biryani 46
Aloo Aur Tamater Ka Pulao 47

Delhi
Purani Dilli ki Ande aur Sabzion ki Biryani 25
Purani Dilli ki Gosht ki Biryani 26
Kofta Biryani 28
Mutton Biryani 29
Babu Shahi's Matka Peer Biryani 30
Santare ki Biryani–I 32
Santare ki Biryani–II 34
Moti Pulao 36
Kabab Biryani 38
Muthanjan Pulao 39
Maya's Biryani 41
Pork Chops Pulao 42
Mewa Pulao 48
Guchchi Biryani 50

Kashmir
Mutton Pulao 44
Mutton Biryani 45

Hyderabad
Gosht Biryani–I 56
Bater ki Biryani 57
Murgh ki Biryani 60
Fenugreek and Chicken Biryani 62
Gosht Biryani–II 64
Dumpokht Biryani 66
Masoor Dal Mutton Biryani 67
Doodh ki Biryani 68
Kairi ki Biryani 70
Korme ki Biryani 72
Paye ka Pulao 75
Katchi Biryani 76
Seviyon ki Biryani 78
Bone Marrow Pulao 80
Keeme ki Khichri 81
Keeme ki Biryani 82

Karonde ki Biryani	84
Boote aur Keeme ki Biryani	86
Zafraan Pilaf	113
Qabooli	114
Jackfruit Biryani-I	117

Tamil Nadu
Salem Biryani	88
Aambur Biryani	89
Egg Biryani	90
Chettinad Mutton Biryani	92
Dindigul Biryani	93
Masoor Dal Biryani (Vegetable version)	118

Karnataka
Mangalore Fish Biryani	94
Karwar Prawn Biryani	95
Coorg Mutton Biryani	96
Belgaum Chicken Biryani	97
South Canara Chicken Biryani	98
Udupi Vegetable Biryani	116

Kerala
Prawn Biryani with Curry leaves and Aniseed	100
Mutton Biryani	101
Chemeen Biryani	102
Meen Choru	104
Whole Fish Biryani	107
Thalassery Chicken Biryani	109
Tellichery Biryani	110
Northern Malabar Kozhi Biryani	111
Jackfruit Biryani–II	121

West Bengal
Fish Biryani with Aloo Bukhara	126
Chicken and Apricot Biryani	129
Kolkata Mutton Biryani	132
Easy Fish Biryani	134

Bangladesh
Ramzan Biryani	135

Bihar
Chicken Biryani	136
Mutton Biryani	137

Assam
Kampuri Biryan	138

Maharashtra
Masala Bhat	176
Mixed Dal Vada Biryani	177
Ravan Bhat	178

Kolhapur
Kolhapuri Biryani	144

Mumbai
Jhinga Biryani	146
Parsi Prawn Pulao	148
Pork Biryani	149
Choozon ka Pulao	152
Mumbai Tawa Biryani	153
Aloo Bukhara Biryani	154
Subzi Gosht Biryani	155
Parsi Pasanda Biryani	156
Bohri Biryani	158
Khoja Biryani	159

Sindh
Machhi Jo Pulao	150
Sindhi Mutton Biryani	161
Teevan Jo Pulao	162

Gujarat
Kutch Khoja Biryani	163

Goa
Goan Special	164
Arroz Con Pollo	166
Chicken Biryani	167
Mutton Biryani Upside Down	168

Rajasthan
Malai ki Biryani	170
Pasande ki Biryani	172
Seviyon ki Biryani	173
Soola Biryani	174

Acknowledgements

Twice over, I have discovered that writing a book (even a cookbook) is an excruciatingly exhilarating exercise. After all, a cookbook is not a one-person thing. Very few persons can claim to be omniscient on cooking, especially if it pertains to a somewhat esoteric subject like biryanis. Apart from a very large number of recipes, which I have collected over the last three decades, I had to draw on several experts.

When I began the project, I wondered if India could have a hundred biryanis. In the course of this project, I discovered that if one takes into account the creativity of the human mind inhabiting various towns and villages, there could be hundreds of biryanis. That is why I was not surprised to learn that in the southern states of Tamil Nadu, Kerala and Karnataka, many towns had their own biryanis. My thanks in the creation of this book go to some friends and some chefs.

Let me start with friends. I must thank Sanjay Khan (Abbas) and his wonderful wife Zarine. They not only parted, most willingly, with a biryani they had lovingly created, called Sabzi-Gosht Biryani, but opened the doors of their dream-like Bangalore spa, Golden Palms, for some Karnataka biryanis. Till they and Chef Francis came to my rescue, I was literally groping for biryanis from Karnataka.

Sunanda Roy gave me an insight into Bengali biryanis, one of them magically named Ramzan Biryani. Thanks, Sunanda and Tarun.

For Maharashtra, I turned to my lovely friend Kunda Mahurkar, herself a very talented cook. Apart from the fiery Kolhapuri Biryani, she also gave me the recipe of the tantalizingly titled Ravan Biryani, a deadly killer of a biryani by any yardstick.

Our friend Ashqin Qureshi, of Purani Dilli, who has again and again sent my husband and children into ecstasies with his home biryani, and his son Zia who prevailed upon his sister, Babli, to give me the recipe.

The daughters of the inimitable Laloo Prasad Yadav, Misa and Anoushka generously gave me the recipes of two Bihari biryanis when I seemed to be drawing a blank in Bihar as well.

Since my husband has always raved about Sindhi non-vegetarian food, which he was able to savour during his university days in Pune, I was very keen to source some good

Sindhi biryanis as well. Help came in the person of the gracious Ritu Uttam from the well-known Uttam family of Delhi.

My thanks, also, to the grand Babu Shahi of Matka Peer, Delhi, for graciously parting with the recipe of his famous biryani.

Finally, I must thank Neelam and Tarun Vadehra for letting me into Maya's biryani.

I have also drawn on chefs and managers from hotels in Mumbai, Kochi and Goa, during my visits to these places. My grateful thanks to M. A. Rashid, Executive Chef, The Gateway Hotel, Ernakulam; to Chef Shivi and Chef Chandru of Meridien, Kochi; to Chef Kedar Bobde of Hotel Grand Hyatt, Mumbai, and to Manager Roland Monteiro of Hotel 360, Goa.

I don't really need to go through the formality of acknowledging the role of my husband and my children. But it needs to be said that they were with me through every step, providing me with unending support, encouragement, and love. Their sincerity, dedication, and innovative ideas have contributed to the overall excellence of this book and I don't think any of this would have been possible without them. It is their passion for food and my love for them that has inspired me to write this book and to constantly create new versions of their favourite dish–The Biryani.

Amit Vadehra, my son-in-law and a multi talented person, helped in designing the cover and structuring the book. My photograph in the book is also his contribution.

Since props in food shots now seem to be more or less passé, I had to mobilize good crockery. For this I must thank Good Earth, my sister Sunita Vadehra and my good friends Ritu Vadehra and Manju Kapoor.

Lastly, I must express my gratitude to Chiki Sarkar and Milee Ashwarya for mooting this book and for being so wonderfully hands-on all the time. Their involvement and commitment spurred me to complete this project in just about a year.

PRATIBHA KARAN

A note on the author

Pratibha Karan retired as Secretary, Ministry of Food Processing Industries, Government of India, in 2003. As an IAS officer, she has worked in Delhi, Puducherry, and Arunachal Pradesh, where her abiding interest in food took her on a long odyssey of culinary experiences. Though herself a vegetarian, she soon started learning and experimenting with non-vegetarian cuisine. Her first book *A Princely Legacy: Hyderabadi Cuisine* received much critical acclaim. Pratibha lives in Delhi with her family.